Sources of
Western Society

**VOLUME 1: FROM ANTIQUITY
TO THE ENLIGHTENMENT**

D1469193

Sources of
Western Society

VOLUME 1: FROM ANTIQUITY TO THE ENLIGHTENMENT

Amy R. Caldwell

CALIFORNIA STATE UNIVERSITY, CHANNEL ISLANDS

SECOND EDITION

BEDFORD/ST. MARTIN'S   BOSTON ◆ NEW YORK

For Bedford/St. Martin's

Publisher for History: Mary V. Dougherty
Executive Editor: Traci Mueller Crowell
Director of Development for History: Jane Knetzger
Senior Editor: Heidi Hood
Developmental Editor: Shannon Hunt
Editorial Assistant: Jennifer Jovin
Production Supervisor: Andrew Ensor
Executive Marketing Manager: Jenna Bookin Barry
Text Design and Project Management: DeMasi Design and Publishing Services
Cover Design: Billy Boardman
Cover Art: Empress Theodora (detail of mosaic), c. 547 AD, San Vitale, Ravenna, Italy
    © Giraudon/Bridgeman Art Library
Composition: Jeff Miller Book Design
Printing and Binding: RR Donnelley & Sons

President: Joan E. Feinberg
Editorial Director: Denise B. Wydra
Director of Marketing: Karen R. Soeltz
Director of Production: Susan W. Brown
Assistant Director, Editorial Production: Elise S. Kaiser
Manager, Publishing Services: Emily Berleth

Manufactured in the United States of America.

7 6 5 4 3
f e

For information, write: Bedford/St. Martin's, 75 Arlington Street, Boston, MA 02116 (617-399-4000)

ISBN-10: 0-312-64079-X
ISBN-13: 978-0-312-64079-8

S*ources of Western Society* is a compilation of primary sources created by those who shaped and experienced the development of the Western world — among them rulers and subjects alike, men and women, philosophers, revolutionaries, economists, and laborers, from ancient times to the present. With a parallel chapter structure and documents handpicked to complement the text, this reader is designed to accompany both *A History of Western Society*, tenth edition, and *Western Society: A Brief History*, second edition. *Sources of Western Society* aspires to animate the past for students, providing resonant accounts of everyday life and the people and events that changed the face of Western history.

While a good textbook offers a clear framework of major historical figures and movements, *Sources* evokes the experiences of historical times at the moments they were lived and creates a dynamic connection for students, bridging the events of the past with their own understandings of power and its abuses, of the ripple effects of human agency, and of the material conditions of life. For example, John Locke's *Second Treatise of Civil Government* is cited in the textbook for its crucial role in the development of citizens' rights. In *Sources*, Locke himself makes a convincing case for the need for individual empowerment, as well as the study of history: "For he that thinks absolute power purifies men's blood, and corrects the baseness of human nature, need read but the history of this, or any other age, to be convinced of the contrary."

With input from the textbook authors, as well as from current instructors of the Western civilization survey course, we have compiled these documents with one goal foremost in mind: to make history's most compelling voices accessible to students, from the most well-known thinkers of their times to the galvanized or introspective commoner. In Chapter 21, for example, Thomas Malthus presents his economic theories on population and sustainability, while a threatening letter from worker Ned Ludd and his followers in Yorkshire protests the replacement of human textile workers by machines. Reformer Robert Owen expresses his views on the value of education for working-class youth, and a magazine illustration depicts the plight of children in a French cotton factory. John Aikin and Friedrich Engels provide very different opinions of the Industrial Revolution's impact on Manchester, England.

We have stepped back from drawing conclusions and instead provide just enough background to facilitate students' own analyses of the sources at hand. Chapter-opening paragraphs briefly review the major events of the time and place the documents that follow within the framework of the corresponding textbook chapter. A concise headnote for each document provides context about the author and the circumstances surrounding the document's creation, while gloss notes supply information to aid comprehension of unfamiliar terms and references. Each document is followed by Reading and Discussion Questions that spur deep student analysis of the material, while chapter-concluding Comparative Questions encourage students to contemplate the harmony and discord among the sources within and among the chapters. The excerpts range widely in length to allow for a range of class assignments.

NEW TO THIS EDITION

The second edition of *Sources* offers new pedagogical tools and provides instructors with greater flexibility in the development of their syllabus. Now expanded to an average of six sources per chapter with over one-third new sources overall, this edition offers a greater variety of topics to explore. Each chapter now features two or three "Viewpoints" selections that allow students to compare and contrast differing accounts of one topic or event, while new visual documents — nineteen in all — challenge students to analyze the historical meaning of art and photographs. In addition, new pronunciation guides make the language of historical documents more accessible. This edition aims for a balance of voices from all social classes and from the perspective of non-Europeans and Europeans alike, such as letters from King Affonso of Congo about the effects of the Portuguese slave trade on his kingdom and Heinrich Hauser's description of being unemployed in Germany during the Great Depression. *Sources of Western Society* now includes excerpts from popular classic sources such as Anna Comnena's *Alexiad*, Voltaire's *A Treatise on Toleration*, the People's Charter of 1838, and Wilfred Owen's *Poems*. Fresh sources include not only speeches and essays but letters, interviews, pamphlets, and poetry.

ACKNOWLEDGMENTS

Thanks to the reviewers whose thoughtful comments helped shape the second edition: Gemma Albanese, Dawson College; Melinda N. Brown,

Hinds Community College, Rankin Campus; David Byrne, Santa Monica College; Shane Caldwell, Zionsville Community High School; Joanna Carraway, Rockhurst University; Marie Therese Champagne, University of West Florida; Andrew Donson, University of Massachusetts Amherst; Robert C. Feinberg, Community College of Rhode Island; Melissa Korycinski, SUNY Onondaga Community College; Lara Kriegel, Florida International University; Andrew E. Larsen, Marquette University and University of Wisconsin-Milwaukee; Carole Levin, University of Nebraska-Lincoln; Nancy McLoughlin, University of California, Irvine; Laura M. Nelson, West Virginia University; Sherri Raney, Oklahoma Baptist University; and Jason L. Ward, Lee University. For their availability and insight, many thanks to the *History of Western Society* authors John P. McKay, John Buckler, Clare Crowston, Merry Wiesner-Hanks, and Joe Perry. We have worked as closely and cooperatively with Shannon Hunt in preparing this edition as we did with Lynn Sternberger for the first. To both we owe a large debt of gratitude for their editorial skills and efficiency, their valuable input and feedback, and, certainly not least of all, their unfailing patience and good humor. Thanks also to Heidi Hood and Jennifer Jovin, who played smaller but nonetheless important roles in the preparation of this edition. Emily Berleth of Bedford/St. Martin's and Linda DeMasi of DeMasi Design and Publishing Services made production of this reader possible with remarkable finesse.

CONTENTS

Sources of
Western Society

**VOLUME 1: FROM ANTIQUITY
TO THE ENLIGHTENMENT**

Origins

ca. 400,000–1100 B.C.E.

B y 3000 B.C.E., two contrasting agricultural societies had developed in Mesopotamia and Egypt. Mesopotamia was located between the great Tigris and Euphrates Rivers, which were a challenge to navigate and needed to be channeled into complicated irrigation systems. The area possessed few natural defenses against invasion. Egypt, on the other hand, was largely protected by desert, and the flooding of the Nile was fairly regular and could be managed with relative ease. The pharaohs were able to create a unified kingdom at an early point in Egypt's history, in part because the current of the Nile made travel up and down the river feasible. In Mesopotamia, various city-states warred against one another for domination. The writings these cultures left are among the earliest records of Western society. The following documents are concerned with two basic questions: how did the gods create and govern the world, and what sort of life should mortals lead to fulfill their duties to the gods and one another?

DOCUMENT 1-1

A Mesopotamian Creation Myth

ca. 2000–1000 B.C.E.

Creation myths offer supernatural explanations for the origins of the earth, heavens, and life in the natural world. This Mesopotamian creation myth, known as the Enuma Elish, *portrays the struggle of the sun-god Marduk, the patron god of Babylon, with Tiamat the sea-goddess, mother of all gods. As Babylon came to dominate the other cities of the Euphrates Valley, however, Marduk defeated Tiamat to become the chief of all the gods.*

From James B. Pritchard, ed., *Ancient Near Eastern Texts Relating to the Old Testament,* 2d ed. (Princeton, N.J.: Princeton University Press, 1955), pp. 61, 64, 67–68.

Naught but primordial Apsu, their begetter,
(And) Mummu-Tiamat, she who bore them all,
Their waters commingling as a single body;
No reed hut had been matted, no marsh land had appeared,
When no gods whatever had been brought into being,
Uncalled by name, their destinies undetermined —
Then it was that the gods were formed within them. . . .
[*Several generations of gods were descendants of Tiamat and Apsu, some of whom, particularly the gods Anu and Nudimmud, surpassed the other gods in strength.*]
The divine brothers [Anu and Nudimmud] banded together
They disturbed Tiamat as they surged back and forth,
Yea, they troubled the mood of Tiamat
By their hilarity in the Abode of Heaven.
Apsu could not lessen their clamor
And Tiamat was speechless at their [ways].
Their doings were loathsome . . .
Unsavory were their ways; they were overbearing.
[*And so begins a war among the gods. Apsu was killed during the war, so Tiamat created monsters to help her destroy her rivals. Ea, a leading god among Tiamat's opponents, asked his son Marduk to join the war.*]
"My son, thou who knowest all wisdom,
Calm [Tiamat] with thy holy spell. . . .
The lord [rejoiced] at the word of his father.
His heart exulting, he said to his father:
"Creator of the gods, destiny of the great gods,
"If I indeed, as your avenger,
Am to vanquish Tiamat and save your lives,
Set up the Assembly [of gods], proclaim supreme my destiny!
When jointly in Ubshukinna[1] you have sat down rejoicing,
Let my word, instead of you, determine the fates.
Unalterable shall be what I may bring into being;
Neither recalled not changed shall be the command of my lips!" . . .
[*Marduk defeats Tiamat's army, and then finally battles the goddess herself.*]
They strove in single combat, locked in battle. . . .
He released the arrow, it tore her belly,
It cut through her insides, splitting the heart.
Having thus subdued her, he extinguished her life.

---

[1] **Ubshukinna**: The meeting hall of the gods.

He cast down her carcass to stand upon it. . . .
He split her like a shellfish into two parts:
Half of her he set up and ceiled it as sky,
Pulled down the bar and posted guards.
He bade them to allow not her waters to escape.
He crossed the heavens and surveyed the regions. . . .
Opening his mouth, he addresses Ea
To impart the plan he had conceived in his heart:
"Blood I will mass and cause bones to be.
I will establish a savage, man shall be his name.
Truly, savage-man I will create.
He shall be charged with the service of the gods
That they might be at ease!"

READING AND DISCUSSION QUESTIONS

1. According to this account, how is the world created?

2. Central to this creation story is a struggle to the death between two gods. What might the focus on battle reveal about Mesopotamian beliefs?

3. How and why were human beings created? What does this story reveal about how Mesopotamians understood the relationship between humans and the gods?

DOCUMENT 1-2

The Epic of Gilgamesh

ca. 2750 B.C.E.

The Epic of Gilgamesh *is one of the oldest surviving stories in world history. Fragments of the story can be found on tablets throughout the Mesopotamian region, but the most complete version of the text comes from twelve tablets written in the Akkadian language and dating to 1300 B.C.E. The epic*

From The Epic of Gilgamesh, trans. Maureen Gallery Kovacs (Stanford, Calif.: Stanford University Press, 1989), pp. 4, 6, 51–56, 84–86, 106–107.

tells the tale of Gilgamesh, the part-human, part-divine king of Uruk. In these excerpts, Gilgamesh meets his friend Enkidu. Together, they confront Ishtar, the goddess of war and fertility. After Enkidu dies, Gilgamesh sets out to find the secret of immortality. On his journey, he encounters Siduri, the tavern keeper, who challenges him to reconsider why he wants eternal life.

[This is the story of]
how Gilgamesh went through every hardship.
Supreme over other kings, lordly in appearance,
he is the hero. . . .
He walks out in front, the leader,
and walks at the rear, trusted by his companions.
Mighty net, protector of his people,
raging flood-wave who destroys even walls of stone! . . .
It was he who crossed the ocean, the vast seas, to the rising sun,
who explored the world regions, seeking life. . . .
Who can say like Gilgamesh: "I am King!"?

[*The legend of Gilgamesh's adventures begins with the people of his king-dom complaining about their king. They accuse him of taking away their sons, possibly as conscripts for his army, and of sexually exploiting young women. The people ask the gods to intervene with Gilgamesh. The goddess Aruru creates Enkidu to distract the king.*]

In the wilderness (?) she created valiant Enkidu,
born of Silence, endowed with strength. . . .
His whole body was shaggy with hair,
he had a full head of hair like a woman,
his locks billowed in profusion. . . .
He knew neither people nor settled living, . . .
He ate grasses with the gazelles,
and jostled at the watering hole with the animals. . . .

[*The local populace was afraid of Enkidu, and eventually Gilgamesh was called upon to defend them from the wild man. After a brief struggle, Gilga-mesh defeats Enkidu in a fight, and the two become the best of friends. They fight monsters and have many adventures together, including the following encounter with the goddess Ishtar.*]

When Gilgamesh placed his crown on his head,
Princess Ishtar raised her eyes to the beauty of Gilgamesh.
    "Come along, Gilgamesh, be you my husband,
        to me grant your lusciousness.

Be you my husband, and I will be your wife. . . .
Bowed down beneath you will be kings, lords, and princes.
The Lullubu people[2] will bring you the produce of the mountains
    and countryside as tribute." . . .
Gilgamesh addressed Princess Ishtar saying:
    "What would I have to give you if I married you?
    Do you need oil or garments for your body?
    Do you lack anything for food or drink?
    I would gladly feed you food fit for a god,
    I would gladly give you wine fit for a king. . . .
    See here now, I will recite the list of your lovers . . .
    Tammuz, the lover of your earliest youth,
    for him you have ordained lamentations year upon year! . . .
    You loved the stallion, famed in battle,
    yet you ordained for him the whip, the goad, and the lash. . . .
When Ishtar heard this,
in a fury she went up to the heavens,
going to Anu, her father, and crying,
going to Anrum, her mother, and weeping:
    "Father, Gilgamesh has insulted me over and over,
    Gilgamesh has recounted despicable deeds about me,
    despicable deeds and curses!"
Anu addressed Princess Ishtar, saying:
    "What is the matter? Was it not you who provoked King Gilgamesh?
    So Gilgamesh recounted despicable deeds about you,
    despicable deeds and curses!"
Ishtar spoke to her father, Anu, saying:
    "Father, give me the Bull of Heaven,
    so he can kill Gilgamesh in his dwelling.
    If you do not give me the Bull of Heaven
    I will knock down the Gates of the Netherworld,
    I will smash the door posts, and leave the doors flat down,
    and will let the dead go up to eat the living!
    And the dead will outnumber the living!"
Anu addressed Princess Ishtar, saying:
    "If you demand the Bull of Heaven from me,
    there will be seven years of empty husks for the land of Uruk.

---

[2] **Lullubu people**: The Lullubi were a wild, nomadic people of the mountains.

Have you collected grain for the people!
Have you made grasses grow for the animals?"
Ishtar addressed Anu, her father, saying:
"I have heaped grain in the granaries for the people,
I made grasses grow for the animals,
in order that they might eat in the seven years of empty husks.
I have collected grain for the people,
I have made grasses grow for the animals." . . .
[About six lines are missing here.]
When Anu heard her words,
he placed the nose rope of the Bull of Heaven in her hand.
Ishtar led the Bull of Heaven down to the earth.
When it reached Uruk it climbed down to the Euphrates . . .
At the snort of the Bull of Heaven a huge pit opened up,
and 100 young men of Uruk fell in.
At his second snort a huge pit opened up,
and 200 young men of Uruk fell in.
At his third snort a huge pit opened up,
and Enkidu fell in up to his waist.
Then Enkidu jumped out and seized the Bull of Heaven by its horns. . . .
Enkidu stalked and *hunted down* the Bull of Heaven.
He grasped it by the thick of its tail
and held onto it with both his hands (?),
while Gilgamesh, like *an expert butcher*,
boldly and *surely approached the Bull of Heaven*. . . .
He thrust his sword.
After they had killed the Bull of Heaven, . . .
Then the brothers sat down together.
Ishtar went up onto the top of the Wall of Uruk-Haven,
cast herself into the pose of mourning, and hurled her woeful curse:
"Woe unto Gilgamesh who slandered me and killed the Bull of
Heaven!"
When Enkidu heard this pronouncement of Ishtar,
he wrenched off the Bull's hindquarter and flung it in her face:
"If I could only get at you I would do the same to you!
I would drape his innards over your arms!"
The men of Uruk gathered together, staring at them.
Gilgamesh said to the palace retainers:
"Who is the bravest of the men?
Who is the boldest of the males?

[*Enkidu reveals to Gilgamesh that he will die soon, and that the afterlife will be a place of sorrow. After Enkidu dies, Gilgamesh goes on a journey to find the secret of eternal life. After traveling for some time, he encounters Siduri, who owns a tavern.*]

Gilgamesh said to the tavern-keeper:

"I am Gilgamesh . . .

I grappled with the Bull that came down from heaven, and killed him."

The tavern-keeper spoke to Gilgamesh, saying:

"*If you are Gilgamesh, . . .* why are your cheeks emaciated, your expression desolate?

Why is your heart so wretched, your features so haggard?

Why is there such sadness deep within you?

Why do you look like one who has been traveling a long distance so that ice and heat have seared your face?" . . .

Gilgamesh spoke to her, to the tavern-keeper he said:

"Tavern-keeper, should not my cheeks be emaciated?

Should my heart not be wretched, my features not haggard?

Should there not be sadness deep within me?

Should I not look like one who has been traveling a long distance, and should ice and heat not have seared my face?

My friend, . . . Enkidu, the wild ass who chased the wild donkey, panther of the wilderness,

we joined together, and went up into the mountain.

We grappled with and killed the Bull of Heaven. . . .

Enkidu, whom I love deeply, who went through every hardship with me,

the fate of mankind has overtaken him.

Six days and seven nights I mourned over him

and would not allow him to be buried

until a maggot fell out of his nose.

I was terrified *by his appearance* (?),

I began to fear death, and so roam the wilderness.

How can I stay silent, how can I be still?

My friend whom I love has turned to clay.

Am I not like him? Will I lie down, never to get up again?"

[*The tavern-keeper sends Gilgamesh to find the one man, Utnapishtim (oot-nuh-PISH-tim), who has been granted immortality by the gods. She warns him, however, about what he will find on the journey.*]

The tavern-keeper spoke to Gilgamesh, saying: . . .

The crossing is difficult, its ways are treacherous —

and in between are the Waters of Death that bar its approaches!
And even if, Gilgamesh, you should cross the sea,
    when you reach the Waters of Death what would you do?
[*After his long, arduous journey Gilgamesh finally finds Utnapishtim, who*
tells him that no human can be immortal. He does, however, tell Gilgamesh
of a plant that will restore his youth. Utnapishtim instructs a ferryman, Ursha-
nabi, to take Gilgamesh back to Uruk, after Gilgamesh finds the plant.]
[Gilgamesh says,] "this plant is a plant against decay
by which a man can attain his survival.
I will bring it to Uruk and have an old man eat the plant to test it.
The plant's name is 'The Old Man Becomes a Young Man.'"
Then I will eat it and return to the condition of my youth." . . .
Seeing a spring and how cool its waters were,
Gilgamesh went down and was bathing in the water.
A snake smelled the fragrance of the plant,
silently came up and carried off the plant. . . .
At that point Gilgamesh sat down, weeping,
his tears streaming over the side of his nose.
"Counsel me, O ferryman Urshanabi!
For whom have my arms labored, Urshanabi!
For whom has my heart's blood roiled!
I have not secured any good deed for myself, . . ."
They arrived in Uruk. Gilgamesh said to Urshanabi, the ferryman:
"Go up, Urshanabi, onto the wall of Uruk and walk around.
Examine its foundation, inspect its brickwork thoroughly. . . .

READING AND DISCUSSION QUESTIONS

1. At the beginning of the epic, what kind of king is Gilgamesh? Does he stay the same in the story, or does he change?

2. What happens when Gilgamesh rejects Ishtar? Who suffers because of her anger? What does this episode reveal about the Mesopotamian understanding of the relationship between humans and the gods?

3. What kind of advice does Gilgamesh get from the tavern keeper? What lesson is she trying to teach him?

4. Why do you think Gilgamesh did not immediately eat the plant of youth? Why is it that after losing the plant, he asks Urshanabi to look at the walls and foundation of Uruk?

DOCUMENT 1-3

The Code of Hammurabi

ca. 1780 B.C.E.

*As king of Babylon, Hammurabi (hahm-moo-RAH-bee; r. ca. 1792–1750
B.C.E.) created an empire that extended throughout Mesopotamia. During
his reign, Babylon was one of the first great cities in the world. Hammurabi
compiled one of the best-known law codes of ancient times and ordered it to
be carved on stone tablets and set up in a public space. The inscriptions were
in Akkadian, the daily language of the people. Although it is not known how
many Babylonians were literate at this time, ordinary people might have
had a general sense of what was written there.*

3. If any one bring an accusation of any crime before the elders, and
   does not prove what he has charged, he shall, if it be a capital offense
   charged, be put to death. . . .
5. If a judge try a case, reach a decision, and present his judgment in
   writing; if later error shall appear in his decision, and it be through
   his own fault, then he shall pay twelve times the fine set by him in
   the case, and he shall be publicly removed from the judge's bench,
   and never again shall he sit there to render judgment. . . .
15. If anyone take a male or female slave of the court, or a male or
    female slave of a freed man, outside the city gates, he shall be put to
    death.
16. If anyone receive into his house a runaway male or female slave of
    the court, or of a freedman, and does not bring it out at the public
    proclamation of the major domus,[3] the master of the house shall be
    put to death.
17. If anyone find runaway male or female slaves in the open country
    and bring them to their masters, the master of the slaves shall pay
    him two shekels of silver. . . .
25. If fire break out in a house, and some one who comes to put it out
    cast his eye upon the property of the owner of the house, and take

From James B. Pritchard, ed., *Ancient Near Eastern Texts Relating to the Old Testament*, 3d ed. (Princeton, N.J.: Princeton University Press, 1969), pp. 176–178.

[3] **major domus:** In this context, an official in charge of overseeing slaves.

the property of the master of the house, he shall be thrown into that self-same fire. . . .

30. If a chieftain or a man leave his house, garden, and field and hires it out, and some one else takes possession of his house, garden, and field and uses it for three years: if the first owner return and claims his house, garden, and field, it shall not be given to him, but he who has taken possession of it and used it shall continue to use it. . . .

108. If a tavern-keeper (feminine) does not accept corn according to gross weight in payment of drink, but takes money, and the price of the drink is less than that of the corn, she shall be convicted and thrown into the water.

109. If conspirators meet in the house of a tavern-keeper, and these conspirators are not captured and delivered to the court, the tavern-keeper shall be put to death.

110. If a sister of a god[4] open a tavern, or enter a tavern to drink, then shall this woman be burned to death. . . .

128. If a man take a woman to wife, but have no intercourse with her, this woman is no wife to him.

129. If a man's wife be surprised with another man, both shall be tied and thrown into the water, but the husband may pardon his wife and the king his slaves.

130. If a man violate the wife (betrothed or child-wife) of another man, who has never known a man, and still lives in her father's house, and sleep with her and be surprised, this man shall be put to death, but the wife is blameless.

131. If a man bring a charge against one's wife, but she is not surprised with another man, she must take an oath and then may return to her house.

132. If the "finger is pointed" at a man's wife about another man, but she is not caught sleeping with the other man, she shall jump into the river for her husband. . . .

137. If a man wish to separate from a woman who has borne him children, or from his wife who has borne him children: then he shall give that wife her dowry, and a part of the usufruct of field, garden, and property, so that she can rear her children. When she has brought up her children, a portion of all that is given to the children, equal as that of one son, shall be given to her. She may then marry the man of her heart.

---

[4] **sister of a god**: A woman dedicated to the service of a god or goddess.

138. If a man wishes to separate from his wife who has borne him no children, he shall give her the amount of her purchase money and the dowry which she brought from her father's house, and let her go.

139. If there was no purchase price he shall give her one mina of gold as a gift of release. . . .

141. If a man's wife, who lives in his house, wishes to leave it, plunges into debt, tries to ruin her house, neglects her husband, and is judicially convicted: if her husband offer her release, she may go on her way, and he gives her nothing as a gift of release. If her husband does not wish to release her, and if he take another wife, she shall remain as servant in her husband's house. . . .

144. If a man take a wife and this woman give her husband a maid-servant, and she bear him children, but this man wishes to take another wife, this shall not be permitted to him; he shall not take a second wife.

145. If a man take a wife, and she bear him no children, and he intend to take another wife: if he take this second wife, and bring her into the house, this second wife shall not be allowed equality with his wife. . . .

195. If a son strike his father, his hands shall be hewn off.

196. If a man put out the eye of another man, his eye shall be put out.

197. If he break another man's bone, his bone shall be broken.

198. If he put out the eye of a freed man, or break the bone of a freed man, he shall pay one gold mina.

199. If he put out the eye of a man's slave, or break the bone of a man's slave, he shall pay one-half of its value.

200. If a man knock out the teeth of his equal, his teeth shall be knocked out.

201. If he knock out the teeth of a freed man, he shall pay one-third of a gold mina.

202. If anyone strike the body of a man higher in rank than he, he shall receive sixty blows with an ox-whip in public.

203. If a free-born man strike the body of another free-born man of equal rank, he shall pay one gold mina.

204. If a freed man strike the body of another freed man, he shall pay ten shekels in money.

205. If the slave of a freed man strike the body of a freed man, his ear shall be cut off. . . .

209. If a man strike a free-born woman so that she lose her unborn child, he shall pay ten shekels for her loss.

210. If the woman die, his daughter shall be put to death.
211. If a woman of the free class lose her child by a blow, he shall pay five shekels in money.
212. If this woman die, he shall pay half a mina.
213. If he strike the maid-servant of a man, and she lose her child, he shall pay two shekels in money.
214. If this maid-servant die, he shall pay one-third of a mina. . . .

READING AND DISCUSSION QUESTIONS

1. What do these laws reveal about the social structure of Babylon? How is the role of social rank in Babylonian society reflected in these laws?

2. What do these laws reveal about contemporary family life? What do they reveal about the status of women and children?

3. What can we surmise about a person's responsibilities to the community as a whole?

DOCUMENT 1-4

The Egyptian Book of the Dead: The Declaration of Innocence

ca. 2100–1800 B.C.E.

The Egyptian Book of the Dead *comprises texts that were placed in tombs and described how a dead person should overcome various obstacles in the afterlife. Although there was no standard* Book of the Dead *(this was not a name used by the Egyptians), many of the same texts appear in tombs dating from shortly after 2000 B.C.E. until the adoption of Christianity. This "Declaration of Innocence," one such text, is remarkable for the detail with which it describes the possible sins of the deceased Egyptian. In listing the undesirable acts, it creates an outline of what Egyptians considered acceptable social behavior.*

From Miriam Lichtheim, trans. and ed., *Ancient Egyptian Literature: A Book of Readings*, vol. 2, The New Kingdom (Berkeley: University of California Press, 1973), 124–26.

To be said on reaching the Hall of the Two Truths[5] so as to purge [name]
 of any sins committed and to see the face of every god:
Hail to you, great God, Lord of the Two Truths!
I have come to you, my Lord,
I was brought to see your beauty.
I know you, I know the names of the forty-two gods
Who are with you in the Hall of the Two Truths,
Who live by warding off evildoers,
Who drink of their blood,
On that day of judging characters before Wennofer [Osiris]. Lo, your
 name is "He-of-Two-Daughters,"
(And) "He-of-Maat's[6]-Two-Eyes."
Lo, I come before you,
Bringing Maat to you,
Having repelled evil for you.
I have not done crimes against people,
I have not mistreated cattle,
I have not sinned in the Place of Truth,
I have not known what should not be known,
I have not done any harm.
I did not begin a day by exacting more than my due,
My name did not reach the bark of the mighty ruler.
I have not blasphemed a god,
I have not robbed the poor.
I have not done what the god abhors,
I have not maligned a servant to his master.
I have not caused pain,
I have not caused tears.
I have not killed,
I have not ordered to kill,
I have not made anyone suffer.
I have not damaged the offerings in the temples,

---

[5] **Hall of the Two Truths**: A place of judgment after death. Upon reaching the Hall of
Two Truths, ancient Egyptians would stand before a jury of gods, hear a recounting
of their life's deeds, and have their hearts literally weighed by the god Osiris on the
scales of justice. A heart heavy with guilt meant the owner would be devoured by the
demon Ammit.
[6] **Maat** (muh-AHT): Egyptian goddess who personified truth, cosmic order, and justice. Her followers were considered upholders of the universal order.

I have not depleted the loaves of the gods,
I have not stolen the cakes of the dead.
I have not copulated nor defiled myself.
I have not increased nor reduced the measure,
I have not diminished the arura [land].
I have not cheated in the fields.
I have not added to the weight of the balance,
I have not falsified the plummet of the scales.
I have not taken milk from the mouths of children,
I have not deprived cattle of their pasture.
I have not snared birds in the reeds of the gods,
I have not caught fish in their ponds.
I have not held back water in its season,
I have not dammed a flowing stream,
I have not quenched a needed fire.
I have not neglected the days of meat offerings,
I have not detained cattle belonging to the god,
I have not stopped a god in his procession.
I am pure, I am pure, I am pure, I am pure!

READING AND DISCUSSION QUESTIONS

1. What kinds of offenses has the speaker not committed? What does each of these reveal about Egyptian social life?

2. Why might the declaration repeatedly state that the Egyptian knows the names of the gods?

3. List two offenses against gods, two offenses against mortals, and two that could offend both mortals and gods. What do these various offenses reveal about Egyptian moral thinking?

Kings and Gods

DOCUMENT 1-5

AKHENATEN

The Hymn to Aton

ca. 1350 B.C.E.

This hymn is attributed to the pharaoh Akhenaten (ah-keh-NAH-tuhn; r. ca. 1367–1350 B.C.E.). When he became pharaoh, Akhenaten abandoned the traditional Egyptian gods, whom he considered frauds, and replaced them with the worship of Aton, a single, universal god. While the details of Akhenaten's religion remain unclear, historians agree that Atenism is one of the oldest known examples of monotheism, the belief in one god. This change was not popular in Egypt and the worship of Aton did not last long after Akhenaten's death.

Your rising is beautiful in the horizon of heaven, O Aton, ordainer of life.
You rise in the eastern horizon, filling every land with your radiance.
You are beautiful, great, splendid, and raised up above every land.
Your rays, like those of Ra,[7] deck every land you have made,
You have taken [the lands], and have made them subject to your son (i.e.,
    Akhenaten).
You are far away, but your beams are on the earth;
You are on [people's] faces, they [admire] your goings.
When you set in the west, the earth is dark as with death.
Men lie down in their cabins shrouded in wrappings;
One cannot see his companion, and if all the goods that are under their
    heads are carried off, they cannot see (the thief). . . .
You rise up in the horizon at dawn
You shine in the disk in the day
You scatter the darkness

From Sir Ernest Alfred Wallis Budge, *The Gods of the Egyptians, or Studies in Egyptian Mythology*, vol. 1 (London: Methuen and Co., 1904), pp. 75–78. Text modernized by Amy R. Caldwell.

[7] **Ra:** Traditional Egyptian god of the sun.

You send out your rays, the Two Lands[8] rejoice,
Men wake up and stand on their feet,
For you raise them.
All beasts and cattle turn into their pastures,
The grass and herbs flourish,
The waterfowl fly over their marshes, their feathers praising your Ka.[9] . . .
How many are the things which you have made! . . .
O God, one who has no counterpart!
You, existing alone, did by your heart create the earth and everything that
    is thereon.
Men, cattle, beasts, and creatures of all kinds that move on feet,
All the creatures of the sky that fly with wings,
The deserts of Syria and Kush, and the land of Egypt
You have assigned to everyone his place,
Providing the daily food, each receiving his destined share;
You decree his span of life.
The speech and characteristics of men vary, as do their skins,
The dwellers in foreign lands having their distinguishing marks. . . .
O Lord of every land, you shine upon them,
O Aton of the day, you mighty one of majesty.
You create the life.
Of the foreign desert, and of all deserts, O Lord of the way
You create their life.
You have set a Nile in heaven, it descends upon them.
It makes on the mountains a flood like the great, green sea,
It waters the fields around their villages.
How perfect, wholly perfect, are your plans, O lord of eternity!
You are a Nile in the sky for all those who dwell in the deserts of foreign
    lands.

READING AND DISCUSSION QUESTIONS

1. What kind of god is Aton? Why does Akhenaten compare him to the
    sun?

2. What benefits does Aton bring? What does he do for Egyptians?

3. What does the author mean by a "Nile in the sky?" Why is it impor-
    tant that Aton brings good things to non-Egyptians?

---

[8] **Two Lands**: Upper and Lower Egypt, which formed one united kingdom at this time.
[9] **Ka**: The soul or spirit.

DOCUMENT 1-6

Sacred Kingship: Set, Rameses II, and Horus

ca. 1244 B.C.E.

In the Egyptian religion, pharaohs were closely associated with the god Horus. In fact, the pharaoh was considered the living incarnation of Horus, making the pharaoh a god-king. Many Egyptian stories about the gods have Horus in conflict with his uncle Set, who had been jealous of his brother Osiris. He killed Osiris, dismembered his body, and scattered the parts all over Egypt. Isis, Osiris's wife, reassembled her husband, brought him back to life, and they conceived their son Horus. Horus fought with Set many times to avenge his father. Set and Horus also represent Upper and Lower Egypt, respectively, and are often seen together with a pharaoh, as in the image below. Set is to the left, and Horus is on the right. Pharaoh Rameses II is in the middle, wearing the crowns of Upper and Lower Egypt.

READING AND DISCUSSION QUESTIONS

1. How would you describe the hand gestures that Set and Horus are making toward the pharaoh? What do the gestures say about the gods' relationship with the pharaoh?

Eric Meola/Getty Images.

2. What is similar about what Horus and Rameses are wearing? Why is that significant?

3. If the pharaoh is Horus incarnate, why is Set in the picture, too?

4. Is there a political message in this image? If so, what is it?

COMPARATIVE QUESTIONS

1. In what ways is the relationship between gods and humans in the Mesopotamian sources different from the relationship in the Egyptian documents?

2. In the "Declaration of Innocence," the writer lists a multitude of crimes against the gods and humanity. In what ways are notions of morality in the *Book of the Dead* and Hammurabi's code similar to or different from other, nonancient "morality lists"?

3. Based on the documents, what would you list as the top priorities of a model Egyptian or Mesopotamian citizen? List at least three priorities each for Egyptians and Mesopotamians.

4. Compare and contrast Akhenaten's "Hymn to Aton" with the image of Rameses II, Set, and Horus. Is Akhenaten's relationship with his god different from Rameses's relationship with the traditional gods?

CHAPTER 2

Small Kingdoms and Mighty Empires in the Near East

ca. 1100–513 B.C.E.

T he following documents describe how the Hebrew people came into being and how they struggled for existence. Sometime between 1700 and 1300 B.C.E., their God handed down the Law to the Hebrews, who were unified under one religion but who had not yet found the "promised land" on which to build their nation. Eventually, they moved into the region of Palestine and built their own kingdom. The kingdom of Israel flourished under Kings David and Solomon, whose heirs split the kingdom into two smaller states — Israel and Judah, around 925 B.C.E. These smaller states had to contend with more powerful empires in the region, and both eventually lost their independence. The northern kingdom, Israel, fell to the Assyrians, while around 586 B.C.E., the remnants of the southern kingdom were defeated by the Babylonian king Nebuchadnezzar (*ne-buh-kuhd-NEH-zuhr*), and exiled to his capital. The Hebrews were forced to reside in Babylon until its capture by the new Persian ruler, Cyrus the Great. Although Cyrus practiced the dualistic religion known as Zoroastrianism, he let the people he conquered maintain their religious traditions, and allowed the Hebrews to return to Jerusalem, their homeland.

DOCUMENT 2-1

Book of Genesis: The Hebrews Explain Creation

ca. 950–450 B.C.E.

The following passage is the beginning of Genesis, the first book of the Hebrew Bible, or Torah. The range of dates in the headnote reveals something about

---

Genesis 1:1–31; 2:1–7.

the hotly debated issue of how the Hebrew Bible was created. Modern histo-
rians believe that by about 450 B.C.E., the book of Genesis existed in some-
thing close to the form we now possess. At the same time, it is known that
some passages of Genesis are much older.

In the beginning God created the heavens and the earth.

Now the earth was formless and empty, darkness was over the surface of the deep, and the Spirit of God was hovering over the waters.

And God said, "Let there be light," and there was light. God saw that the light was good, and He separated the light from the darkness. God called the light "day," and the darkness he called "night." And there was evening, and there was morning — the first day.

And God said, "Let there be an expanse between the waters to separate water from water." So God made the expanse and separated the water under the expanse from the water above it. And it was so. God called the expanse "sky." And there was evening, and there was morning — the second day.

And God said, "Let the water under the sky be gathered to one place, and let dry ground appear." And it was so. God called the dry ground "land," and the gathered waters he called "seas." And God saw that it was good.

Then God said, "Let the land produce vegetation: seed-bearing plants and trees on the land that bear fruit with seed in it, according to their various kinds." And it was so. The land produced vegetation: plants bearing seed according to their kinds and trees bearing fruit with seed in it according to their kinds. And God saw that it was good. And there was evening, and there was morning — the third day.

And God said, "Let there be lights in the expanse of the sky to separate the day from the night, and let them serve as signs to mark seasons and days and years, and let them be lights in the expanse of the sky to give light on the earth." And it was so. God made two great lights — the greater light to govern the day and the lesser light to govern the night. He also made the stars. God set them in the expanse of the sky to give light on the earth, to govern the day and the night, and to separate light from darkness. And God saw that it was good. And there was evening, and there was morning — the fourth day.

And God said, "Let the water teem with living creatures, and let birds fly above the earth across the expanse of the sky." So God created the great creatures of the sea and every living and moving thing with which the water teems, according to their kinds, and every winged bird according to its kind. And God saw that it was good. God blessed them and said, "Be fruitful and increase in number and fill the water in the seas, and let the birds increase on the earth." And there was evening, and there was morning — the fifth day.

And God said, "Let the land produce living creatures according to their kinds: livestock, creatures that move along the ground, and wild animals, each according to its kind." And it was so. God made the wild animals according to their kinds, the livestock according to their kinds, and all the creatures that move along the ground according to their kinds. And God saw that it was good.

Then God said, "Let us make man in our image, in our likeness, and let them rule over the fish of the sea and the birds of the air, over the livestock, over all the earth, and over all the creatures that move along the ground."

So God created man in his own image, in the image of God he created him; male and female he created them.

God blessed them and said to them, "Be fruitful and increase in number; fill the earth and subdue it. Rule over the fish of the sea and the birds of the air and over every living creature that moves on the ground."

Then God said, "I give you every seed-bearing plant on the face of the whole earth and every tree that has fruit with seed in it. They will be yours for food. And to all the beasts of the earth and all the birds of the air and all the creatures that move on the ground — everything that has the breath of life in it — I give every green plant for food." And it was so.

God saw all that he had made, and it was very good. And there was evening, and there was morning — the sixth day.

Thus the heavens and the earth were completed in all their vast array. By the seventh day God had finished the work he had been doing; so on the seventh day he rested from all his work. And God blessed the seventh day and made it holy, because on it he rested from all the work of creating that he had done.

This is the account of the heavens and the earth when they were created. When the Lord God made the earth and the heavens — and no shrub of the field had yet appeared on the earth and no plant of the field had yet sprung up, for the Lord God had not sent rain on the earth and there was no man to work the ground, but streams came up from the earth and watered the whole surface of the ground — the Lord God formed the man from the dust of the ground and breathed into his nostrils the breath of life, and the man became a living being.

READING AND DISCUSSION QUESTIONS

1. Consider the stages of creation. What does their order reveal about the Hebrew faith?

2. God creates man on the sixth day, but a few verses later the text states that "there was not a man to till the ground," then a mist watered the earth and God formed man from the dust of the ground. Why does God seem to create man twice, and what could this indicate about the way the text was created?

3. Explain the following passage: "Be fruitful and increase in number; fill the earth and subdue it." What does this indicate about how the Hebrews understood the relationship between their God and humanity?

4. Why does the text state that at the end of various stages of creation, God "saw that it was good"?

DOCUMENT 2-2

Exodus and Deuteronomy:
The Hebrew Law and Covenant

ca. 950–450 B.C.E.

Moses was the greatest of the Hebrew prophets, and is revered by Jews, Christians, and Muslims alike. After Moses led his people out of bondage in Egypt, the Hebrew God revealed a series of commandments to Moses on Mount Sinai. This was not the first occasion when their God handed down moral commandments to his people, but it was here that He forbade His people to worship other gods. The passage establishes monotheism, the worship of only one god, as a tenet of the Hebrew religion. Their God also promises the Hebrews substantial benefits in exchange for their obedience.

On the morning of the third day there was thunder and lightning, with a thick cloud over the mountain, and a very loud trumpet blast. Everyone in the camp trembled. Then Moses led the people out of the camp to meet

---

Exodus 19:16–25; 20:1–21. Deuteronomy 28:1–9; 15–26.

with God, and they stood at the foot of the mountain. Mount Sinai was covered with smoke, because the Lord descended on it in fire. The smoke billowed up from it like smoke from a furnace, the whole mountain trembled violently, and the sound of the trumpet grew louder and louder. Then Moses spoke and the voice of God answered him.

The Lord descended to the top of Mount Sinai and called Moses to the top of the mountain. So Moses went up and the Lord said to him, "Go down and warn the people so they do not force their way through to see the Lord and many of them perish. Even the priests, who approach the Lord, must consecrate themselves, or the Lord will break out against them."

Moses said to the Lord, "The people cannot come up Mount Sinai, because you yourself warned us, 'Put limits around the mountain and set it apart as holy.'"

The Lord replied, "Go down and bring Aaron[1] up with you. But the priests and the people must not force their way through to come up to the Lord, or he will break out against them."

So Moses went down to the people and told them.

And God spoke all these words:

"I am the Lord your God, who brought you out of Egypt, out of the land of slavery.

"You shall have no other gods before me.

"You shall not make for yourself an idol in the form of anything in heaven above or on the earth beneath or in the waters below. You shall not bow down to them or worship them; for I, the Lord your God, am a jealous God, punishing the children for the sin of the fathers to the third and fourth generation of those who hate me, but showing love to a thousand [generations] of those who love me and keep my commandments.

"You shall not misuse the name of the Lord your God, for the Lord will not hold anyone guiltless who misuses his name.

"Remember the Sabbath day by keeping it holy. Six days you shall labor and do all your work, but the seventh day is a Sabbath to the Lord your God. On it you shall not do any work, neither you, nor your son or daughter, nor your manservant or maidservant, nor your animals, nor the alien within your gates. For in six days the Lord made the heavens and the earth, the sea, and all that is in them, but he rested on the seventh day. Therefore the Lord blessed the Sabbath day and made it holy.

---

[1] **Aaron**: Moses's brother and high priest of the Hebrews.

"Honor your father and your mother, so that you may live long in the land the Lord your God is giving you.

"You shall not murder.

"You shall not commit adultery.

"You shall not give false testimony against your neighbor.

"You shall not covet your neighbor's house. You shall not covet your neighbor's wife, or his manservant or maidservant, his ox or donkey, or anything that belongs to your neighbor."

When the people saw the thunder and lightning and heard the trumpet and saw the mountain in smoke, they trembled with fear. They stayed at a distance and said to Moses, "Speak to us yourself and we will listen. But do not have God speak to us or we will die."

Moses said to the people, "Do not be afraid. God has come to test you, so that the fear of God will be with you to keep you from sinning."

The people remained at a distance, while Moses approached the thick darkness where God was.

[*After giving the Hebrews the law, Moses also tells the Hebrews what will happen if they obey or disobey their God.*]

If you fully obey the Lord your God and carefully follow all his commands I give you today, the Lord your God will set you high above all the nations on earth. All these blessings will come upon you and accompany you if you obey the Lord your God:

You will be blessed in the city and blessed in the country.

The fruit of your womb will be blessed, and the crops of your land and the young of your livestock — the calves of your herds and the lambs of your flocks.

Your basket and your kneading trough will be blessed.

You will be blessed when you come in and blessed when you go out.

The Lord will grant that the enemies who rise up against you will be defeated before you. They will come at you from one direction but flee from you in seven.

The Lord will send a blessing on your barns and on everything you put your hand to. The Lord your God will bless you in the land he is giving you.

The Lord will establish you as his holy people, as he promised you on oath, if you keep the commands of the Lord your God and walk in his ways. . . .

However, if you do not obey the Lord your God and do not carefully follow all his commands and decrees I am giving you today, all these curses will come upon you and overtake you:

You will be cursed in the city and cursed in the country.

Your basket and your kneading trough will be cursed.

The fruit of your womb will be cursed, and the crops of your land, and the calves of your herds and the lambs of your flocks.

You will be cursed when you come in and cursed when you go out.

The Lord will send on you curses, confusion and rebuke in everything you put your hand to, until you are destroyed and come to sudden ruin because of the evil you have done in forsaking him. The Lord will plague you with diseases until he has destroyed you from the land you are entering to possess. The Lord will strike you with wasting disease, with fever and inflammation, with scorching heat and drought, with blight and mildew, which will plague you until you perish. The sky over your head will be bronze, the ground beneath you iron. The Lord will turn the rain of your country into dust and powder; it will come down from the skies until you are destroyed.

The Lord will cause you to be defeated before your enemies. You will come at them from one direction but flee from them in seven, and you will become a thing of horror to all the kingdoms on earth. Your carcasses will be food for all the birds of the air and the beasts of the earth, and there will be no one to frighten them away.

READING AND DISCUSSION QUESTIONS

1. Consider the description of God's descent upon Mount Sinai and the following passage: "And the Lord said to [Moses], 'Go down and warn the people so they do not force their way through to see the Lord and many of them perish.'" What does this passage reveal about the Hebrews' conception of their God's power?

2. Why does God forbid the creation and worship of idols?

3. What incentives are there for the Hebrews to obey their God's commands?

DOCUMENT 2-3

Book of 2 Kings: Jerusalem Saved

701 B.C.E.

King Hezekiah's (heh-zeh-KAI-ah) predecessors had agreed to pay tribute to the Assyrians in exchange for peace. After Hezekiah took the throne, he started a series of religious and political reforms. In order to ensure that the Hebrew God was worshipped according to Hebrew Law, he destroyed any temples outside of Jerusalem. His refusal to pay tribute to King Sennacherib of Assyria and his alliance with Egypt was part of a larger strategy meant to restore the independence of his kingdom, and perhaps recapture the glories of the kingdom of David and Solomon. In his own account, Sennacherib claims victory over Hezekiah and his people. The Hebrew Bible, however, tells a different story.

In the fourteenth year of King Hezekiah's reign, Sennacherib king of Assyria attacked all the fortified cities of Judah and captured them. So Hezekiah king of Judah sent this message to the king of Assyria at Lachish: "I have done wrong. Withdraw from me, and I will pay whatever you demand of me." . . . So Hezekiah gave him all the silver that was found in the temple of the Lord and in the treasuries of the royal palace. . . .

The king of Assyria sent his supreme commander, his chief officer and his field commander with a large army, from Lachish to King Hezekiah at Jerusalem. . . . The field commander said to them, "Tell Hezekiah: This is what the great king, the king of Assyria, says: 'On what are you basing this confidence of yours? You say you have strategy and military strength — but you speak only empty words. On whom are you depending, that you rebel against me? Look now, you are depending on Egypt, that splintered reed of a staff, which pierces a man's hand and wounds him if he leans on it! Such is Pharaoh king of Egypt to all who depend on him.'" . . .

Then the commander stood and called out in Hebrew: "Hear the word of the great king, the king of Assyria! This is what the king says: Do not let Hezekiah deceive you. He cannot deliver you from my hand. Do not let Hezekiah persuade you to trust in the Lord when he says, 'The Lord will surely deliver us; this city will not be given into the hand of the king of Assyria.' Do not listen to Hezekiah. This is what the king of Assyria

---

2 Kings 18:13–15; 19:1–19, 35–37.

says: 'Make peace with me and come out to me. Then every one of you will eat from his own vine and fig tree and drink water from his own cistern, until I come and take you to a land like your own, a land of grain and new wine, a land of bread and vineyards, a land of olive trees and honey. Choose life and not death!'"

Then Eliakim son of Hilkiah the palace administrator, Shebna the secretary, and Joah son of Asaph the recorder went to Hezekiah, with their clothes torn, and told him what the field commander had said.

Now Sennacherib received a report that Tirhakah, the king of Egypt, was marching out to fight against him. So he again sent messengers to Hezekiah with this word: "Say to Hezekiah king of Judah: Do not let the god you depend on deceive you when he says, 'Jerusalem will not be handed over to the king of Assyria.' Surely you have heard what the kings of Assyria have done to all the countries, destroying them completely. And will you be delivered? Did the gods of the nations that were destroyed by my forefathers deliver them: the gods of Gozan, Haran, Rezeph, and the people of Eden who were in Tel Assar?" . . .

Hezekiah received the letter from the messengers and read it. Then he went up to the temple of the Lord and spread it out before the Lord. And Hezekiah prayed to the Lord: "O Lord, God of Israel, enthroned between the cherubim,[2] you alone are God over all the kingdoms of the earth. You have made heaven and earth. Give ear, O Lord, and hear; open your eyes, O Lord, and see; listen to the words Sennacherib has sent to insult the living God. It is true, O Lord, that the Assyrian kings have laid waste these nations and their lands. They have thrown their gods into the fire and destroyed them, for they were not gods but only wood and stone, fashioned by men's hands. Now, O Lord our God, deliver us from his hand, so that all kingdoms on earth may know that you alone, O Lord, are God." . . .

That night the angel of the Lord went out and put to death a hundred and eighty-five thousand men in the Assyrian camp. When the people got up the next morning — there were all the dead bodies! So Sennacherib king of Assyria broke camp and withdrew. He returned to Nineveh and stayed there.

One day, while he was worshiping in the temple of his god Nisroch,[3] his sons Adrammelech and Sharezer cut him down with the sword, and they escaped to the land of Ararat. And Esarhaddon his son succeeded him as king.

---

[2] **cherubim**: Angels.
[3] **Nisroch**: The Assyrian god of agriculture.

READING AND DISCUSSION QUESTIONS

1. How does Sennacherib try to make Hezekiah submit to the Assyrians?

2. What prevented the Assyrian army from taking Jerusalem?

3. How do the Hebrews explain their deliverance from Sennacherib's forces?

VIEWPOINTS

The Legacy of Cyrus

DOCUMENT 2-4

CYRUS OF PERSIA
Ruling an Empire
ca. 550 B.C.E.

Cyrus the Great (r. 559–530 B.C.E.) was a king of Persia who expanded his rule to create one of the largest empires in the world up to that time. He conquered the Medes (MEEDS), to whom the Persians had been subject; the Lydians in what is now western Turkey; and the Neo-Babylonians in the heart of Mesopotamia. He also established his rule over vast areas of central Asia. Cyrus followed a policy of fair treatment for conquered peoples, freeing the Jews from their "Babylonian captivity" and allowing them to return to their homeland. The following selection is Cyrus's account of his legacy.

I am Cyrus, king of the world, great king, legitimate king, king of Babylon, king of Sumer and Akkad, king of the four rims [of the earth], son of Cambyses, great king, king of Anshan, grandson of Cyrus, great king, king of Anshan, descendant of Teispes, great king, king of Anshan, of a family [which] always [exercised] kingship; whose rule Bel and Nabu[4] love, whom they want as king to please their hearts.

From James B. Pritchard, ed., *Ancient Near Eastern Texts Relating to the Old Testament*, 3d ed. (Princeton, N.J.: Princeton University Press, 1969), pp. 315–316.

[4] **Bel and Nabu:** Babylonian gods.

When I entered Babylon as a friend and [when] I established the seat of government in the palace of the ruler under jubilation and rejoicing. Marduk,[5] the great lord (induced) the magnanimous inhabitants of Babylon (to love me), and I was daily endeavoring to worship him. My numerous troops walked around in Babylon in peace, I did not allow anybody to terrorize [any place] of the [country of Sumer] and Akkad. I strove for peace in Babylon, [I abolished] the [labor tribute] which was against their [social] standing. I brought relief to their dilapidated housings, putting an end to their complaints. Marduk, the great Lord, was well pleased with my deeds and sent friendly blessings to myself, Cyrus, the king who worships him, to Cambyses, my son, the offspring of my loins, as well as to all my troops, and we all [praised] his great [godhead] joyously, standing before him in peace.

All the kings of the entire world from the Upper to the Lower Sea, those who are seated in throne rooms, [those who] live in other [types of buildings as well as] all the kings of the West land living in tents, brought their heavy tributes and kissed my feet in Babylon. [As to the region] from . . . as far as Ashur and Susa, Agade, Eshnuna, the towns of Zamban, Me-Turnu, Der, as well as the region of the Gutium, I returned to [these] sacred cities on the other sides of the Tigris, the sanctuaries of which have been ruins for a long time, the images which [used] to live therein and established for them permanent sanctuaries. I [also] gathered all their [former] inhabitants and returned [to them] their habitations. Furthermore, I resettled upon the command of Marduk, the great lord, all the gods of Sumer and Akkad who Nabonidus[6] has brought into Babylon to the anger of the lord of the gods, unharmed, in the [former] chapels, the places which make them happy.

May all the gods whom I have resettled in their sacred cities ask daily Bel and Nabu for a long life for me and may they recommend me [to him]; to Marduk, my lord, they may say this: "Cyrus, the king who worships you, and Cambyses, his son, ... all of them I settled in a peaceful place . . . ducks and doves . . . I endeavored to repair their dwelling places. . . ."

---

[5] **Marduk**: The Mesopotamian god who created humans. See Document 1-1.
[6] **Nabonidus**: The last king of the Neo-Babylonian Empire, whom Cyrus overthrew.

READING AND DISCUSSION QUESTIONS

1. Why does Cyrus claim that he entered Babylon as a friend, and what orders did he give his troops about how to treat the Babylonians?

2. What reforms and improvements did Cyrus bring to Babylon? Why would Cyrus solve problems that he had not created in the first place?

3. How did Cyrus treat people who had been displaced from their homes? How did he treat the gods of the people he conquered?

DOCUMENT 2-5

Book of Isaiah: Blessings for Cyrus

ca. 550 B.C.E.

The Hebrews had been exiles in Babylon since King Nebuchadnezzar conquered Jerusalem in 586 B.C.E. After Cyrus and his Persian troops conquered Babylon, Cyrus allowed the Hebrews to return to Jerusalem to rebuild the city and the temple to their God. In the Hebrew Bible, he is included as one who did the work of their God, knowingly or not.

"This is what the Lord says to his anointed,
  to Cyrus, whose right hand I take hold of
  to subdue nations before him
  and to strip kings of their armor,
  to open doors before him
  so that gates will not be shut:
I will go before you
  and will level the mountains;
  I will break down gates of bronze
  and cut through bars of iron.
I will give you the treasures of darkness,
  riches stored in secret places,
  so that you may know that I am the Lord,
  the God of Israel, who summons you by name.

Isaiah 45:1–8; 13–14.

For the sake of Jacob[7] my servant,
>   of Israel my chosen,
>   I summon you by name
>   and bestow on you a title of honor,
>   though you do not acknowledge me. . . .
I am the Lord, and there is no other;
>   apart from me there is no God.
>   I will strengthen you,
>   though you have not acknowledged me,
so that from the rising of the sun
>   to the place of its setting
>   men may know there is none besides me.
>   I am the Lord and there is no other.
I form the light and create darkness,
>   I bring prosperity and create disaster;
>   I, the Lord, do all these things.
"You heavens above, rain down righteousness;
>   let the clouds shower it down.
>   Let the earth open wide,
>   let salvation spring up,
>   let righteousness grow with it;
>   I, the Lord, have created it . . .
I will raise up Cyrus in my righteousness:
>   I will make all his ways straight.
>   He will rebuild my city
>   and set my exiles free,
>   but not for a price or reward,
>   says the Lord Almighty."
This is what the LORD says:
>   "The products of Egypt and the merchandise of Cush,[8]
>   and those tall Sabeans[9] —
>   they will come over to you
>   and will be yours;
>   they will trudge behind you,
>   coming over to you in chains.
>   They will bow down before you

---

[7] **Jacob**: One of the Hebrew ancestors; also known as Israel.
[8] **Cush**: A region in what is now Sudan.
[9] **Sabeans**: Inhabitants of the southern Arabian peninsula.

and plead with you, saying,
'Surely God is with you, and there is no other;
there is no other god.'"

READING AND DISCUSSION QUESTIONS

1. Why is the Hebrew God pleased with Cyrus?
2. What promises does this God make to Cyrus?
3. What reasons does the Hebrew God have for helping Cyrus?

DOCUMENT 2-6

ZOROASTER

Gatha 30: Good Thoughts, Good Words, Good Deeds

ca. 600 B.C.E.

The Persian priest Zoroaster (zo-ro-ASS-tuhr), also known as Zarathustra (zar-uh-THUH-struh), reformed the religion of his people, separating the traditional deities into two groups. One group, led by Ahuramazda (ah-HOOR-uh-MAZ-duh), promoted goodness and ethical behavior; the other, led by Ahriman (AH-ree-mahn), was the force behind all evil. The names of the other gods were often personifications of an inner quality, such as Good Thought and Piety. Embraced by King Darius (dah-REE-uhs; r. 521–486 B.C.E.), Zoroastrianism (zo-ro-ASS-tree-uh-nihz-uhm) remained a dominant belief in Persia for centuries. The passage below is Gatha 30, one of seventeen poems believed to be written by Zoroaster himself. The Gathas are part of a larger text known as the Yasna, which contains liturgical services, prayers, and hymns to the good gods.

From Charles F. Horne, ed., *The Sacred Books and Early Literature of the East* (New York and London: Park, Austin, and Lipscombe, 1917), pp. 23–25.

Now will I proclaim to those who will hear the things that the understanding man should remember, for hymns unto Ahura and prayers to Good Thought; also the joy that is with the heavenly lights, which through Right shall be beheld by him who wisely thinks.

Hear with your ears the best things; look upon them with clear-seeing thought, for decision between the two Beliefs, each man for himself before the Great Consummation,[10] bethinking you that it be accomplished to our pleasure.

Now the two primal Spirits, who revealed themselves in vision as Twins, are the Better and the Bad in thought and word and action. And between these two the wise once chose aright, the foolish not so.

And when these twin Spirits came together in the beginning, they established Life and Not-Life, and that at the last the Worst Existence shall be to the followers of the Lie, but the Best Thought to him that follows Right.

Of these twin Spirits he that followed the Lie chose doing the worst things; the holiest Spirit chose Right, he that clothes himself with the heavens as a garment. So likewise they that are eager to please Ahura Mazda [choose] dutiful actions.

Between these two the demons also chose not aright, for infatuation came upon them as they took counsel together, so that they chose the Worst Thought. Then they rushed together to Violence, that they might enfeeble the world of man.

And to them (humans) came Dominion, Good Thought, and Right; and Piety gave continued life of their bodies and indestructibility. . . .

So when there comes the punishment of these evil ones, then, O Mazda, at thy command shall Good Thought establish the Dominion. . . .

So may we be those that make this world advance! O Mazda, and you other Ahuras,[11] gather together the Assembly, . . . that thoughts may meet where Wisdom is at home.

Then truly on the Lie shall come destruction [but those who choose good] shall be partakers in the promised reward in the fair abode of Good Thought, of Mazda, and of Right.

If, O mortals, you follow those commandments that Mazda hath ordained — of happiness and pain, the long punishment for the liars, and blessings for the righteous — then hereafter shall ye have bliss.

---

[10] **Great Consummation**: The end of the world.

[11] **Ahuras**: The good gods.

READING AND DISCUSSION QUESTIONS

1. How does Zoroaster explain the creation of all things that exist? What role do humans play in creation?

2. What are the attributes of the good gods and the evil gods?

3. How does a person become a follower of either the good gods or the bad gods? What happens to the good people and the evil people at the end of the world?

COMPARATIVE QUESTIONS

1. What are some differences or similarities between the Mesopotamian (Document 1-1), Hebrew, and Zoroastrian explanations for creation? How do the tones of each document compare?

2. What, if any, differences can you find between man as created by God in Genesis and man as commanded by God in Exodus and Deuteronomy? What kind of God is the God in each document?

3. How do the "Hymn to Aton" (Document 1-5) and the Hebrew Law compare in their attitudes toward foreign peoples?

4. How could the Hebrew Law be used to explain the Hebrews' deliverance from the Assyrians? How could it explain Cyrus's restoration of Jerusalem to the Hebrews?

5. On what points do the two documents on Cyrus agree? What do their differences suggest about the differences between the Hebrew and Persian peoples?

CHAPTER 3

The Development of Classical Greece

ca. 2000–338 B.C.E.

The earliest literature of the Greek civilization reflects the Greeks' intense interest in examining the world as a way to understand themselves, their gods, and their surroundings. Through their epic poems, written around 800 B.C.E., Homer and Hesiod provided explanations for how the gods worked in the world and how humans should behave. Around this time the Greeks developed the polis system, in which independent communities defined their own political systems and societies. The poleis differed widely in their ideas of what made for an effective government, however, and their independent spirit made alliances with other communities difficult to maintain. Conflict between the two greatest poleis, Athens and Sparta, eventually led to the destruction of much of Greece's progress. However, the warfare also marked a time of intellectual and cultural flourishing, as philosophers sought rational explanations for human nature and the world around them, lyric poets explored human thoughts and emotions in verse, and historians recorded the triumphs and failures of their civilization. The documents in this chapter address the Greek interest in individuals and communities, and the proper relationship between the two. In a related theme, they also discuss the proper definition of justice in a civilized world.

DOCUMENT 3-1

HOMER

The Odyssey: *Odysseus and the Sirens*

ca. 800 B.C.E.

Homer's Odyssey, a masterwork of Western literature and an important cultural, religious, and social record of Greek civilization, is one of the few historical documents that survive from the early period of Greek history. Composed in dactylic hexameter, a form of verse that is usually sung, the Odyssey was probably passed down orally. It tells the story of hero Odysseus's ten-year journey home to Ithaca after his victory in the Trojan War (possibly 1200 or 1100 B.C.E.). The Odyssey begins in the middle of this journey, and Homer uses flashback to supply background information as his protagonist's struggles unfold. In the following passage, Odysseus tells his men how the goddess Circe (sir-SEE) warned him about the dangers they will encounter on their journey.

At last, and sore at heart, I told my shipmates,
"Friends . . . it's wrong for only one or two
to know the revelations that lovely Circe
made to me alone. I'll tell you all,
so we can die with our eyes wide open now
or escape our fate and certain death together.
First, she warns, we must steer clear of the Sirens,
their enchanting song, their meadow starred with flowers.
I alone was to hear their voices, so she said,
but you must bind me with tight chafing ropes
so I cannot move a muscle, bound to the spot,
erect at the mast-block, lashed by ropes to the mast.
And if I plead, commanding you to set me free,
then lash me faster, rope pressing on rope.

So I informed my shipmates point by point,
all the while our trim ship was speeding toward

From Homer, *The Odyssey*, trans. Robert Fagles (London: Penguin Books, 1996), pp. 276–279.

the sirens' island, driven by the brisk wind.
But then — the wind fell in an instant,
all glazed to a dead calm . . .
a mysterious power hushed the heaving swells.
The oarsmen leapt to their feet, struck the sail,
stowed it deep in the hold and sat to the oarlock,
thrashing with polished oars, frothing the water white.
Now with a sharp sword I sliced an ample wheel of beeswax
down into pieces, kneaded them in my two strong hands
and the wax grew soft, worked by my strength
and Helios'[1] burning rays, the sun at high noon,
and I stopped the ears of my comrades one by one.
They bound me hand and foot in the tight ship —
erect at the mast-block, lashed by ropes to the mast —
and rowed and churned the whitecaps stroke on stroke.
We were just offshore as far as a man's shout can carry,
scudding close, when the Sirens sensed at once a ship
was racing past and burst in their high, thrilling song:
"Come closer, famous Odysseus — Achaea's[2] pride and glory —
moor your ship on our coast so you can hear our song!
Never has any sailor passed our shores in his black craft
until he has heard the honeyed voices pouring from our lips,
and once he hears to his heart's content sails on, a wiser man.
We know all the pains that the Greeks and Trojans once endured
on the spreading plain of Troy when the gods willed it so —
all that comes to pass on the fertile earth, we know it all!"

So they sent their ravishing voices out across the air
and the heart inside me throbbed to listen longer.
I signaled the crew with frowns to set me free —
they flung themselves at the oars and rowed on harder,
Perimedes and Eurylochus springing up at once
to bind me faster with rope chafing on rope.
But once we'd left the Sirens fading in our wake,
once we could hear their song no more, their urgent call —
my steadfast crew was quick to remove the wax I'd used
to seal their ears and loosed the bonds that lashed me.

---

[1] **Helios**: Greek sun god.
[2] **Achaea**: Greece.

[*Now Odysseus must decide how to navigate his ship past two monsters,*
Scylla, who is close to the rocks, and Charybdis, who creates a whirlpool.
Circe warned him that if he avoids one, he will come too close to the other.
She suggested sailing past Scylla as quickly as possible, instructing Odys-
seus not to waste time putting on armor.]

We'd scarcely put that island astern when suddenly
I saw smoke and heavy breakers, heard their booming thunder.
The men were terrified — oarblades flew from their grip,
clattering down to splash in the vessel's wash.
She lay there, dead in the water . . .
no hands to tug the blades that drove her on.
But I strode down the decks to rouse my crewmen,
halting beside each one with a bracing, winning word:
"Friends, we're hardly strangers at meeting danger —
and this is no worse than what we faced
when Cyclops penned us up in his vaulted cave
with crushing force! But even from there my courage,
my presence of mind and tactics saved us all,
and we will live to remember *this* someday,
I have no doubt. Up now, follow my orders,
all of us work as one! . . .
You, helmsman, here's your order — burn it in your mind,
the steering-oar of our rolling ship is in your hands.
Keep her clear of that smoke and surging breakers,
head for those crags or she'll catch you off guard,
she'll yaw over there — you'll plunge us all in ruin!"

So I shouted. They snapped to each command.
No mention of Scylla — how to fight that nightmare? —
for fear the men would panic, desert their oars
and huddle down and stow themselves away.
But now I cleared my mind of Circe's orders —
cramping my style, urging me not to arm at all.
I donned my heroic armor, seized long spears
in both my hands and marched out on the half-deck,
forward, hoping from there to catch the first glimpse
of Scylla, ghoul of the cliffs, swooping to kill my men.
But nowhere could I make her out — and my eyes ached
scanning that mist-bound rock face top to bottom.

* * *

Now wailing in fear, we rowed on up those straits,
Scylla to starboard, dreaded Charybdis off to port,
her horrible whirlpool gulping the sea-surge down, down
but when she spewed it up — like a cauldron over a raging fire,
all her churning depths would seethe and heave — exploding spray
showering down to splatter the peaks of both crags at once!
But when she swallowed the sea-surge down her gaping maw
the whole abyss lay bare and the rocks around her roared,
terrible, deafening —
                 bedrock showed down deep, boiling
black with sand —
                and ashen terror gripped the men.
But now, fearing death, all eyes fixed on Charybdis —
now Scylla snatched six men from our hollow ship,
the toughest, strongest hands I had, and glancing
backward over the decks, searching for my crew
I could see their hands and feet already hoisted,
flailing, high, higher, over my head, look —
wailing down at me, comrades riven in agony,
shrieking out my name for one last time! . . . so now they writhed,
gasping as Scylla swung them up her cliff and there
at her cavern's mouth she bolted them down raw —
screaming out, flinging their arms toward me,
lost in that mortal struggle. . . .
Of all the pitiful things I've had to witness,
suffering, searching out the pathways of the sea,
this wrenched my heart the most.

READING AND DISCUSSION QUESTIONS

1. What kind of a leader is Odysseus? How do his decisions affect his men? How does he balance their needs with his own plans?

2. Why does Odysseus ignore Circe's advice about Scylla and Charybdis, even though her plan for escaping the Sirens worked?

3. Of all the Greek heroes, Odysseus is described as the most resourceful. In what ways does this passage support that assessment?

4. Why might Homer have composed this story? Is it meant to be a history lesson, or is it for instruction, entertainment, or some other purpose?

DOCUMENT 3-2

HESIOD

Works and Days

ca. 800 B.C.E.

Hesiod, along with Homer, is one of the earliest known sources for Greek civilization. His Theogony *covers the history of the gods, while his* Works and Days *addresses how humans should act. Along with moral instructions, Hesiod also provides recommendations on how to manage farms and households. The text is addressed to his younger brother, Perses, who cheated Hesiod out of his inheritance. When Hesiod took the matter to the judges, Perses bribed them to decide in his favor.*

But you, Perses, listen to right and do not foster violence; for violence is bad for a poor man. Even the prosperous cannot easily bear its burden, but is weighed down under it when he has fallen into delusion. The better path is to go by on the other side towards justice. . . .

But they who give straight judgments to strangers and to the men of the land, and go not aside from what is just, their city flourishes, and the people prosper in it: Peace, the nurse of children, is abroad in their land, and all-seeing Zeus[3] never decrees cruel war against them. Neither famine nor disaster ever haunt men who do true justice; but lightheartedly they tend the fields which are all their care. The earth bears them victual in plenty, and on the mountains the oak bears acorns upon the top and bees in the midst. Their woolly sheep are laden with fleeces; their women bear children like their parents. They flourish continually with good things, and do not travel on ships, for the grain-giving earth bears them fruit. . . .

And there is virgin Justice, the daughter of Zeus, who is honored and reverenced among the gods who dwell on Olympus, and whenever anyone hurts her with lying slander, she sits beside her father, Zeus the son of Cronos, and tells him of men's wicked heart, until the people pay for the mad folly of their princes who, evilly minded, pervert judgment and give sentence crookedly. Keep watch against this, you princes, and make

---

From Hesiod, Homer, and Hugh Gerald Evelyn-White, *Hesiod, the Homeric Hymns, and Homerica* (New York: G. P. Putnam's Sons, 1920), pp. 19–33.

[3] **Zeus**: Leading god in the Greek pantheon.

straight your judgments, you who devour bribes; put crooked judgments altogether from your thoughts. . . .

To you, foolish Perses, I will speak good sense. Badness can be got easily . . . : the road to her is smooth, and she lives very near us. But between us and Goodness the gods have placed the sweat of our brows: long and steep is the path that leads to her, and it is rough at the first; but when a man has reached the top, then is she easy to reach, though before that she was hard.

That man is altogether best who considers all things himself and marks what will be better afterwards and at the end; and he, again, is good who listens to a good adviser; but whoever neither thinks for himself nor keeps in mind what another tells him, he is an unprofitable man. But do you at any rate, always remembering my charge, work, high-born Perses, that Hunger may hate you, and venerable Demeter[4] richly crowned may love you and fill your barn with food; for Hunger is altogether a good comrade for the sluggard. Both gods and men are angry with a man who lives idle, for in nature he is like the stingless drones who waste the labor of the bees, eating without working; but let it be your care to order your work properly, that in the right season your barns may be full of victual. Through work men grow rich in flocks and substance, and working they are much better loved by the immortals. Work is no disgrace: it is idleness which is a disgrace. . . .

Let the wage promised to a friend be fixed; . . . and get a witness; for trust and mistrust, alike ruin men. . . .

First of all, get a house, and a woman and an ox for the plough — a slave woman and not a wife, to follow the oxen as well — and make everything ready at home, so that you may not have to ask of another, and he refuse you, and so, because you are in lack, the season pass by and your work come to nothing. Do not put your work off till tomorrow and the day after; for a sluggish worker does not fill his barn, nor one who puts off his work: industry makes work go well, but a man who puts off work is always at hand-grips with ruin.

READING AND DISCUSSION QUESTIONS

1. Based on this document, what kind of society do the Greeks have? What ranks does Greek society include?

---

[4] **Demeter**: Goddess of agriculture and fertility.

2. According to Hesiod, what sort of behavior do the gods expect of humanity?

3. What qualities does Hesiod value in a person?

4. How does Hesiod define justice?

DOCUMENT 3-3

ARCHILOCHUS OF PAROS, SAPPHO OF LESBOS, ANACREON OF TEOS

Lyric Poems

ca. 700–450 B.C.E.

One of the literary forms that developed after the age of Homer and Hesiod was the lyric poem. These poems show that Greek literature extended beyond just tales of the gods or the deeds of heroes long gone. The lyric poems reflect the Greek interest in oneself as an individual. Not much is known about these authors. Archilochus of Paros (ca. 680–652 B.C.E.) was a soldier from a noble family. He is generally considered the first of the lyric poets. The only source of information about the life of Sappho of Lesbos (ca. 620–550 B.C.E.) is her fragmented poetry. The references to love between women in her work has led to her association with homosexuality. Anacreon of Teos (563–478 B.C.E.) fled his home city after it was captured by the Persian army in 540. He served the tyrant Polycrates after he captured the city of Samos, then moved to Athens after his patron died. It is believed that he returned to Teos later in life and died there.

ARCHILOCHUS OF PAROS

Some barbarian is waving a shield, since I was obliged to
leave that perfectly good piece of equipment behind
under a bush. But I got away, so what does it matter?
Let the shield go; I can buy another one equally good.

Archilochus of Paros: From Richard Lattimore, *Greek Lyrics* (Chicago: University of Chicago Press, 1960), p. 2.

Sappho of Lesbos

I have not one word from her
Frankly I wish I were dead
When she left, she wept
a great deal; she said to me, "This parting must be
endured, Sappho. I go unwillingly."
I said, "Go, and be happy
but remember (you know
well) whom you leave shackled by love
"If you forget me, think
of our gifts to Aphrodite
and all the loveliness that we shared
"all the violet tiaras,
braided rosebuds, dill and
crocus twined around your young neck
"myrrh poured on your head
and on soft mats girls with
all that they most wished for beside them
"while no voices chanted
choruses without ours,
no woodlot bloomed in spring without song . . ."

Anacreon of Teos

"Old Age"
The women tell me every day
That all my bloom has past away.
"Behold," the pretty wantons cry,
"Behold this mirror with a sigh;
The locks upon thy brow are few,
And, like the rest, they're withering too!"
Whether decline has thinned my hair,
I'm sure I neither know, nor care;
But this I know and this I feel,
As onward to the tomb I steal,
That still as death approaches nearer,

Sappho of Lesbos: From Sappho, *Sappho*, trans. Mary Barnard (Berkeley: University of California Press, 1958), p. 42.

Anacreon of Teos: From John Henry Wright, ed., *Masterpieces of Greek Literature* (Boston: Houghton Mifflin, 1902), pp. 60–61.

The joys of life are sweeter, dearer;
And had I but an hour to live,
That little hour to bliss I'd give.

READING AND DISCUSSION QUESTIONS

1. What topics concern these poets?
2. How do these poems demonstrate the Greek interest in individuality?

VIEWPOINTS

Political Philosophy

DOCUMENT 3-4

THUCYDIDES

The History of the Peloponnesian War:
Pericles' Funeral Oration

ca. 400 B.C.E.

Thucydides (thoo-SIH-dih-deez) was an Athenian general who lost a battle in the early years of the Peloponnesian War (431–404 B.C.E.). Exiled from Athens, he spent the remainder of the war tracking the progress of the conflict and ultimately wrote its history. Thucydides's work is one of the earliest examples of historical writing in Western civilization, as well as an in-depth look at how the war affected Greek civilization. The selection that follows is from the first years of the war, when Pericles (PEHR-uh-kleez), the leading Athenian statesman, gave this eulogy in memory of those who died in the war.

But before I praise the dead, I should like to point out by what principles of action we rose to power, and under what institutions and through what manner of life our empire became great. . . .

From Thucydides, *The History of the Peloponnesian War*, 2d ed., trans. Benjamin Jowett (London: Henry Frowde, 1900), pp. 126–132.

Our form of government does not enter into rivalry with the institutions of others. Our government does not copy our neighbors, but is an example to them. It is true that we are called a democracy, for the administration is in the hands of the many and not of the few. But while the law secures equal justice to all alike in their private disputes, the claim of excellence is also recognized; and when a citizen is in any way distinguished, he is preferred to the public service, not as a matter of privilege, but as the reward of merit. Neither is poverty a bar, but a man may benefit his country whatever the obscurity of his condition. There is no exclusiveness in our public life, and in our private intercourse we are not suspicious of one another, nor angry with our neighbor if he does what he likes; we do not put on sour looks at him which, though harmless, are not pleasant. While we are thus unconstrained in our private intercourse, a spirit of reverence pervades our public acts; we are prevented from doing wrong by respect for the authorities and for the laws, having an especial regard to those which are ordained for the protection of the injured as well as those unwritten laws which bring upon the transgressor of them the reprobation of the general sentiment.

And we have not forgotten to provide for our weary spirits many relaxations from toil; we have regular games and sacrifices throughout the year; our homes are beautiful and elegant; and the delight which we daily feel in all these things helps to banish melancholy. Because of the greatness of our city the fruits of the whole earth flow in upon us; so that we enjoy the goods of other countries as freely as our own.

Then, again, our military training is in many respects superior to that of our adversaries. Our city is thrown open to the world, and we never expel a foreigner and prevent him from seeing or learning anything of which the secret if revealed to an enemy might profit him. We rely not upon management or trickery, but upon our own hearts and hands. And in the matter of education, whereas they from early youth are always undergoing laborious exercises which are to make them brave, we live at ease, and yet are equally ready to face the perils which they face. And here is the proof: The Lacedaemonians[5] come into Attica not by themselves, but with their whole confederacy following; we go alone into a neighbor's country; and although our opponents are fighting for their homes and we on a foreign soil, we have seldom any difficulty in overcoming them. Our enemies have never yet felt our united strength, the care of a navy divides our attention, and on land we are obliged to send our own citizens everywhere. But

---

[5] **Lacedaemonians**: Spartans.

they, if they meet and defeat a part of our army, are as proud as if they had routed us all, and when defeated they pretend to have been vanquished by us all.

If then we prefer to meet danger with a light heart but without laborious training, and with a courage which is gained by habit and not enforced by law, are we not greatly the gainers? Since we do not anticipate the pain, although, when the hour comes, we can be as brave as those who never allow themselves to rest; thus too our city is equally admirable in peace and in war. For we are lovers of the beautiful, yet simple in our tastes, and we cultivate the mind without loss of manliness. Wealth we employ, not for talk and ostentation, but when there is a real use for it. To avow poverty with us is no disgrace; the true disgrace is in doing nothing to avoid it. An Athenian citizen does not neglect the state because he takes care of his own household; and even those of us who are engaged in business have a very fair idea of politics. We alone regard a man who takes no interest in public affairs, not as a harmless, but as a useless character; and if few of us are orignators, we are all sound judges of a policy. The great impediment to action is, in our opinion, no discussion, but the want of that knowledge which is gained by discussion preparatory to action. For we have a peculiar power of thinking before we act, and of acting, too, whereas other men are courageous from ignorance but hesitate upon reflection. And they are surely to be esteemed the bravest spirits who, having the clearest sense both of the pains and pleasures of life, do not on that account shrink from danger. In doing good, again, we are unlike others; we make our friends by conferring, not by receiving favors. . . .

To sum up: I say that Athens is the school of Hellas,[6] and that the individual Athenian in his own person seems to have the power of adapting himself to the most varied forms of action with the utmost versatility and grace. This is no passing and idle word, but truth and fact; and the assertion is verified by the position to which these qualities have raised the state. For in the hour of trial Athens alone among her contemporaries is superior to the report of her. . . .

I have dwelt upon the greatness of Athens because I want to show you that we are contending for a higher prize than those who enjoy none of these privileges, and to establish by manifest proof the merit of these men whom I am now commemorating. Their loftiest praise has been already spoken. For in magnifying the city I have magnified them, and men like them whose virtues made her glorious.

---

[6] **Hellas**: Greece.

READING AND DISCUSSION QUESTIONS

1. According to Pericles, what makes Athens so great? What does democracy mean to him?

2. How is Athens different from other Greek cities? What do Athenians care about that other Greeks don't?

3. What is the relationship between the individual and the community in Athens? Which is more important to Pericles?

DOCUMENT 3-5

PLATO

The Republic: *The Allegory of the Cave*

ca. 360 B.C.E.

The Peloponnesian War ended badly for the Athenians: they lost to the Spartans, the Athenian democracy fell, and the city came under the rule of tyrants. The Athenian democracy was eventually restored, but was unstable. During that time, the philosopher Socrates (SOK-ruh-teez; ca. 470–399 B.C.E.) gathered a following of young Athenians as he pointed out the shortcomings of the wealthy, powerful, and wise. Socrates was put on trial and executed for impiety and corrupting the youth. After his death, his student Plato (PLAY-toh; 427–347 B.C.E.) wrote The Republic, *a study of the ideal state. Much of the book is written in the form of an imagined dialogue. The section below is a discussion between Socrates, who does most of the talking, and Plato's older brother Glaucon, who provides the short responses.*

SOCRATES: And now, let me show in a figure how far our nature is enlightened or unenlightened: — Behold! human beings living in a underground den, which has a mouth open towards the light and reaching all along the den; here they have been from their childhood, and have their legs and necks chained so that they cannot move, and can only see before them, being prevented by the chains from turning round their heads. Above and behind them a fire is blazing at a distance, and

From Plato, *The Dialogues of Plato*, vol. 2, trans. Benjamin Jowett (New York: Charles Scribner's Sons, 1914), pp. 265–274.

between the fire and the prisoners there is a raised way; and you will see, if you look, a low wall built along the way, like the screen which marionette players have in front of them, over which they show the puppets.

GLAUCON: I see.

SOCRATES: And do you see men passing along the wall carrying all sorts of vessels, and statues and figures of animals made of wood and stone and various materials, which appear over the wall? Some of them are talking, others silent.

GLAUCON: You have shown me a strange image, and they are strange prisoners.

SOCRATES: Like ourselves, and they see only their own shadows, or the shadows of one another, which the fire throws on the opposite wall of the cave?

GLAUCON: True; how could they see anything but the shadows if they were never allowed to move their heads?

SOCRATES: And of the objects which are being carried in like manner they would only see the shadows?

GLAUCON: Yes.

SOCRATES: And if they were able to converse with one another, would they not suppose that they were naming what was actually before them?

GLAUCON: Very true.

SOCRATES: And suppose further that the prison had an echo which came from the other side, would they not be sure to fancy when one of the passers-by spoke that the voice which they heard came from the passing shadow?

GLAUCON: No question.

SOCRATES: To them . . . the truth would be literally nothing but the shadows of the images.

GLAUCON: That is certain.

SOCRATES: And now look again, and see what will naturally follow if the prisoners are released and disabused of their error. At first, when any of them is liberated and compelled suddenly to stand up and turn his neck round and walk and look towards the light, he will suffer sharp pains; the glare will distress him, and he will be unable to see the realities of which in his former state he had seen the shadows; and then conceive some one saying to him, that what he saw before was an illusion, but that now, when he is approaching nearer to being and his eye is turned towards more real existence, he has a clearer vision, — what will be his reply? And you may further imagine that his instructor is pointing to the objects as they pass and requiring him to name them, —

will he not be perplexed? Will he not fancy that the shadows which he formerly saw are truer than the objects which are now shown to him?

GLAUCON: Far truer.

SOCRATES: And if he is compelled to look straight at the light, will he not have a pain in his eyes which will make him turn away to take refuge in the objects of vision which he can see, and which he will conceive to be in reality clearer than the things which are now being shown to him?

GLAUCON: True.

SOCRATES: And suppose once more, that he is reluctantly dragged up a steep and rugged ascent, and held fast until he's forced into the presence of the sun himself, is he not likely to be pained and irritated? When he approaches the light his eyes will be dazzled, and he will not be able to see anything at all of what are now called realities.

GLAUCON: Not all in a moment.

SOCRATES: He will require to grow accustomed to the sight of the upper world. And first he will see the shadows best, next the reflections of men and other objects in the water, and then the objects themselves; then he will gaze upon the light of the moon and the stars and the spangled heaven; and he will see the sky and the stars by night better than the sun or the light of the sun by day?

GLAUCON: Certainly.

SOCRATES: Last of all he will be able to see the sun, and not mere reflections of him in the water, but he will see him in his own proper place, and not in another; and he will contemplate him as he is.

GLAUCON: Certainly.

SOCRATES: He will then proceed to argue that this is he who gives the season and the years, and is the guardian of all that is in the visible world, and in a certain way the cause of all things which he and his fellows have been accustomed to behold?

GLAUCON: Clearly . . . he would first see the sun and then reason about it.

SOCRATES: And when he remembered his old habitation, and the wisdom of the den and his fellow-prisoners, do you not suppose that he would felicitate himself on the change, and pity them?

GLAUCON: Certainly, he would.

SOCRATES: And if they were in the habit of conferring honors among themselves on those who were quickest to observe the passing shadows and to remark which of them went before, and which followed after, and which were together; and who were therefore best able to draw conclusions as to the future, do you think that he would care for such honors and glories, or envy the possessors of them? . . .

GLAUCON: Yes, I think that he would rather suffer anything than entertain these false notions and live in this miserable manner.

SOCRATES: Imagine once more . . . such a one coming suddenly out of the sun to be replaced in his old situation; would he not be certain to have his eyes full of darkness?

GLAUCON: To be sure.

SOCRATES: And if there were a contest, and he had to compete in measuring the shadows with the prisoners who had never moved out of the den, while his sight was still weak, and before his eyes had become steady . . . would he not be ridiculous? Men would say of him that up he went and down he came without his eyes; and that it was better not even to think of ascending; and if any one tried to loose another and lead him up to the light, let them only catch the offender, and they would put him to death.

GLAUCON: No question.

SOCRATES: The prison-house is the world of sight, the light of the fire is the sun, and you will not misapprehend me if you interpret the journey upwards to be the ascent of the soul into the intellectual world according to my poor belief, which, at your desire, I have expressed whether rightly or wrongly God knows. But, whether true or false, my opinion is that in the world of knowledge the idea of good appears last of all, and is seen only with an effort; and, when seen, is also inferred to be the universal author of all things beautiful and right, parent of light and of the lord of light in this visible world, and the immediate source of reason and truth in the intellectual; and that this is the power upon which he who would act rationally, either in public or private life must have his eye fixed.

GLAUCON: I agree as far as I am able to understand you.

SOCRATES: Moreover . . . you must not wonder that those who attain to this beatific vision are unwilling to descend to human affairs; for their souls are ever hastening into the upper world where they desire to dwell; which desire of theirs is very natural, if our allegory may be trusted.

GLAUCON: Yes, very natural.

SOCRATES: And is there anything surprising in one who passes from divine contemplations to the evil state of man, behaving himself in a ridiculous manner; if, while his eyes are blinking and before he has become accustomed to the surrounding darkness, he is compelled to fight in courts of law, or in other places, about the images or the shadows of images of justice, and is endeavoring to meet the conceptions of those who have never yet seen absolute justice?

GLAUCON: Anything but surprising. . . .

SOCRATES: Whereas, our argument shows that the power and capacity of learning exists in the soul already; and that just as the eye was unable to turn from darkness to light without the whole body, so too the instrument of knowledge can only by the movement of the whole soul be turned from the world of becoming into that of being, and learn by degrees to endure the sight of being, and of the brightest and best of being, or in other words, of the good.

And there is another thing which is likely or rather a necessary inference from what has preceded, that neither the uneducated and uninformed of the truth, nor yet those who never [finish] their education, will be able ministers of State. . . .

GLAUCON: Very true.

SOCRATES: Then . . . the business of us who are the founders of the State will be to compel the best minds to attain that knowledge which we have already shown to be the greatest of all — they must continue to ascend until they arrive at the good; but when they have ascended and seen enough we must not allow them to do as they do now.

GLAUCON: What do you mean?

SOCRATES: I mean that they remain in the upper world: but this must not be allowed; they must be made to descend again among the prisoners in the den, and partake of their labors and honors, whether they are worth having or not.

GLAUCON: But is not this unjust; ought we to give them a worse life, when they might have a better?

SOCRATES: You have again forgotten, my friend . . . the intention of the legislator, who did not aim at making any one class in the State happy above the rest; the happiness was to be in the whole State, and he held the citizens together by persuasion and necessity, making them benefactors of the State, and therefore benefactors of one another; to this end he created them, not to please themselves, but to be his instruments in binding up the State. . . .

And will our pupils, when they hear this, refuse to take their turn at the toils of State, when they are allowed to spend the greater part of their time with one another in the heavenly light?

GLAUCON: Impossible, for they are just men, and the commands which we impose upon them are just; there can be no doubt that every one of them will take office as a stern necessity, and not after the fashion of our present rulers of State.

SOCRATES: Yes, my friend . . . ; and there lies the point. You must contrive for your future rulers another and a better life than that of a ruler, and then you may have a well-ordered State; for only in the State which offers this, will they rule who are truly rich, not in silver and gold, but in virtue and wisdom, which are the true blessings of life. Whereas if they go to the administration of public affairs, poor and hungering after their own private advantage, thinking that hence they are to snatch the chief good, order there can never be; for they will be fighting about office, and the civil and domestic broils which thus arise will be the ruin of the rulers themselves and of the whole State.

GLAUCON: Most true.

READING AND DISCUSSION QUESTIONS

1. What is the condition of the people in the cave? How does their condition affect the way they understand the world?

2. How does the one who leaves the cave react to the things he encounters? Why does he go back into the cave?

3. How do the people in the cave treat the one who left? Why?

4. What kind of people are like those in the cave? What kind of people are like the one who leaves the cave? What kind of people leave the cave and then go back?

5. What is Plato saying about the balance between the needs of an individual and the needs of the state? How does he think justice can be found for both individuals and states?

DOCUMENT 3-6

ARISTOTLE
Politics: *Democracy*
ca. 340 B.C.E.

Aristotle (EH-ruh-STAH-tuhl; 384–322 B.C.E.), a student of Plato's, is one of the most important philosophers in Western civilization — in the Middle Ages he was known simply as "The Philosopher." His extensive body of work attempts to classify and study all things known to exist, but he was particu-

From *The Politics of Aristotle*, trans. Benjamin Jowett (Oxford: Clarendon Press, 1885), pp. 126–129.

larly well known for his ideas about science, ethics, and politics. The Politics *explains the types of state that exist as well as their merits and shortfalls. In the passage that follows he considers which kind of state is best.*

We have now to inquire what is the best constitution for most states, and the best life for most men, neither assuming a standard of virtue which is above ordinary persons, nor an education which is exceptionally favored by nature and circumstances, nor yet an ideal state which is an aspiration only, but having regard to the life in which the majority are able to share, and to the form of government which states in general can attain. . . .

Now in all states there are three elements: one class is very rich, another very poor, and a third in a mean.[7] It is admitted that moderation and the mean are best, and therefore it will clearly be best to possess the gifts of fortune in moderation; for in that condition of life men are most ready to follow rational principle. But he who greatly excels in beauty, strength, birth, or wealth, or on the other hand who is very poor, or very weak, or very much disgraced, finds it difficult to follow rational principle. Of these two the one sort grow into violent and great criminals, the others into rogues and petty rascals. And two sorts of offenses correspond to them, the one committed from violence, the other from roguery. Again, the middle class is least likely to shrink from rule, or to be over-ambitious for it; both of which are injuries to the state. Again, those who have too much of the goods of fortune, strength, wealth, friends, and the like, are neither willing nor able to submit to authority. The evil begins at home; for when they are boys, by reason of the luxury in which they are brought up, they never learn, even at school, the habit of obedience. On the other hand, the very poor, who are in the opposite extreme, are too degraded. So that the one class cannot obey, and can only rule despotically; the other knows not how to command and must be ruled like slaves. Thus arises a city, not of freemen, but of masters and slaves, the one despising, the other envying; and nothing can be more fatal to friendship and good fellowship in states than this: for good fellowship springs from friendship; when men are at enmity with one another, they would rather not even share the same path. But a city ought to be composed, as far as possible, of equals and similars; and these are generally the middle classes. . . .

Thus it is manifest that the best political community is formed by citizens of the middle class, and that those states are likely to be well-administered in which the middle class is large, and stronger if possible

---

[7] **in a mean:** Average; neither rich nor poor.

than both the other classes, or at any rate than either singly; for the addition of the middle class turns the scale, and prevents either of the extremes from being dominant. Great then is the good fortune of a state in which the citizens have a moderate and sufficient property; for where some possess much, and the others nothing, there may arise an extreme democracy, or a pure oligarchy; or a tyranny may grow out of either extreme — either out of the most rampant democracy, or out of an oligarchy; but it is not so likely to arise out of the middle constitutions and those akin to them. . . .

These considerations will help us to understand why most governments are either democratical or oligarchical. The reason is that the middle class is seldom numerous in them, and whichever party, whether the rich or the common people, transgresses the mean and predominates, draws the constitution its own way, and thus arises either oligarchy or democracy. There is another reason — the poor and the rich quarrel with one another, and whichever side gets the better, instead of establishing a just or popular government, regards political supremacy as the prize of victory, and the one party sets up a democracy and the other an oligarchy. Further, both the parties which had the supremacy in Hellas looked only to the interest of their own form of government, and established in states, the one, democracies, and the other, oligarchies; they thought of their own advantage, of the public not at all. . . . But it has now become a habit among the citizens of states, not even to care about equality; all men are seeking for dominion, or, if conquered, are willing to submit.

What then is the best form of government, and what makes it the best, is evident; and of other constitutions, since we say that there are many kinds of democracy and many of oligarchy, it is not difficult to see which has the first and which the second or any other place in the order of excellence, now that we have determined which is the best. For that which is nearest to the best must of necessity be better, and that which is furthest from it worse, if we are judging absolutely and not relatively to given conditions: I say "relatively to given conditions," since a particular government may be preferable, but another form may be better for some people.

READING AND DISCUSSION QUESTIONS

1. What happens to a state dominated by the rich?
2. What happens to a state dominated by the poor?
3. Which kind of state is best? What makes it the best?

COMPARATIVE QUESTIONS

1. Compare and contrast the characteristics of a Greek hero, as seen in Homer, with the characteristics of a good person as seen in Hesiod. How do Greek heroes compare with Mesopotamian heroes (Document 1-1)?

2. What do these documents reveal about the Greek understandings of the relationship between the individual and the community?

3. What does Archilochus think of losing his shield, and what do you think Homer or Hesiod would say to a soldier who lost his part of his armor? What about their writing styles makes you think that? How does the style of their epics compare to that of the lyric poems?

4. How do Pericles's definition of justice and Hesiod's definition of justice compare? How are their concerns about justice different from or similar to those of the civilizations in Chapters 1 and 2?

5. Compare and contrast Pericles, Plato, and Aristotle. How would each one define good government? Is Plato's notion of ideal justice compatible with the beliefs of Pericles or Aristotle? Do Pericles and Aristotle have the same definition of democracy?

CHAPTER 4

The Hellenistic World

336–30 B.C.E.

I n 338 B.C.E., Philip II, king of Macedonia, defeated the armies of Athens and Thebes at the battle of Chaeronea (kehr-uh-NEE-uh) and established a Common Peace, a new political system that maintained each Greek city-state's right to its own laws and customs. Following Philip II's assassination in 336 B.C.E., his young son Alexander set about to finish his father's plans and conquer Persia. By the time of his premature death in 323 B.C.E., Alexander had conquered the entire Persian Empire and taken his army through Afghanistan into what is now northwestern India. The newly connected reaches of the expanded Greek Empire became a melting pot of culture in what is commonly referred to as the Hellenistic Period (336–30 B.C.E.). Although Alexander's empire quickly broke up into smaller states, Greek rulers dominated most of the eastern Mediterranean and spread Greek culture, or Hellenism, far into the East. New schools of philosophy took root and gained followers, and educated people throughout the Mediterranean world adopted the Greek language. Yet the divided empire never regained the strength and stability it had possessed under Alexander, and the Hellenistic Period was characterized by constant warfare.

On the Burial of Alexander and Hephaestion: Ephippus of Olynthus Remembers Alexander the Great

ca. 323 B.C.E.

Even before his death in 323 B.C.E., Alexander the Great had become a legend. A former student of Aristotle's, Alexander was known not for his philosophical inquiry but for his prolific military conquests for Greece, including vast stretches of the Persian-ruled Middle East, Central Asia, and India. Many writers and historians deified Alexander — who thought of himself as the son of Zeus — although some tried to describe him as the flawed mortal he was. Alexander is known to have appointed a certain Ephippus as a superintendent in Egypt, but it is uncertain whether this man was the Ephippus of Olynthus mentioned in the following passage.

Concerning the luxury of Alexander the Great, Ephippus of Olynthus, in his treatise *On the Burial of Alexander and Hephaestion*, relates that he had in his park a golden throne and couches with silver feet, on which he used to sit while transacting business with his companions. Nicobule[1] says, moreover, that while he was at supper all the dancers and athletes sought to amuse the king. At his very last banquet, Alexander, remembering an episode in the *Andromeda*[2] of Euripides, recited it in a declamatory manner, and then drank a cup of unmixed wine with great zest, and compelled all the rest to do the same. Ephippus tells us, too, that Alexander used to wear at his entertainments even the sacred vestments. Sometimes he would put on the purple robe, cloven sandals, and horns of Ammon,[3] as if he had

---

From G. W. Botsford and E. G. Sihler, eds., *Hellenic Civilization* (New York: Columbia University Press, 1915), pp. 682–683.

[1] **Nicobule**: Greek female historian to whom a biography of Alexander is ascribed.

[2] **Andromeda**: Euripides' play of approximately 412 B.C.E., in which the hero Perseus saves Andromeda from being sacrificed to a sea monster.

[3] **horns of Ammon**: Symbolized the Greco-Egyptian "composite god" Zeus-Ammon, a king of all other gods.

been the god. Sometimes he would imitate Artemis,[4] whose dress he often wore while driving in his chariot; at the same time he had on a Persian robe, which displayed above his shoulders the bow and javelin of the goddess. At times also he would appear in the guise of Hermes;[5] at other times, and in fact nearly every day, he would wear a purple cloak, a chiton shot with white, and a cap with a royal diadem attached. When too he was in private with his friends he wore the sandals of Hermes, with the petasus[6] on his head and the caduceus[7] in hand. Often however he wore a lion's skin and carried a club like Heracles.[8] . . .

Alexander used also to have the floor sprinkled with exquisite perfumes and with fragrant wine; and myrrh and other kinds of incense were burned before him, while all the bystanders kept silence or spoke words only of good omen because of fear. For he was an extremely violent man with no regard for human life, and gave the impression of a man of choleric temperament.

READING AND DISCUSSION QUESTIONS

1. According to this source, in what ways did Alexander seek to glorify himself? What do Alexander's choices reveal about Greek attitudes toward the gods?

2. Why would Alexander recite from the *Andromeda* during the banquet Ephippus describes? What does his selection suggest about Alexander's attitudes toward himself and his subjects?

3. How would you describe the author's (or authors') view of Alexander? Point to specific passages to support your argument.

---

[4] **Artemis**: Daughter of Zeus and goddess of fertility and the hunt.

[5] **Hermes**: Messenger of the gods.

[6] **petasus**: Flat hat, typically worn by the god Mercury.

[7] **caduceus**: Wand of the god Hermes, a staff with two serpents wrapping around it.

[8] **Heracles**: A half-god and the son of Zeus, Heracles was worshipped for his incomparable strength, courage, and cleverness.

DOCUMENT 4-2

Religious and Political Mixing: The Ptolemies of Egypt

ca. 270–246 B.C.E.

No matter how great his military conquests, Alexander in the end was merely mortal. He died young, and his empire was divided among his generals. Egypt was claimed by Ptolemy I (TAH-luh-mee), whose descendants would reign until the death of Cleopatra in 30 B.C.E. The Ptolemaic dynasty made their capital Alexandria, a cosmopolitan city on the Nile Delta, which many Greeks and Hebrews called home. The Ptolemies blended both Greek and Egyptian religious and political systems, as seen in these coins depicting Ptolemy VI Philometer (ca. 186–145 B.C.E.).

READING AND DISCUSSION QUESTIONS

1. What kind of clothes does the king wear in each image?

2. What is significant about the crowns the emperor wears (see Document 1-6)?

3. What is the political message of these images? What is the religious message of these images?

Réunion des Musées Nationaux/Art Resource, N.Y.

VIEWPOINTS

Living the Good Life

DOCUMENT 4-3

DIOGENES LAERTIUS

The Lives and Opinions of Eminent Philosophers:
Diogenes of Sinope, the Cynic

ca. 300–200 B.C.E.

Though the ideas of most Hellenistic philosophers can be traced back to classical Greek thought, the Cynics took a particularly radical approach. Unlike their contemporaries, the Epicureans and Stoics, they did not form an actual school. Doing so would have violated their basic principle, which was to live ethically, not develop a rational, systematic philosophy. Their name, cynic, comes from the Greek word for dog. Some of them took that literally, even barking at their opponents. One of the best-known Cynics was Diogenes of Sinope, who lived in Athens.

And when he saw a mouse running about and not seeking for a bed, nor taking care to keep in the dark, nor looking for any of those things which appear enjoyable to such an animal, he found a remedy for his own poverty. He was, according to the account of some people, the first person who doubled up his cloak out of necessity, and who slept in it; and who carried a wallet, in which he kept his food; and who used whatever place was near for all sorts of purposes, eating, and sleeping, and conversing in it. . . . He took a cask[9] . . . for his house, as he himself tells us in his letters. And during the summer he used to roll himself in the warm sand, but in winter he would embrace statues all covered with snow, practicing himself, on every occasion, to endure anything. . . .

From Diogenes Laertius, *The Lives and Opinions of Eminent Philosophers*, trans. C. D. Yonge (London: George Bell and Sons, 1901), pp. 224–248.

[9] **took a cask . . . for his house**: He lived in a large barrel.

He often condemned those who praise the just for being superior to money, but who at the same time are eager themselves for great riches. He was also very indignant at seeing men sacrifice to the Gods to procure good health, and yet at the sacrifice eating in a manner injurious to health. He often expressed his surprise at slaves, who, seeing their masters eating in a gluttonous manner, still do not themselves lay hands on any of the eatables. . . .

Once, while he was sitting in the sun, . . . Alexander was standing by, and said to him, "Ask any favor you choose of me." And he replied, " Cease to shade me from the sun." . . .

Plato defined man thus: "Man is a two-footed, featherless animal," and was much praised for the definition; so Diogenes plucked a cock and brought it into his school, and said, "This is Plato's man." On which account this addition was made to the definition, "With broad flat nails." . . . When people were speaking of the happiness of Callisthenes,[10] and saying what splendid treatment he received from Alexander, he replied, "The man is wretched, for he is forced to breakfast and dine whenever Alexander chooses."

READING AND DISCUSSION QUESTIONS

1. How does Diogenes live his life? Why does he choose to live this way?
2. What is Diogenes' attitude toward the famous and powerful? Why does he treat them the way he does?
3. Does Diogenes exhibit any of the qualities that were valued by the classical Greeks? If, so which ones?

---

[10] **Callisthenes**: Greek historian and advisor to Alexander.

DOCUMENT 4-4

EPICURUS

The Principal Doctrines of Epicureanism

ca. 306 B.C.E.

Epicurus (eh-pih-KYOUR-uhs), founder of the Epicurean school of philosophy, lived from 340 to 270 B.C.E., primarily in Athens. The central principle of his teachings was to live a life that was free of pain and fear (the bad), and filled with pleasure and friendship (the good). He presented arguments that helped establish numerous principles of scientific and religious study, including the idea that you should believe only that which can be observed. His sometimes unpopular theories challenged Greek notions of the gods' power in their lives. Few of his works survive — the quotes that follow were recorded by Diogenes Laertius, the great Greek biographer and a likely Epicurean.

1. The blessed and immortal nature knows no trouble itself nor causes trouble to any other, so that it is never constrained by anger or favor. For all such things exist only in the weak.

2. Death is nothing to us: for that which is dissolved is without sensation; and that which lacks sensation is nothing to us. . . .

4. Pain does not last continuously in the flesh, but the acutest pain is there for a very short time, and even that which just exceeds the pleasure in the flesh does not continue for many days at once. But chronic illnesses permit a predominance of pleasure over pain in the flesh.

5. It is not possible to live pleasantly without living prudently and honorably and justly, nor again to live a life of prudence, honor, and justice without living pleasantly. And the man who does not possess the pleasant life, is not living prudently and honorably and justly, and the man who does not possess the virtuous life, cannot possibly live pleasantly. . . .

7. Some men wished to become famous and conspicuous, thinking that they would thus win for themselves safety from other men. Wherefore if the life of such men is safe, they have obtained the

From Whitney H. Oates, ed., *The Stoic and Epicurean Philosophers* (New York: Modern Library, 1940), pp. 35–39.

good which nature craves; but if it is not safe, they do not possess that for which they strove at first by the instinct of nature.

8. No pleasure is a bad thing in itself: but the means which produce some pleasures bring with them disturbances many times greater than the pleasures. . . .

10. If the things that produce the pleasures of profligates[11] could dispel the fears of the mind about the phenomena of the sky and death and its pains, and also teach the limits of desires and of pains, we should never have cause to blame them: for they would be filling themselves full with pleasures from every source and never have pain of body or mind, which is the evil of life. . . .

12. A man cannot dispel his fear about the most important matters if he does not know what is the nature of the universe but suspects the truth of some mythical story. So that without natural science it is not possible to attain our pleasures unalloyed.[12] . . .

15. The wealth demanded by nature is both limited and easily procured; that demanded by idle imaginings stretches on to infinity. . . .

17. The just man is most free from trouble, the unjust most full of trouble. . . .

21. He who has learned the limits of life knows that that which removes the pain due to want and makes the whole of life complete is easy to obtain; so that there is no need of actions which involve competition. . . .

27. Of all the things which wisdom acquires to produce the blessedness of the complete life, far the greatest is the possession of friendship. . . .

31. The justice which arises from nature is a pledge of mutual advantage to restrain men from harming one another and save them from being harmed. . . .

33. Justice never is anything in itself, but in the dealings of men with one another in any place whatever and at any time it is a kind of compact not to harm or be harmed.

READING AND DISCUSSION QUESTIONS

1. According to Epicurus, what is the relationship between pain and pleasure? What is true pleasure?

---

[11] **profligates**: Wasteful and extravagant people.
[12] **unalloyed**: Purely and completely.

2. How does natural science contribute to true pleasure?

3. How does Epicurus define justice?

4. What principles should a human being follow to lead a fulfilled life? Which of Epicurus's principles might have upset his contemporaries, and why?

DOCUMENT 4-5

EPICTETUS

Encheiridion, *or* The Manual

ca. 100 C.E.

Epictetus, a Greek slave and philosopher, wrote his manual for living as a Stoic during the height of the Roman Empire. After his owner freed him, Epictetus opened a school of Stoic philosophy in Rome. Stoics, like Epicureans and Cynics, believed that they were followers of Socrates' philosophy. Of the Hellenistic philosophies, Stoicism was the most popular. Rather than inspiring people to change political or social systems so that they conform to an ideal, it taught people that the best way to live was to accept things as they were.

I.

Of things some are in our power, and others are not. In our power are opinion, movement towards a thing, desire, aversion; and in a word, whatever are our own acts: not in our power are the body, property, reputation, offices (magisterial power), and in a word, whatever are not our own acts. And the things in our power are by nature free, not subject to restraint nor hindrance: but the things not in our power are weak, slavish, subject to restraint, in the power of others. Remember then that if you think the things which are by nature slavish to be free, and the things which are in the power of others to be your own, you will be hindered, you will

From George Long, trans., *The Discourses of Epictetus: With the Encheiridion and Fragments* (London: George Bell and Sons, 1888), pp. 379–404.

lament, you will be disturbed, you will blame both gods and men: but if you think that only which is your own to be your own, and if you think that what is another's, as it really is, belongs to another, no man will ever compel you, no man will hinder you, you will never blame any man, you will accuse no man, you will do nothing involuntarily (against your will), no man will harm you, you will have no enemy, for you will not suffer any harm.

If then you desire (aim at) such great things, remember that you must not (attempt to) lay hold of them with a small effort; but you must leave alone some things entirely, and postpone others for the present. But if you wish for these things also (such great things), and power (office) and wealth, perhaps you will not gain even these very things (power and wealth) because you aim also at those finer things (such great things); certainly you will fail in those things through which alone happiness and freedom are secured. Straightway then practice saying to every harsh appearance, "You are an appearance, and in no manner what you appear to be." Then examine it by the rules which you possess, and by this first and chiefly, whether it relates to the things which are in our power or to things which are not in our power: and if it relates to any thing which is not in our power, be ready to say, that it does not concern you. . . .

III.

In every thing which pleases the soul, or supplies a want, or is loved, remember to add this to the (description); what is the nature of each thing, beginning from the smallest? If you love an earthen vessel, say it is an earthen vessel which you love; for when it has been broken, you will not be disturbed. If you are kissing your child or wife, say that it is a human being whom you are kissing, for when the wife or child dies, you will not be disturbed. . . .

V.

Men are disturbed not by the things which happen, but by the opinions about the things: for example, death is nothing terrible, for if it were, it would have seemed so to Socrates; for the opinion about death, that it is terrible, is the terrible thing. When then we are impeded or disturbed or grieved, let us never blame others, but ourselves, that is, our opinions. It is the act of an ill-instructed man to blame others for his own bad condition; it is the act of one who has begun to be instructed, to lay the blame on himself; and of one whose instruction is completed, neither to blame another, nor himself. . . .

VII.

As on a voyage when the vessel has reached a port, if you go out to get water, it is an amusement by the way to pick up a shell fish or some bulb, but your thoughts ought to be directed to the ship, and you ought to be constantly watching if the captain should call, and then you must throw away all those things, that you may not be bound and pitched into the ship like sheep: so in life also, if there be given to you instead of a little bulb and a shell a wife and child, there will be nothing to prevent [you from taking them]. But if the captain should call, run to the ship, and leave all those things without regard to them. But if you are old, do not even go far from the ship, lest when you are called you make default. . . .

XI.

Never say about anything, I have lost it, but any I have restored it. Is your child dead? It has been restored. Is your wife dead? She has been restored. Has your estate been taken from you? Has not then this also been restored? But he who has taken it from me is a bad man. But what is it to you, by whose hands the giver demanded it back? So long as he may allow you, take care of it as a thing which belongs to another, as travellers do with their inn.

XII.

If you intend to improve, throw away such thoughts as these: if I neglect my affairs, I shall not have the means of living: unless I chastise my slave, he will be bad. For it is better to die of hunger and so to be released from grief and fear than to live in abundance with perturbation; and it is better for your slave to be bad than for you to be unhappy. Begin then from little things. Is the oil spilled? Is a little wine stolen? Say on the occasion, at such price is sold freedom from perturbation; at such price is sold tranquillity, but nothing is got for nothing. And when you call your slave, consider that it is possible that he does not hear; and if he does hear, that he will do nothing which you wish. But matters are not so well with him, but altogether well with you, that it should be in his power for you to be not disturbed. . . .

XX.

Remember that it is not he who reviles you or strikes you, who insults you, but it is your opinion about these things as being insulting. When then a man irritates you, you must know that it is your own opinion which has irritated you. Therefore especially try not to be carried away by the appearance. For if you once gain time and delay, you will more easily master yourself. . . .

XXII.

If you desire philosophy, prepare yourself from the beginning to be ridiculed, to expect that many will sneer at you, and say, He has all at once returned to us as a philosopher; and whence does he got this supercilious look for us? Do you not show a supercilious look; but hold on to the things which seem to you best as one appointed by God to this station. And remember that if you abide in the same principles, these men who first ridiculed will afterwards admire you: but if you shall have been overpowered by them, you will bring on yourself double ridicule.

READING AND DISCUSSION QUESTIONS

1. What things can a person control? What things are out of one's control?

2. How should one respond to events, both good and bad?

3. What is the point of life according to the Stoics?

DOCUMENT 4-6

The Maccabee Revolt

ca. 175 B.C.E.

The cultural fusion of the Hellenistic era was capable of producing new and exciting ideas in politics, religion, culture, and the arts. On the other hand, the exchanges of power and collision of different societies also produced religious, political, and ethnic conflict. Cyrus had allowed the Jews to rebuild their capital, Jerusalem, and their temple, the center of their religion (see Document 2-5). Their homeland became a province of the Persian Empire,

---

1 Maccabees 1–2.

and remained so until Alexander conquered the Persians. After Alexander died, most of the Asian part of the empire, including the Jewish lands (now known as Judah or the Kingdom of Judea), passed into the hands of his general Seleucus. Seleucid control of the region lasted for centuries, sometimes peacefully, but not always. In the events chronicled in 1 Maccabees, the Jews revolted against their Greek rulers.

And it happened, after that Alexander son of Philip, the Macedonian, . . . had smitten Darius king of the Persians and Medes, that he reigned in his stead, the first over Greece,

And made many wars, and won many strong holds, and slew the kings of the earth,

And went through to the ends of the earth, and took spoils of many nations, insomuch that the earth was quiet before him; whereupon he was exalted and his heart was lifted up.

And he gathered a mighty strong host and ruled over countries, and nations, and kings, who became tributaries unto him.

And after these things he fell sick, and perceived that he should die.

Wherefore he called his servants, such as were honorable, and had been brought up with him from his youth, and parted his kingdom among them, while he was yet alive.

So Alexander reigned twelve years, and then died.

And his servants bare rule every one in his place.

And after his death they all put crowns upon themselves; so did their sons after them many years: and evils were multiplied in the earth.

And there came out of them a wicked root Antiochus surnamed Epiphanes, . . .

In those days went there out of Israel wicked men, who persuaded many, saying, Let us go and make a covenant with the heathen that are round about us: for since we departed from them we have had much sorrow.

So this device pleased them well.

Then certain of the people were so forward herein, that they went to the king, who gave them license to do after the ordinances of the heathen:

Whereupon they built a place of exercise at Jerusalem according to the customs of the heathen:

And made themselves uncircumcised, and forsook the holy covenant, and joined themselves to the heathen, and were sold to do mischief. . . .

[*Meanwhile, Antiochus invaded Egypt.*]

And after that Antiochus had smitten Egypt, he returned again in the hundred forty and third year, and went up against Israel and Jerusalem with a great multitude,

And entered proudly into the sanctuary, and took away the golden altar, and the candlestick of light, and all the vessels thereof,

And the table of the shewbread,[13] and the pouring vessels, and the vials, and the censers[14] of gold, and the veil, and the crown, and the golden ornaments that were before the temple, all which he pulled off.

He took also the silver and the gold, and the precious vessels: also he took the hidden treasures which he found.

And when he had taken all away, he went into his own land, having made a great massacre, and spoken very proudly.

Therefore there was a great mourning in Israel. . . .

And after two years fully expired the king sent his chief collector of tribute unto the cities of Judah, who came unto Jerusalem with a great multitude,

And spake peaceable words unto them, but all was deceit: for when they had given him credence, he fell suddenly upon the city, and smote it very sore, and destroyed much people of Israel.

And when he had taken the spoils of the city, he set it on fire, and pulled down the houses and walls thereof on every side.

But the women and children took they captive, and possessed the cattle.

Then builded they the city of David with a great and strong wall, and with mighty towers, and made it a strong hold for them. . . .

Thus they shed innocent blood on every side of the sanctuary, and defiled it: Insomuch that the inhabitants of Jerusalem fled because of them: whereupon the city was made an habitation of strangers, and became strange to those that were born in her; and her own children left her. . . .

Moreover king Antiochus wrote to his whole kingdom, that all should be one people,

And every one should leave his [own] laws: so all the heathen agreed according to the commandment of the king.

Yea, many also of the Israelites consented to his religion, and sacrificed unto idols, and profaned the sabbath.

For the king had sent letters by messengers unto Jerusalem and the cities of Judah that they should follow the strange laws of the land,

---

[13] **shewbread**: Loaves of bread left as an offering to God in the temple.

[14] **censers**: Vessels used to burn incense.

And forbid burnt offerings, and sacrifice, and drink offerings, in the temple; and that they should profane the sabbaths and festival days:

And pollute the sanctuary and holy people:

Set up altars, and groves, and chapels of idols, and sacrifice swine's flesh, and unclean beasts:

That they should also leave their children uncircumcised, and make their souls abominable with all manner of uncleanness and profanation:

To the end they might forget the law, and change all the ordinances.

And whosoever would not do according to the commandment of the king, he said, he should die. . . .

Then many of the people were gathered unto them, to wit every one that forsook the law; and so they committed evils in the land;

And drove the Israelites into secret places, even wheresoever they could flee for succor. . . .

And there was very great wrath upon Israel.

In those days arose Mattathias the son of John, the son of Simeon, a priest of the sons of Joarib, from Jerusalem, and dwelt in Modin.

And when he saw the blasphemies that were committed in Judah and Jerusalem,

He said, Woe is me! wherefore was I born to see this misery of my people, and of the holy city, and to dwell there, when it was delivered into the hand of the enemy, and the sanctuary into the hand of strangers? . . .

Then Mattathias and his sons rent their clothes, and put on sackcloth, and mourned very sore.

In the mean while the king's officers, such as compelled the people to revolt, came into the city Modin, to make them sacrifice.

And when many of Israel came unto them, Mattathias also and his sons came together.

Then answered the king's officers, and said to Mattathias on this wise, Thou art a ruler, and an honorable and great man in this city, and strengthened with sons and brethren:

Now therefore come thou first, and fulfill the king's commandment, like as all the heathen have done, yea, and the men of Judah also, and such as remain at Jerusalem: so shalt thou and thy house be in the number of the king's friends, and thou and thy children shall be honored with silver and gold, and many rewards.

Then Mattathias answered and spake with a loud voice, Though all the nations that are under the king's dominion obey him, and fall away every one from the religion of their fathers, and give consent to his commandments:

Yet will I and my sons and my brethren walk in the covenant of our fathers.

God forbid that we should forsake the law and the ordinances.

We will not hearken to the king's words, to go from our religion, either on the right hand, or the left.

Now when he had left speaking these words, there came one of the Jews in the sight of all to sacrifice on the altar which was at Modin, according to the king's commandment.

Which thing when Mattathias saw, he was inflamed with zeal, and his reins trembled, neither could he forbear to shew his anger according to judgment: wherefore he ran, and slew him upon the altar.

Also the king's commissioner, who compelled men to sacrifice, he killed at that time, and the altar he pulled down.

READING AND DISCUSSION QUESTIONS

1. How, according to the author, have the Jews changed while under Greek rule?

2. What new laws did King Antiochus introduce? What reasons might he have had for those changes?

3. Why does Mattathias refuse to comply with the king's law?

COMPARATIVE QUESTIONS

1. How would you compare Alexander as described by Diogenes with Alexander as described by Ephippus? How is Alexander like the Greeks described in Chapter 3? How is he different from those Greeks?

2. After Alexander conquers his empire, how do the Greeks adapt to the people they rule? What actions do they take to rule effectively? What actions make ruling over other people problematic?

3. All three Hellenistic philosophies mentioned in this chapter offer a way to live a good life. How does each philosophy tell its followers to find happiness in this life? How does each view the gods and immortality?

CHAPTER 5

The Rise of Rome

ca. 750–31 B.C.E.

Founded around 750 B.C.E., Rome was first ruled by kings. Whoever was king was expected to rule according to law and with the assistance of the senate, whose members were the heads of the leading Roman families. In the sixth century B.C.E., a dynasty from the foreign Etruscan peoples took over the monarchy and established a series of kings, the Tarquins, who did not always rule according to law. In 509 B.C.E. the last king was expelled and Rome became a republic. Over the next two hundred years, Rome gained rule of the whole Italian peninsula, partly by conquest and partly in alliance with other states. In the course of three wars (264 to 146 B.C.E.) the Romans destroyed Carthage, the greatest power in the western Mediterranean. The wealth that came with the expanding empire allowed Roman culture to flourish and created more opportunities for leisure and the arts. It also increased conflicts between the rich and poor and created a large enslaved population. By the time of Julius Caesar's assassination in 44 B.C.E., Rome ruled the whole of the Mediterranean basin and much of western Europe. Unlike the empire of Alexander, however, the Roman Empire would endure for another five hundred years in the West and fifteen hundred years in the East.

DOCUMENT 5-1

LIVY

The Rape of Lucretia

ca. 27–25 B.C.E.

The story of Lucretia, excerpted from Livy's (59 B.C.E.–17 C.E.) comprehensive history of Rome, is a foundational myth that describes how the Roman

From Livy, *Ab Urbe condita (History)*, vol. 1, trans. George Baker (Philadelphia: T. Wardle, 1840), pp. 58–59.

republic came into being. The story illustrates complicated Roman attitudes
toward both suicide and female virtue. For example, Roman generals who
were defeated in battle sometimes killed themselves, essentially taking respon-
sibility for their military failures. The Romans believed this was a noble
gesture. Lucretia's story has long been an important theme in Western art.
Titian, Rembrandt, Dürer, Raphael, Botticelli, Shakespeare, Handel, and
many others subsequently created works in her honor.

A few days after, Sextus Tarquinius,[1] without the knowledge of Collatinus,[2]
went to Collatia, with only a single attendant: he was kindly received by
the family, who suspected not his design, and, after supper, conducted to
the chamber where guests were lodged. Then, burning with desire, as
soon as he thought that everything was safe, and the family all at rest, he
came with his sword drawn to Lucretia, where she lay asleep, and, holding
her down, with his left hand pressed on her breast, said, "Lucretia, be
silent: I am Sextus Tarquinius; my sword is in my hand, if you utter a word,
you die."

Terrified at being thus disturbed from sleep, she saw no assistance
near, and immediate death threatening her. Tarquinius then acknowledged his passion, entreated, mixed threats with entreaties, and used every
argument likely to have effect on a woman's mind: but finding her inflex-
ible, and not to be moved, even by the fear of death, he added to that fear,
the dread of dishonor, telling her that, after killing her he would murder a
slave, and lay him naked by her side, that she might be said to have been
slain in base adultery. The shocking apprehension, conveyed by this men-
ace, overpowering her resolution in defending her chastity, his lust became
victorious; and Tarquinius departed, applauding himself for this triumph
over a lady's honor.

But Lucretia plunged by such a disaster into the deepest distress, dispatched a messenger to Rome to her father, with orders to proceed to
Ardea to her husband, and to desire them to come to her, each with one
faithful friend; to tell them, that there was a necessity for their doing so,
and speedily, for that a dreadful affair had happened. Spurius Lucretius
came with Publius Valerius, the son of Volesus; Collatinus with Lucius
Junius Brutus, in company with whom he chanced to be returning to
Rome, when he was met by his wife's messenger.

---

[1] **Sextus Tarquinius**: Prince of Rome, son of King L. Tarquinius Superbus (r. 535–
510 B.C.E.).
[2] **Collatinus**: Lucretia's husband.

They found Lucretia sitting in her chamber, melancholy and dejected: on the arrival of her friends, she burst into tears, and on her husband's asking, "Is all well?" "Far from it," said she, "for how can it be well with a woman who has lost her chastity? Collatinus, the impression of another man is in your bed; yet my person only has been violated, my mind is guiltless as my death will testify. But give me your right hands, and pledge your honor that the adulterer shall not escape unpunished. He is Sextus Tarquinius, who, under the appearance of a guest, disguising an enemy, obtained here last night, by armed violence, a triumph deadly to me, and to himself also, if ye be men."

They all pledged their honor, one after another, and endeavored to comfort her distracted mind, acquitting her of blame, as under the compulsion of force, and charging it on the violent perpetrator of the crime, told her, that "the mind alone was capable of sinning, not the body, and that where there was no such intention, there could be no guilt."

"[It is] your concern," said she, "to consider what is due to him; as to me, though I acquit myself of the guilt, I cannot dispense with the penalty, nor shall any woman ever plead the example of Lucretia, for surviving her chastity." Thus saying, she plunged into her heart a knife which she had concealed under her garment, and falling forward on the wound, dropped lifeless. The husband and father shrieked aloud.

But Brutus, while they were overpowered by grief, drawing the knife, from the wound of Lucretia, and holding it out, reeking with blood, before him, said, "By this blood, most chaste until injured by royal insolence, swear, and call you, O ye gods, to witness, that I will prosecute to destruction, by sword, fire, and every forcible means in my power, both Lucius Tarquinius the proud, and his impious wife, together with their entire race, and never will suffer one of them, nor any other person whatsoever, to be king in Rome." He then delivered the knife to Collatinus, afterwards to Lucretius, and Valerius, who were filled with amazement, as at a prodigy, and at a loss to account for this unusual elevation of sentiment in the mind of Brutus.

However, they took the oath as directed, and converting their grief into rage, followed Brutus, who put himself at their head, and called on them to proceed instantly to abolish kingly power.

They brought out the body of Lucretia from the house, conveyed it to the forum, and assembled the people, who came together quickly, in astonishment, as may be supposed at a deed so atrocious and unheard of. Every one exclaimed with vehemence against the villainy and violence of the prince: they were deeply affected by the grief of her father, and also by the discourse of Brutus, who rebuked their tears and ineffectual complaints, and advised them, as became men, as became Romans, to take up arms against those who had dared to treat them as enemies. The most spirited among the youth offered themselves with their arms, and the rest followed their example. On which, leaving half their number at the gates to defend Collatia, and fixing guards to prevent any intelligence of the commotion being carried to the princes, the rest, with Brutus at their head, marched to Rome.

When they arrived there, the sight of such an armed multitude spread terror and confusion wherever they came: but, in a little time, when people observed the principal men of the state marching at their head, they concluded, that whatever the matter was, there must be good reason for it. Nor did the heinousness of the affair raise less violent emotions in the minds of the people at Rome, than it had at Collatia: so that, from all parts of the city, they hurried into the forum; where, as soon as the party arrived, a crier summoned the people to attend the tribune of the celeres,[3] which office happened at that time to be held by Brutus.

He there made a speech, no way consonant to that low degree of sensibility and capacity, which until that day, he had counterfeited; recounting the violence and lust of Sextus Tarquinius, the shocking violation of Lucretia's chastity, and her lamentable death; the misfortune of Tricipitinus,[4] in being left childless, who must feel the cause of his daughter's death as a greater injury and cruelty, than her death itself: to these representations he added the pride of the king himself, the miseries and toils of the commons, buried under ground to cleanse sinks and sewers, saying, that ". . . citizens of Rome, the conquerors of all the neighboring nations, were, from warriors, reduced to laborers and stone cutters"; mentioned the barbarous murder of King Servius Tullius,[5] his abominable daughter driving in her carriage over the body of her father, and invoked the gods to avenge the cause of parents.

By descanting on these and other, I suppose, more forcible topics, which the heinousness or present injuries suggested at the time, but which it is difficult for writers to repeat, he inflamed the rage of the multitude to such a degree, that they were easily persuaded to deprive the king of his government, and to pass an order for the banishment of Lucius Tarquinius, his wife, and children. Brutus himself, having collected and armed

---

[3] **tribune of the celeres**: Commander of the king's body guard.
[4] **Tricipitinus**: Spurius Tricipitinus Lucretius; Lucretia's father.
[5] **Servius Tullius**: King of Rome (r. 578–535 B.C.E.), who reorganized the Roman constitution to expand the political rights of the lower classes. He was killed by patrician conspirators, including his daughter Tullia.

such of the young men as voluntarily gave in their names, set out for the camp at Ardea, in order to excite the troops there to take part against the king. The command in the city he left to Lucretius, who had some time before been appointed by the king to the office of prefect of the city. During this tumult Tullia fled from her house; both men and women, wherever she passed, imprecating curses on her head, and invoking the furies, the avengers of parents.

READING AND DISCUSSION QUESTIONS

1. How did Tarquinius frighten Lucretia into having sex with him?
2. How did the men in Lucretia's family react to what had happened to her?
3. What reason did Lucretia give for killing herself? What other motive may also have driven her?
4. Describe the speech that Brutus gave to the multitude. What parts of the speech angered the people?

DOCUMENT 5-2

A Roman Wedding

ca. 160 C.E.

The family was at the heart of the Roman social and political organization. Families were part of tribes, which were represented in the Tribal Assembly (comitia tributa), which held elections for political office. Choice of marriage partners was, therefore, not personal, but a way for families to advance their political status or business relationships. A wife was subject to her husband or her father (depending on the specific form of the marriage agreement) throughout her life. She could inherit property, which usually was part of the dowry she received when she married. The image below is from a Roman wedding. The groom holds his wife with one hand and the marriage contract in another. The woman behind them is the matron of honor and the man beside the groom is a witness.

READING AND DISCUSSION QUESTIONS

1. Why do you think the marriage contract is displayed so prominently between the bride and groom?

2. Why does he hold the contract, not the bride?

3. How does this presentation of marriage compare or contrast with Lucretia's marriage?

DOCUMENT 5-3

Manumissions of Hellenistic Slaves: The Process of Freedom

ca. 167–101 B.C.E.

In the ancient world, slavery was not always a permanent condition. The father of the Roman poet Horace, for example, had been born a slave but was eventually freed and became a rich man. The documents that follow illustrate the often blurry boundaries between servitude and freedom in Roman society. In the first case, one of unconditional manumission (emancipation), the slave Sosus is released immediately and forever. In the second instance, one of conditional manumission, the slaves Maiphatas and Ammia are required to stay with their owner Critodamus until he dies, at which point they will become free persons.

UNCONDITIONAL MANUMISSION

In the archonship of Tharres, in the month of Panagyrius, as reckoned by the people of Amphissa, and in the archonship of Damostratus at Delphi, in the month of Poitropius (144 B.C.E.), Telon and Cleto, with the approval of their son Straton, sold to Pythian Apollo a male slave whose name is Sosus, of Cappadocian origin, for the price of 3 minas of silver. Accordingly Sosus entrusted the sale to the god, on condition of his being free and not to be claimed as a slave by anyone for all time. Guarantor in accordance with the law and the contract: Philoxenus son of Dorotheus of Amphissa. The previous sale of Sosus to Apollo which took place in the archonship of Thrasycles at Delphi, and the provisions of the sale, namely that Sosus should remain with Telon and Cleto for as long as they live, shall be null and void. Witnesses: the priests of Apollo, Praxias and Andronicus, and the archon Pyrrhias son of Archelaus, and the Amphissians Charixenus son of Ecephylus, Polycritus, Aristodamus son of Callicles, Euthydamus son of Polycritus, Dorotheus son of Timesius, Demetrius son of Monimus. The contract is kept by the priest Praxias and Andronicus, and the Amphissians Polycritus and (Charixenus) son of Ecephylus.

From M. M. Austin, ed., *The Hellenistic World from Alexander to the Roman Conquest: A Selection of Ancient Sources in Translation* (Cambridge: Cambridge University Press, 1981), pp. 221–222.

CONDITIONAL MANUMISSION

When Panaetolus and Phytaeus were generals of the Aetolians, in the month of Homoloius, and in the archonship of Xeneas at Delphi and the month Bysius (167 B.C.E.), Critodamus son of Damocles, of Physce, sold to Pythian Apollo a male slave whose name is Maiphatas, of Galatian origin, and a female (slave) whose name is Ammia, of Illyrian origin, for the price of seven minas of silver. Maiphatas and Ammia shall remain with Critodamus for as long as Critodamus lives, doing for Critodamus what they are told to; if they do not remain and do what they are told to, the sale shall be null and void. When Critodamus dies, Maiphatas and Ammia shall be free and the sale shall remain with the god on condition that they are free and not to be claimed as slaves by anyone for their whole life, doing whatever they wish and going wherever they wish. Guarantors in accordance with the law and the contract: Philon son of Aristeas, Astoxenus son of Dionysius. Witnesses: the priests Amyntas and Tarantinus; private citizens: Dexicrates, Sotimus, Callimachus, Euangelus, . . . chaeus, of Delphi, Lyciscus and Menedamus, of Physce.

READING AND DISCUSSION QUESTIONS

1. Why do you think it is mentioned that Telon and Cleto's son Straton also approved of Solus's manumission?

2. Why might there be so many witnesses to these transactions?

3. Based on these documents, what seems to be the main difference between conditional and unconditional manumission?

> DOCUMENT 5-4

SENECA

The Sounds of a Roman Bath

ca. 50 C.E.

Personal cleanliness was imperative to both Greeks and Romans. The Greeks in particular frequently complained that barbarians were dirty. Public baths

From Naphtali Lewis and Meyer Reinhold, eds., *Roman Civilization: Selected Readings*, vol. 2 (New York: Columbia University Press, 1951), p. 228.

were central gathering places for Romans of many classes. The well-off frequently had baths in their own houses, but even so they might visit the public baths to meet friends or partake in other activities. The baths had a questionable reputation, in part because prostitutes often sought clients there. Seneca (ca. 4 B.C.E.–65 C.E.), who recorded this sketch of a bath's commotion, was a philosopher, orator, and eventually the chief adviser to the emperor.

I live over a bath. Imagine the variety of voices, enough noise to make you sick. When the stronger fellows are working out with heavy weights, when they are working hard or pretending to work hard, I hear their grunts; and whenever they exhale, I hear their hissing and panting. Or when some lazy type is getting a cheap rubdown, I hear the slap of the hand pounding his shoulders. . . . If a serious ballplayer comes along and starts keeping score out loud, that's the end for me. . . . And there's the guy who always likes to hear his own voice when washing, or those people who jump into the swimming pool with a tremendous splash. . . . The hair plucker keeps up a constant chatter to attract customers, except when he is plucking armpits and making his customer scream instead of screaming himself. It would be disgusting to list all the cries from the sausage seller, and the fellow hawking cakes, and all the food vendors yelling out what they have to sell, each with own special intonation.

READING AND DISCUSSION QUESTIONS

1. What other activities took place at the public baths besides bathing?
2. In what ways do all these activities go together?
3. How would you describe Roman notions of privacy and personal space?
4. What does it reveal about Roman urban life that someone like Seneca would live so close to the public baths?

Political Unrest in Rome

DOCUMENT 5-5

APPIAN OF ALEXANDRIA
The Civil Wars
ca. 100 C.E.

Rome's success in building an empire led to some unintended consequences. After they conquered the Italian peninsula, Romans had to decide what to do with the land they had acquired, even as they were conquering and acquiring more land. The expansion of political rights to the plebeians (lower classes) that began centuries before did not mean that full political or economic equality had developed. In the second century B.C.E., the social, political, and economic problems facing the Republic spilled over into violence. One faction of politicians, led by Tiberius Gracchus (163–133 B.C.E.), had a controversial plan to resolve the tensions. This account of the rise in political problems comes from the historian Appian of Alexandria (ca. 95–165 C.E.).

The Romans, as they subdued the Italian nations successively in war, seized a part of their lands and built towns there, or established their own colonies in those already existing, and used them in place of garrisons. Of the land acquired by war they assigned the cultivated part forthwith to settlers, or leased or sold it. Since they had no leisure as yet to allot the part which then lay desolated by war (this was generally the greater part), they made proclamation that in the meantime those who were willing to work it might do so for a share of the yearly crops — a tenth of the grain and a fifth of the fruit. From those who kept flocks was required a share of the animals, both oxen and small cattle. They did these things in order to multiply the Italian race, which they considered the most laborious[6] of

---

From Appian of Alexandria, *The Roman History of Appian of Alexandria*, vol. II., trans. Horace White (New York: Macmillan Company, 1899), pp. 5–14.

[6] **laborious**: Hardworking.

peoples, so that they might have plenty of allies at home. But the very opposite thing happened; for the rich, getting possession of the greater part of the undistributed lands, and being emboldened by the lapse of time to believe that they would never be dispossessed, and adding to their holdings the small farms of their poor neighbors, partly by purchase and partly by force, came to cultivate vast tracts instead of single estates, using for this purpose slaves as laborers and herdsmen, lest free laborers should be drawn from agriculture into the army. The ownership of slaves itself brought them great gain from the multitude of their progeny, who increased because they were exempt from military service. Thus the powerful ones became enormously rich and the race of slaves multiplied throughout the country, while the Italian people dwindled in numbers and strength, being oppressed by penury, taxes, and military service. If they had any respite from these evils they passed their time in idleness, because the land was held by the rich, who employed slaves instead of freemen as cultivators.

For these reasons the [Roman] people became troubled lest they should no longer have sufficient allies of the Italian stock, and lest the government itself should be endangered by such a vast number of slaves. . . . At length Tiberius Sempronius Gracchus, an illustrious man, eager for glory, a most powerful speaker, and for these reasons well known to all, delivered an eloquent discourse, while serving as tribune, concerning the Italian race, lamenting that a people so valiant in war, and blood relations to the Romans, were declining little by little in pauperism and paucity of numbers without any hope of remedy. He inveighed against the multitude of slaves as useless in war and never faithful to their masters, and adduced the recent calamity brought upon the masters by their slaves in Sicily,[7] where the demands of agriculture had greatly increased the number of the latter; recalling also the war waged against them by the Romans, which was neither easy nor short, but long-protracted and full of vicissitudes and dangers. After speaking thus he again brought forward the law, providing that nobody should hold more than 500 jugera[8] of the public domain. But he added a provision to the former law, that the sons of the present occupiers might each hold one-half of that amount, and that the remainder should be divided among the poor. . . .

This was extremely disturbing to the rich because, . . . they could no longer disregard the law as they had done before; nor could they buy the allotments of others, because Gracchus had provided against this by for-

---

[7] **recent calamity . . . Sicily**: a slave revolt was under way in Sicily at this time.

[8] **jugera**: Plural of *jugerum*. A jugerum is approximately two-thirds of an acre.

bidding sales. They collected together in groups, and made lamentation, and accused the poor of appropriating the results of their tillage, their vineyards, and their dwellings. Some said that they had paid the price of the land to their neighbors. Were they to lose the money with the land? Others said that the graves of their ancestors were in the ground, which had been allotted to them in the division of their fathers' estates. Others said that their wives' dowries had been expended on the estates, or that the land had been given to their own daughters as dowry. Money-lenders could show loans made on this security. All kinds of wailing and expressions of indignation were heard at once. On the other side were heard the lamentations of the poor — that they had been reduced from competence to extreme penury, and from that to childlessness, because they were unable to rear their offspring. They recounted the military services they had rendered, by which this very land had been acquired, and were angry that they should be robbed of their share of the common property. They reproached the rich for employing slaves, who were always faithless and ill-tempered and for that reason unserviceable in war, instead of freemen, citizens, and soldiers. While these classes were lamenting and indulging in mutual accusations, a great number of others, composed of colonists, or inhabitants of the free towns, or persons otherwise interested in the lands and who were under like apprehensions, flocked in and took sides with their respective factions. Emboldened by numbers and exasperated against each other they attached themselves to turbulent crowds, and waited for the voting on the new law, some trying to prevent its enactment by all means, and others supporting it in every possible way. . . .

What Gracchus had in his mind in proposing the measure was not wealth, but an increase of efficient population. Inspired greatly by the usefulness of the work, and believing that nothing more advantageous or admirable could ever happen to Italy, he took no account of the difficulties surrounding it. When the time for voting came he advanced many other arguments at considerable length and also asked them whether it was not just to divide among the common people what belonged to them in common; whether a citizen was not worthy of more consideration at all times than a slave; whether a man who served in the army was not more useful than one who did not; and whether one who had a share in the country was not more likely to be devoted to the public interests. He did not dwell long on this comparison between freemen and slaves, which he considered degrading, but proceeded at once to a review of their hopes and fears for the country, saying that the Romans had acquired most of their territory by conquest, and that they had hopes of occupying the rest of the habitable world, but now the question of greatest hazard was, whether they should gain the rest by having plenty of brave men, or whether, through their weakness and mutual jealousy, their enemies should take away what they already possessed. After exaggerating the glory and riches on the one side and the danger and fear on the other, he admonished the rich to take heed, and said that for the realization of these hopes they ought to bestow this very land as a free gift, if necessary, on men who would rear children, and not, by contending about small things, overlook larger ones; especially since they were receiving an ample compensation for labor expended in the undisputed title to 500 jugera each of free land, in a high state of cultivation, without cost, and half as much more for each son of those who had sons. After saying much more to the same purport and exciting the poor, as well as others who were moved by reason rather than by the desire for gain, he ordered the scribe to read the proposed law. . . .

[*Eventually the law was passed, but only after great difficulty.*]

Gracchus became immensely popular by reason of the law and was escorted home by the multitude as though he were the founder, not of a single city or race, but of all the nations of Italy. After this the victorious party returned to the fields from which they had come to attend to this business. The defeated ones remained in the city and talked the matter over, feeling bitterly, and saying that as soon as Gracchus should become a private citizen he would be sorry that he had done despite to the sacred and inviolable office of tribune, and had opened such a fountain of discord in Italy.

[*Tension between the wealthy landowners and Gracchus' supporters eventually led to violence.*]

When [the landowners' faction] arrived at the temple and advanced against the partisans of Gracchus they yielded to the reputation of a foremost citizen, for they saw the Senate following with him. The latter wrested clubs out of the hands of the Gracchans themselves, or with fragments of broken benches or other apparatus that had been brought for the use of the assembly, began beating them, and pursued them. . . . In the tumult many of the Gracchans perished, and Gracchus himself was caught near a temple, and was slain at the door close by the statues of the kings. All the bodies were thrown by night into the Tiber. . . .

On the subject of the murder of Gracchus the city was divided between sorrow and joy. Some mourned for themselves and for him, and deplored the present condition of things, believing that the commonwealth no longer existed, but had been supplanted by force and violence. Others considered that everything had turned out for them exactly as they wished.

READING AND DISCUSSION QUESTIONS

1. What specific problems were created by the acquisition of the Italian lands?
2. What were the provisions of the new law?
3. What reasons did the landowners give for opposing the law?
4. What does this episode reveal about the strengths and weaknesses of the Roman government?

DOCUMENT 5-6

PLUTARCH

On Julius Caesar, a Man of Unlimited Ambition

ca. 44 B.C.E.

The Greek historian Plutarch (ca. 46–120 C.E.) wrote long after Caesar's death, but he seems to have drawn on contemporary accounts. By 44 B.C.E., Rome had suffered generations of civil war, and Caesar had become dictator for life. Throughout his political career, Caesar and his family had been partisans of the popular party, and he was generally well-liked among the Roman populace. However, by the time of his death, Caesar's individual powers overshadowed the Roman polity, and not all citizens tolerated having their governments usurped. One of the most telling points is that some of Caesar's closest associates became his assassins.

But that which brought upon him the most apparent and mortal hatred was his desire of being king; which gave the common people the first occasion to quarrel with him, and proved the most specious pretence to those who had been his secret enemies all along. Those who would have procured him that title gave it out that it was foretold in the Sibyls' books[9] that the Romans should conquer the Parthians when they fought against them under the conduct of a king, but not before. And one day, as Caesar was

---

From A. H. Clough, trans., *Plutarch's Lives*, vol. 4 (Boston: Little, Brown and Company, 1859), pp. 316–320.

[9] **Sibyls' books**: Prophetic writings, widely read in ancient Rome.

coming down from Alba to Rome, some were so bold as to salute him by the name of king; but he, finding the people disrelish it, seemed to resent it himself, and said his name was Caesar, not king. Upon this there was a general silence, and he passed on looking not very well pleased or contented. Another time, when the senate had conferred on him some extravagant honors, he chanced to receive the message as he was sitting on the rostra,[10] where, though the consuls[11] and praetors[12] themselves waited on him, attended by the whole body of the senate, he did not rise, but behaved himself to them as if they had been private men, and told them his honors wanted rather to be retrenched then increased. This treatment offended not only the senate, but the commonalty too, as if they thought the affront upon the senate equally reflected upon the whole republic; so that all who could decently leave him went off, looking much discomposed. Caesar, perceiving the false step he had made, immediately retired home; and laying his throat bare, told his friends that he was ready to offer this to any one would give the stroke. But afterwards he made the malady from which he suffered (epilepsy) the excuse for his sitting, saying that those who are attacked by it lose their presence of mind if they talk much standing; that they presently grow giddy, fall into convulsions, and quite lose their reason. But this was not the reality, for he would willingly have stood up to the senate, had not Cornelius Balbus, one of his friends, or rather flatterers, hindered him. "Will you not remember," said he, "you are Caesar, and claim the honor which is due to your merit?"

He gave a fresh occasion of resentment by his affront to the tribunes. The Lupercalia were then celebrated, a feast at the first institution belonging, as some writers say, to the shepherds, and having some connection with the Arcadian Lycae. Many young noblemen and magistrates run up and down the city with their upper garments off, striking all they meet with thongs of hide, by way of sport; and many women, even of the highest rank, place themselves in the way, and hold out their hands to the lash, as boys in a school do to the master, out of a belief that it procures an easy labor to those who are with child, and makes those conceive who are barren. Caesar, dressed in a triumphal robe, seated himself in a golden chair at the rostra to view this ceremony. Antony, as consul, was one of those who ran this course, and when he came into the forum, and the people made way for him, he went up and reached to Caesar a diadem wreathed

---

[10] **rostra**: Platform from which politicians often addressed the Roman people.
[11] **consuls**: Highest elected officials in the Republic. Two served each year.
[12] **praetors**: Magistrates.

with laurel. Upon this there was a shout, but only a slight one, made by the few who were planted there for that purpose; but when Caesar refused it, there was universal applause. Upon the second offer, very few, and upon the second refusal, all again applauded. Caesar finding it would not take, rose up, and ordered the crown to be carried into the capitol. Caesar's statues were afterwards found with royal diadems on their heads. Flavius and Marullus, two tribunes of the people, went presently and pulled them off, and having apprehended those who first saluted Caesar as king committed them to prison. The people followed them with acclamations, and called them by the name of Brutus,[13] because Brutus was the first who ended the succession of kings, and transferred the power which before was lodged in one man into the hands of the senate and people. Caesar so far resented this, that he displaced Marullus and Flavius; and in urging his charges against them, at the same time ridiculed the people, by himself giving the men more than once the names of Bruti and Cumaei.[14]

This made the multitude turn their thoughts to Marcus Brutus, who, by his father's side, was thought to be descended from that first Brutus, and by his mother's side from the Servilii, another noble family, being besides nephew and son-in-law to Cato.[15] But the honors and favors he had received from Caesar took off the edge from the desires he might himself have felt for overthrowing the new monarchy. For he had not only been pardoned himself after Pompey's defeat at Pharsalia, and had procured the same grace for many of his friends, but was one in whom Caesar had a particular confidence. He had at that time the most honorable praetorship for the year, and was named for the consulship four years after, being preferred before Cassius, his competitor. Upon the question as to the choice, Caesar, it is related, said that Cassius had the fairer pretensions, but that he could not pass by Brutus. Nor would he afterwards listen to some who spoke against Brutus, when the conspiracy against him was already afoot, but laying his hand on his body, said to the informers, "Brutus will wait for this skin of mine," intimating that he was worthy to bear rule on account of his virtue, but would not be base and ungrateful to gain it. Those who

---

[13] **Brutus:** A reference to Marcus Brutus's ancestor, who had been instrumental in the Roman rebellion against Etruscan domination in the fifth century B.C.E. See Document 5-1.

[14] **Bruti and Cumaei:** In Latin, the word *brutus* (plural: *bruti*) means stupid, though it can also refer to the family that descends from the Brutus who opposed the last Tarquin king. *Cumaei* refers to the people from Cumae, who were considered dull and boring.

[15] **Cato:** Senator known for his strict adherence to tradition.

desired a change, and looked on him as the only, or at least the most proper, person to effect it, did not venture to speak with him; but in the night-time laid papers about his chair of state, where he used to sit and determine causes, with such sentences in them as, "You are asleep, Brutus," "You are no longer Brutus." Cassius, when he perceived his ambition a little raised upon this, was more instant than before to work him yet further, having himself a private grudge against Caesar for some reasons that we have mentioned in the "Life of Brutus." Nor was Caesar without suspicions of him, and said once to his friends, "What do you think Cassius is aiming at? I don't like him, he looks so pale." And when it was told him that Antony and Dolabella[16] were in a plot against him, he said he did not fear such fat, luxurious men, but rather the pale, lean fellows, meaning Cassius and Brutus.

READING AND DISCUSSION QUESTIONS

1. Which segments of the Roman population wanted Caesar to become king, and why?

2. How did Caesar treat those who had taken the side of his enemy Pompey earlier in the civil wars?

3. Why is it significant that Caesar did not conceal his epilepsy?

4. What were the motives of the conspirators against Caesar?

COMPARATIVE QUESTIONS

1. What attitudes about appropriate social behaviors are illustrated in the first four documents?

2. Describe Roman society as depicted in these documents. How many different social levels appear? How do they treat each other?

3. The Brutus who took part in the assassination of Caesar was a descendant of the Brutus who gave the speech in the first document. How does this illuminate the ways in which the conspirators may have thought of themselves?

---

[16] **Dolabella**: A general.

4. Compare and contrast Gracchus and Caesar. Are their methods or goals in any way alike? What is similar and different about the problems faced by the republic during Gracchus's life and during Caesar's? How do these men deal with these problems?

5. Compare and contrast Caesar's behavior in the senate as illustrated in Document 5-6 to the behavior of Alexander the Great as described in Document 4-1.

CHAPTER 6

The Pax Romana

31 B.C.E.–284 C.E.

T he social, political, and cultural changes that accompanied the pax Romana had a lasting impact on Western civilization. As the empire grew, its rulers gradually decided to extend the benefits of citizenship to select non-Romans. This process was completed in 212 C.E., when citizenship was granted to all free men in the empire. As they incorporated new peoples into the empire, Romans did not simply impose their culture on others, but allowed a fusion of traditions. As the documents in this chapter show, such cultural blending proved both beneficial and problematic. While the Romans were generally tolerant of different religions, at times they persecuted Christians, and sometimes Jews, because they would not participate in the imperial cult. In the late fourth century C.E., this tolerant view shifted as Christianity became the state religion of Rome, and Christians, who believed that the entire world should convert, began to persecute non-Christians.

VIEWPOINTS

Romans and Others

DOCUMENT 6-1

JUVENAL
The Third Satire: What Is There to Do in Rome?
ca. 100 C.E.

The first-century Roman author Juvenal is remembered for his sharp wit and biting satire. Little is known about the author, but he may have been the son

From Juvenal, *The Sixteen Satires*, trans. Peter Green (London: Penguin Books, 1998), pp. 14–19.

of a former slave. He is mostly known through his sixteen Satires, which pro-
vide commentary on the morals and behavior of Romans in his day. The
third Satire, written in the form of a speech by Juvenal's friend Umbricius,
provides insight into how some Romans might have felt seeing foreigners
attain citizenship in their empire.

"There's no room in this city," [Umbricius] said,
"for the decent professions. . . .
My resources have shrunk since yesterday, and tomorrow
will eat away more of what's left. So I am going . . .
While as yet
I'm in vigorous middle age, while active years are left me,
while my white hairs are still few, and I need no stick
to guide my tottering feet. So farewell Rome, I leave you
to sanitary engineers and municipal architects, fellows
who by swearing black is white find it easy to land
contracts for a new temple, swamp-drainage, harbor-works,
river-clearance, undertaking, the lot — then pocket the profit
and fraudulently file their petition in bankruptcy. . . .
What can I do in Rome? I'm a hopeless liar. Supposing
a book is bad, I can't puff it, and beg for a copy. . . .
I won't be an accomplice
in larceny — ergo [therefore], no governor will take me on his staff. . . .
Now let me turn to that race which goes down so sweetly
with our millionaires, but remains my special pet aversion,
and not mince my words. I cannot, citizens, stomach
a Greek Rome. . . . They flock in from [all over the empire],
all of them lighting out for the City's classiest districts
and burrowing into great houses, with plans to take them over.
Quick wit, unlimited nerve, a gift of the gab that outsmarts
a professional public speaker — that's them. So what do you take
that fellow to be? He's brought every profession with him —
schoolmaster, rhetorician, surveyor, artist, masseur,
diviner, tightrope-walker, magician, or quack, your hungry
Greekling is all by turns. Tell him to fly — he's airborne!
Time to get out . . . when louts blown into Rome . . .
precede me at dinner-parties . . . *me*, who drew my first breath
among these Roman hills, and was nourished on Sabine[1] olives!

---

[1] **Sabine**: Region north of Rome.

What's more, there's none can match their talent for flattery:
dummies they laud as eloquent, the ugly they call handsome. . . .
They're a nation of actors. Laugh and they'll out-guffaw you,
split their sides. When faced with a friend's tears, they weep too,
though totally unmoved. . . .
Besides, nothing's sacred to him and his randy urges,
neither the housewife, nor her virgin daughter, nor her
daughter's still beardless fiancé, nor her hitherto virtuous son —
and if none of these is to hand, he'll lay his friend's grandmother.
But in Rome we must toe the line of fashion, spending
beyond our means, and often on borrowed credit.
It's a universal failing: here we all live in pretentious
poverty. To cut a long story short, there's a price-tag
on everything in Rome."

READING AND DISCUSSION QUESTIONS

1. Why is the speaker leaving Rome?
2. What does the speaker think of the Greeks?
3. What does the author think of the Romans of his generation?

DOCUMENT 6-2

TACITUS

Germania: *Rome Encounters the Noble Savages*

ca. 100 C.E.

Tacitus (ca. 56–117), the greatest Roman historian, wrote at a time when Rome had reached the zenith of its power. In addition to his works on imperial politics, the Annals *and the* Histories, *Tacitus wrote a study of the Germanic tribes who lived beyond the borders of the empire. In his studies of Roman politics, he described abundant examples of corruption and tyranny, but among the Germanic tribes he found a good deal to admire.*

From Tacitus, *Agricola and Germania*, trans. Anthony R. Birley (Oxford: Oxford University Press, 1999), pp. 39–50.

Tacitus never lived among Germanic peoples but obtained his information from writers who had.

The land may vary a certain amount in its appearance, but in general it either bristles with forests or festers with marshes. It is wetter on the side facing the Gauls, windier opposite Noricum and Pannonia.[2] It is fertile for sown crops but will not grow fruit trees. It is rich in livestock, but these are mostly undersized. Even on their foreheads the cattle lack their proper distinction and glory. The people take pride in their quantity, for their cattle are their sole, greatly prized wealth.

Silver and gold have been denied them by the gods, whether as a sign of favor or of anger I cannot say. . . .

Their kings they choose for their noble birth, their army commanders for their valor. Even the kings do not have absolute or unrestricted power, and their commanders lead by example rather than by issuing orders, gaining respect if they are energetic, if they stand out, if they are on the front of the line. Executions, imprisonment, even floggings, are allowed to no one other than the priests, and are not carried out as a punishment or on the orders of the commander, but as it were at the behest of the deity whom they believe to be present as they wage war. They actually bring with them into battle certain images and symbols taken from the sacred groves.

It is a particular incitement to valor that their squadrons and wedges are not formed at random or by chance mustering but are composed of families and kinship groups. They have their nearest and dearest close by, as well, so that they can hear the shrieks of their women and the crying of their children. For each man these are the most sacred witnesses, their praise is the most highly valued. It is to their mothers and their wives, who do not shrink from examining their cuts, that they go with their wounds. They also bring food and words of encouragement to the men as they fight. It is recorded that some armies that were already wavering and on the point of collapse have been rallied by women pleading steadfastly, blocking their path with bared breasts, and reminding their men how near they themselves are to being taken captive. This they fear by a long way more desperately for their women than for themselves. . . . They even believe that there is something holy and an element of the prophetic in women, hence they neither scorn their advice nor ignore their predictions. . . .

---

[2] **Noricum and Pannonia**: What is today Austria, Hungary, and Croatia.

On minor matters only the chiefs decide, on major questions the whole community. But even cases where the decision lies with the commons are considered in advance by the chiefs. Except when there is some chance or sudden happening, they assemble on fixed days, either just before the new moon or just after the full moon. This they reckon to be the most auspicious starting point for transacting business. Indeed, they do not reckon time by days, as we do, but by nights. All their decisions, all their agreements, are made in this way: night is seen as ushering in the day.

Their freedom of spirit involves a drawback, in that they do not assemble all at the same time or as if commanded, but take two or three days over it, hanging back. When the assembled crowd is ready, they take their seats, carrying arms. Silence is commanded by the priests, who have on these occasions the right to enforce obedience. Then the king or the chiefs are heard, in accordance with each one's age, nobility, military distinction, or eloquence. The power of persuasion counts for more than the right to give orders. If a proposal displeases them, they shout out their dissent. If they approve, they clash their spears. Showing approval with weapons is the most honorable way to express assent.

One may also bring in an accusation in the assembly, including a capital charge. The penalty varies according to the crime. Traitors and deserters are hanged on trees. Cowards, those who will not fight, . . . are plunged into a boggy mire. . . .

They transact no business, public or private, except under arms. But it is their practice that no one may bear arms until the community has recognized him as fit to use them. Then in the assembly itself either one of the chiefs or his own father or his kinsmen present the young man with shield and spear. . . .

When they are not waging war they occupy a little of their time in hunting but a good deal is spent without occupation: they devote themselves to sleeping and eating. . . .

It is well known that none of the German peoples live in cities, and that they cannot even bear to live in adjoining houses. They dwell apart from one another, scattered about, wherever a spring, a plain, or a wood attracts them. They do not lay out their villages in our style, with buildings joined and connected together. Each of them leaves an open space around his house, wither as a protection against the risk of fire, or because they lack skill in building. They do not use stones or bricks. They employ timber for all purposes, roughly cut, for they are not concerned to achieve a pleasant external appearance. . . .

The marriage code is strict there, and there is no aspect of their morality that deserves higher praise. They are almost the only barbarians who are content with a single wife, except for a very few, who are not motivated by sexual appetite — it is, rather, that they are courted with numerous offers of marriage on account of their noble rank. The dowry is not brought by the wife to the husband but by the husband to the wife. . . . They live a life of sheltered chastity, uncorrupted by the temptations of public shows or the excitements of banquets. Men and women alike know nothing of clandestine letters. Considering the great size of the population, adultery is very rare. The penalty for it is instant and left to the husband. He cuts off her hair, strips her naked in the presence of her kinsmen, and flogs her all through the village. They have no mercy on a woman who prostitutes her chastity. . . . [A wife] must love not so much the husband himself as their marriage. To limit the number of their children or to kill one of the later-born is regarded as a crime. Good morality is more effective there than good laws elsewhere.

In every household the children grow up, naked and dirty, to that size of limb and stature which we admire in them. Each mother breastfeeds her own child and does not hand them over to maids or nurses. . . . The young men are slow to mate, and reach manhood with unimpaired vigor. Nor are the virgins hurried into marriage. Being as old and as tall as the men, they are equal to their mates in age and strength, and the children inherit the robustness of their parents. . . .

It is an obligation to take over the father's or kinsman's feuds and friendships. But feuds do not go on with no reconciliation. In fact, even homicide can be atoned for with a fixed number of cattle or sheep. The whole family receives this compensation. This is an advantage for the community, since feuds are rather dangerous where freedom exists. . . .

The practice of lending out capital and stretching it out into interest is unknown: ignorance is a surer protection than any prohibition. Lands are occupied by the whole people to be cultivated, the quantity determined by the number of cultivators. They then divide the lands out among themselves according to rank. The great extent of the land makes the division easy. They plough different fields every year and there is still spare land available.

READING AND DISCUSSION QUESTIONS

1. According to Tacitus, why do the Germans fight with their families close by? What does this reveal about Germanic society?

2. What does the following passage tell you about *both* Germanic *and* Roman society: "To limit the number of their children or to kill one of

the later-born is regarded as a crime. Good morality is more effective there than good laws elsewhere"?

3. Describe the most important features of the Germanic economy.

4. What in particular does Tacitus admire about the Germans?

DOCUMENT 6-3

APULEIUS

The Golden Ass: *The Veneration of Isis*

ca. 170 C.E.

In the Hellenistic era, the worship of the Egyptian goddess Isis (see Document 1-6) spread across the Mediterranean. In the Roman Empire, her followers formed one of the most popular mystery cults. Worshippers in these mystery cults, which offered an alternative to the official gods of the Roman state, believed that the god or goddess of the cult took an interest in their individual lives. The Golden Ass illustrates this personal aspect to the cults. Apuleius (ah-puh-LAY-us) tells the story of a young man, Lucius, who avoids adult responsibilities but is fascinated by magic. While spying on a witch who turns herself into a bird, he attempts to do the same, but turns himself into a donkey instead. After suffering many misadventures as a donkey, in despair he finally calls on Isis for assistance. Born in a Roman colony of North Africa about 125 C.E., Apuleius likely based his tale on an older Greek text. His is the only complete Latin novel that survives.

About the first watch of the night I awoke in sudden terror and saw the full orb of the moon just rising from the waves; exceeding bright it was and of unwonted splendor. All about me was the silent mystery of the dark night. I knew that the supreme goddess was now in the [fullness] of her power

---

From Apuleius, *The Metamorphoses: or Golden Ass of Apuleius of Madaura*, vol. 2, trans. Harold Edgeworth Butler (Oxford: Clarendon Press, 1910), pp. 126–132. Text modernized by Amy R. Caldwell.

and that the lives of men were governed by her providence; I knew that not only all cattle and creatures of the wild, but even things inanimate were given new life by her divine splendor and the power of her godhead. . . . I resolved to address my prayers to the august vision of the goddess now present in power, and straightway shaking off sluggish slumber nimbly arose . . . and thus made I my supplication to the all-powerful goddess, my face bathed in tears:

Queen of heaven, whether you be Ceres,[3] the kindly mother from whom in the beginning spring the fruits of earth, . . . or be you Venus the heavenly one, who at the first beginning of things did unite the diversity of the sexes in the power of Love that is born of you, . . . or be you Phoebus's sister,[4] who with gentle healing brings relief to women in travail and has reared such multitudes, . . . or be you Proserpine,[5] to whom men render shuddering reverence with howls by night, . . . by whatever name, by whatever rite, in whatever semblance man may invoke you, do you now aid me in my utter woe. . . . Take from me the foul semblance of a four-footed beast, restore me to the sight of those I love, restore to me the Lucius that I knew. . . .

Thus had I outpoured my supplication and added thereto much woeful wailing, when once more slumber was shed about me on that same couch of sand and overcame my fainting soul. Yet scarce had I closed my eyes in sleep, [when the goddess appeared and spoke to me]. . . .

"Lo, Lucius, I am come, moved by your supplication, I, nature's mother, mistress of all the elements, the first-begotten offspring of the ages, of deities mightiest, queen of the dead, first of heaven's denizens, in whose aspect are blended the aspects of all gods and goddesses. With my rod I rule the shining heights of heaven, the health-giving breezes of the sea, the mournful silence of the underworld. The whole earth worships my godhead, one and individual, under many a changing shape, with varied rites and by many diverse names. There the Phrygians,[6] first-born of men, call me the mother of the gods; . . . there the Athenians, sprung from the soil they till, know me as Cecropian Minerva;[7] . . . Cretans, Diana of

---

[3] **Ceres**: Roman agricultural goddess.

[4] **Phoebus's sister**: Artemis, Greek goddess of fertility, childbirth, and the hunt.

[5] **Proserpine**: Roman goddess of springtime.

[6] **Phrygians**: People from Anatolia, the central region in the modern Republic of Turkey.

[7] **Minerva**: Roman equivalent of Athena, the Greek goddess of wisdom.

the hunter's net;[8] . . . Others call me Juno,[9] others Bellona,[10] others Hecate,[11] . . . and the Egyptians mighty in ancient lore, honor me with my peculiar rites and call me by my true name, Isis the Queen. I am come in pity for your woes. I am come propitious and strong to aid. . . . You must await [my] festival with heart untroubled and profane thoughts banished far from you. For the priest who shall assist in the celebration of the procession, forewarned by me, will bear . . . in his right hand a wreath of roses. Then delay not, but brush aside the crowds and lightly join my procession, relying on my goodwill. Draw nigh and gently, as though you wouldst kiss the priest's hand, pluck the roses and put off from you straightway the hide of that vile beast, that hath ever been hateful to me. And shrink not from any of these things as too hard for you. . . . At my bidding the people that throng you about will part and leave clear a path for you. Nor amid those merry sights and those gay ceremonies will any one shudder at that foul aspect you wear, nor will any interpret to your shame your sudden change of shape nor make malign accusation against you. But you must remember surely and keep hidden in your inmost soul this — that the rest of your life's course, to the term of your last breath, is dedicated to me. Nor is it unjust that you should, so long as you shalt live, owe all your life to her who brought you back to mankind. But you shalt live blessed, you shalt live crowned with glory beneath my protection, and when your life is run and you go down to the nether world, there also in that nether hemisphere you shall see me shining through the darkness of Acheron[12] and reigning in the inmost halls of Styx;[13] and you shall dwell in the Elysian fields,[14] and continually make offering of worship to me, and I will smile on you.

READING AND DISCUSSION QUESTIONS

1. Why did Lucius pray to Isis?
2. What does Isis do? Who is she?

---

[8] **Diana of the hunter's net**: Roman goddess of virginity and the hunt.

[9] **Juno**: Queen of the Roman gods.

[10] **Bellona**: Roman goddess of warfare.

[11] **Hecate**: Goddess of magic and witchcraft.

[12] **Acheron**: One of five rivers in the Greek underworld.

[13] **Styx**: One of five rivers in the Greek underworld.

[14] **Elysian fields**: Home in the afterlife for those who lived a virtuous life.

3.   What benefits does she offer her followers in this life? What about the afterlife?

4.   What else, other than the assistance of a goddess, does the cult of Isis offer? What appeal might it have beyond its religious aspects?

DOCUMENT 6-4

The Gospel According to Matthew:
The Sermon on the Mount

28 C.E.

The Sermon on the Mount is perhaps the best-known summary of Jesus' moral teachings. The themes in this sermon appear throughout the Gospels of the New Testament. In Matthew's retelling, while Jesus' disciples were in attendance, the audience was mainly comprised of Jews. Jesus uses the basic ideas of Hebrew law (Document 2-2), but reinterprets them for his audience.

Now when he saw the crowds, he went up on a mountainside and sat down. His disciples came to him, and he began to teach them saying:

"Blessed are the poor in spirit, for theirs is the kingdom of heaven.

"Blessed are those who mourn, for they will be comforted.

"Blessed are the meek, for they will inherit the earth.

"Blessed are those who hunger and thirst for righteousness, for they will be filled.

"Blessed are the merciful, for they will be shown mercy.

"Blessed are the pure in heart, for they will see God.

"Blessed are the peacemakers, for they will be called sons of God.

"Blessed are those who are persecuted because of righteousness, for theirs is the kingdom of heaven.

"Blessed are you when people insult you, persecute you and falsely say all kinds of evil against you because of me. Rejoice and be glad, because great is your reward in heaven, for in the same way they persecuted the prophets who were before you.

Matthew 5.

"You are the salt of the earth. But if the salt loses its saltiness, how can it be made salty again? It is no longer good for anything, except to be thrown out and trampled by men.

"You are the light of the world. A city on a hill cannot be hidden. Neither do people light a lamp and put it under a bowl. Instead they put it on its stand, and it gives light to everyone in the house. In the same way, let your light shine before men, that they may see your good deeds and praise your Father in heaven.

"Do not think that I have come to abolish the Law or the Prophets; I have not come to abolish them but to fulfill them. I tell you the truth, until heaven and earth disappear, not the smallest letter, not the least stroke of a pen, will by any means disappear from the Law until everything is accomplished. Anyone who breaks one of the least of these commandments and teaches others to do the same will be called least in the kingdom of heaven, but whoever practices and teaches these commands will be called great in the kingdom of heaven. For I tell you that unless your righteousness surpasses that of the Pharisees and the teachers of the law, you will certainly not enter the kingdom of heaven.

"You have heard that it was said to the people long ago, 'Do not murder, and anyone who murders will be subject to judgment.' But I tell you that anyone who is angry with his brother will be subject to judgment. Again, anyone who says to his brother, 'Raca,'[15] is answerable to the Sanhedrin.[16] But anyone who says, 'You fool!' will be in danger of the fire of hell.

"Therefore, if you are offering your gift at the altar and there remember that your brother has something against you, leave your gift there in front of the altar. First go and be reconciled to your brother; then come and offer your gift.

"Settle matters quickly with your adversary who is taking you to court. Do it while you are still with him on the way, or he may hand you over to the judge, and the judge may hand you over to the officer, and you may be thrown into prison. I tell you the truth, you will not get out until you have paid the last penny.

"You have heard that it was said, 'Do not commit adultery.' But I tell you that anyone who looks at a woman lustfully has already committed adultery with her in his heart. If your right eye causes you to sin, gouge it out and throw it away. It is better for you to lose one part of your body than

---

[15] **Raca**: Aramaic for "worthless person."
[16] **Sanhedrin**: A Jewish judicial body.

for your whole body to be thrown into hell. And if your right hand causes you to sin, cut it off and throw it away. It is better for you to lose one part of your body than for your whole body to go into hell.

"It has been said, 'Anyone who divorces his wife must give her a certificate of divorce.' But I tell you that anyone who divorces his wife, except for marital unfaithfulness, causes her to become an adulteress, and anyone who marries the divorced woman commits adultery.

"Again, you have heard that it was said to the people long ago, 'Do not break your oath, but keep the oaths you have made to the Lord.' But I tell you, Do not swear at all: either by heaven, for it is God's throne; or by the earth, for it is his footstool; or by Jerusalem, for it is the city of the Great King. And do not swear by your head, for you cannot make even one hair white or black. Simply let your 'Yes' be 'Yes,' and your 'No,' 'No'; anything beyond this comes from the evil one.

"You have heard that it was said, 'Eye for eye, and tooth for tooth.' But I tell you, Do not resist an evil person. If someone strikes you on the right cheek, turn to him the other also. And if someone wants to sue you and take your tunic, let him have your cloak as well. If someone forces you to go one mile, go with him two miles. Give to the one who asks you, and do not turn away from the one who wants to borrow from you.

"You have heard that it was said, 'Love your neighbor and hate your enemy.' But I tell you: Love your enemies and pray for those who persecute you, that you may be sons of your Father in heaven. He causes his sun to rise on the evil and the good, and sends rain on the righteous and the unrighteous. If you love those who love you, what reward will you get? Are not even the tax collectors doing that? And if you greet only your brothers, what are you doing more than others? Do not even pagans do that? Be perfect, therefore, as your heavenly Father is perfect.

READING AND DISCUSSION QUESTIONS

1. Why might Jesus' teaching be seen as a threat to Roman law and order?

2. How do you think Jesus expected his teachings to be received by both Jews and Roman authorities?

The Alexamenos Graffito

ca. 100 C.E.

Graffiti was a common sight in Roman cities, and historians have learned much about daily Roman life from the examples they have found. This image was found carved into the wall of a police barracks. The caption, written in Greek, reads, "Alexamenos worships [his] god." The picture shows

Alinari/Art Resource, N.Y.

Jesus, with the head of a donkey, being crucified. The man next to the cross, probably meant to be Alexamenos, lifts an arm in worship. This posture with one arm raised was common among Roman mystery cults. At the time, it was widely rumored that Christians worshipped a god with a donkey's head.

READING AND DISCUSSION QUESTIONS

1. Who is being mocked in this image? Why?
2. How well does the person who created this image understand Christianity? What does that reveal about the relationship between Romans and Christians at this time?

COMPARATIVE QUESTIONS

1. Juvenal and Tacitus provide commentary on non-Roman peoples and their behavior. How does each author respond to new things? Why do you think their responses are different?
2. Compare and contrast the Sermon on the Mount and the veneration of Isis. What elements in Jesus' teachings might have appealed to Romans?
3. How is the Sermon on the Mount based on Hebrew law (Document 2-2)? On which points is Jesus' message different from traditional Roman law?
4. In what ways is Christianity different from Roman religion and society? What kinds of misunderstandings arise between Romans and Christians?

CHAPTER 7

Late Antiquity

250–600

W ith the conversion of the emperor Constantine in 312, Christianity was legally accepted as a religion in the Roman Empire. At the
end of the fourth century, Emperor Theodosius I made Christianity the
official religion of the empire, leading to a new relationship between spiritual and secular leaders. The alliance between church and state had the
potential to strengthen both partners, but at times the two struggled for dom-
inance. Beginning in the second half of the second century, the Roman
Empire found itself resisting an influx of Germanic tribes, most of whom
practiced pagan religions. Many of them adopted Christianity and some elements of Roman civilization as they advanced into Roman territory. After a
series of disasters in the fifth century, the last Roman emperor in the West
was deposed in 476. As the Western Roman Empire disintegrated into a collection of smaller states, the Christian church, already a powerful institution
in its own right, increasingly became a center of learning and security. The
eastern half of the empire, based in Constantinople, retained considerable
strength. The emperor Justinian reconquered considerable portions of Italy
and North Africa, although these conquests were generally short-lived.

DOCUMENT 7-1

SAINT AMBROSE OF MILAN
Emperor Theodosius Brought to Heel
390

*Saint Ambrose (ca. 339–397) was the bishop of Milan and one of the most
important religious figures of his time. He was an administrator, a theologian,*

From *Translations and Reprints from the Original Sources of European History*, vol. 4
(Philadelphia: University of Pennsylvania Press, 1897), pp. 23–24.

and a significant political voice. In 390, Emperor Theodosius I had seven thousand people massacred in the Greek city of Thessalonica after they staged a rebellion against the imperial garrison. As punishment, Ambrose refused to admit the emperor to the church until he had done penance for several months. Although Ambrose was not the only church leader to chastise an emperor, he was one of the most successful.

surprise/
^ confuse

I have written these things, indeed, not to confound you, but that the example of these kings might induce you to put away this sin from your kingdom, which you will accomplish by humiliating your soul to God. You are a man and temptation has come to you; confess it. Sin is not put away except by tears and penitence. Neither an angel can do it nor an archangel; the Lord himself, who alone can say, "I am with you," does not forgive us if we have sinned except we be penitent.

I persuade, I beg, I exhort, I admonish; because it is a grief to me that you who were an example of unusual piety, who were the very personification of clemency, who would not allow guilty individuals to be brought into danger, that you do not grieve at the death of so many innocent persons. Although you have fought battles most successfully, although in other things also you are worthy of praise, yet the crown of all your work was always piety. This the devil envied you, since it was your ever present possession. Conquer him while as yet you have wherewith you may conquer. Do not add another sin to your sin, that you may practice what it has injured many to practice.

I, indeed, though in all other things a debtor to your kindness which I can never be ungrateful for, which kindness surpassed that of many emperors and was equalled by the kindness of one only, I, I say, have no cause for a charge of contumacy [resistance to authority] against you, but I have a cause for fear; I dare not offer the sacrifice if you will to be present. Is that which is not allowed after shedding the blood of one innocent person to be allowed after shedding the blood of many? I do not think so.

READING AND DISCUSSION QUESTIONS

1. How would you describe the tone of Ambrose's letter? How does this tone fit the actual content of the letter?

2. What does it mean that Ambrose does not dare to offer the sacrifice if the emperor is present?

3. That Ambrose was able to take the actions described implies what about the power of the church?

DOCUMENT 7-2

SAINT BENEDICT OF NURSIA
The Rule of Saint Benedict
529

By the time of Saint Benedict (ca. 480–543), monasticism was a long-established institution. Some monks (eremites, or hermits) lived on their own; others (cenobites) lived in communities. Benedict's rule for monks living in communities was adopted throughout the Christian world. The Rule was widely praised for both its spirituality and its practicality. Benedict was well aware of the need for harmony within monastic communities. According to legend, some of the monks in Benedict's first community tried to murder him, and on one occasion he was saved when a raven made away with a loaf of poisoned bread.

Concerning the daily manual labor. Idleness is the enemy of the soul. And therefore, at fixed times, the brothers ought to be occupied in manual labor; and again, at fixed times, in sacred reading. Therefore we believe that, according to this disposition, both seasons ought to be arranged; so that, from Easter until the Calends of October,[1] going out early, from the first until the fourth hour they shall do what labor may be necessary. Moreover, from the fourth hour until about the sixth, they shall be free for reading. After the meal of the sixth hour, moreover, rising from table, they shall rest in their beds with all silence; or, perchance, he that wishes to read may so read to himself that he do not disturb another. And the nona [the second meal] shall be gone through with more moderately about the middle of the eighth hour; and again they shall work at what is to be done

---

From E. F. Henderson, ed., *Select Historical Documents of the Middle Ages* (London: G. Bell, 1892), pp. 297–298.

[1] **Calends of October:** October 1.

until Vespers.[2] But, if the exigency or poverty of the place demands that they be occupied by themselves in picking fruits, they shall not be dismayed: for then they are truly monks if they live by the labors of their hands; as did also our fathers and the apostles. Let all things be done with moderation, however, on account of the faint-hearted. . . . [There follows a slightly different schedule for the winter months from October to Easter.] But in the days of Lent,[3] from dawn until the third full hour, they shall be free for their readings; and, until the tenth full hour, they shall do the labor that is enjoined on them. In which days of Lent they shall all receive separate books from the library; which they shall read entirely through in order. These books are to be given out on the first day of Lent. Above all there shall certainly be appointed one or two elders, who shall go round the monastery at the hours in which the brothers are engaged in reading, and see to it that no troublesome brother chance to be found who is open to idleness and trifling, and is not intent on his reading; being not only of no use to himself, but also stirring up others. If such a one — may it not happen — be found, he shall be admonished once and a second time. If he do not amend, he shall be subject under the Rule to such punishment that the others may have fear. . . . On feeble or delicate brothers such a labor or art is to be imposed, that they shall neither be idle, nor shall they be so oppressed by the violence of labor as to be driven to take flight. Their weakness is to be taken into consideration by the abbot.

READING AND DISCUSSION QUESTIONS

1. From this account, describe three practical problems of life in a monastery, and outline how Benedict tries to deal with them.

2. Why does Benedict think it important that monks should work with their hands?

3. In what ways does the *Rule* promote learning?

4. What provisions are made for "feeble or delicate brothers"? Why do they need to be treated carefully?

---

[2] **Vespers**: Evening prayers.
[3] **Lent**: The season of fasting before Easter.

DOCUMENT 7-3

SAINT AUGUSTINE

City of God: *The Two Cities*

413–426

Saint Augustine (354–430), bishop of Hippo Regius in what is now Algeria, was one of the most important early church leaders. In 410, Rome was sacked by Alaric the Visigoth. By this time, most of the emperors had been Christian for nearly a hundred years, but pagan religion was still influential, especially in the countryside and among some of the upper classes. Many pagans claimed that Rome had fallen because Christianity had turned people away from the old gods who had once protected the city. The City of God, *among its other purposes, was Augustine's answer to these claims.*

The glorious city of God is my theme in this work, which you, my dearest son Marcellinus,[4] suggested, and which is due to you by my promise. I have undertaken its defense against those who prefer their own gods to the Founder of this city, — a city surpassingly glorious, whether we view it as it still lives by faith in this fleeting course of time, and sojourns as a stranger in the midst of the ungodly, or as it shall dwell in the fixed stability of its eternal seat, which it now with patience waits for, expecting until "righteousness shall return unto judgment," and it obtain, by virtue of its excellence, final victory and perfect peace. A great work this, and an arduous; but God is my helper. For I am aware what ability is requisite to persuade the proud how great is the virtue of humility, which raises us, not by a quite human arrogance, but by a divine grace, above all earthly dignities that totter on this shifting scene. For the King and Founder of this city of which we speak, has in Scripture uttered to His people a dictum of the divine law in these words: "God resisteth the proud, but giveth grace unto the humble." But this, which is God's prerogative, the inflated ambition of a proud spirit also affects, and dearly loves that this be numbered among

From Rev. Marcus Dods, ed., *The City of God* (Edinburgh: T. & T. Clark, 1888), 1:1–2, 2:47–48.

[4] **Marcellinus**: Marcellinus of Carthage (d. 413), a friend of Augustine.

its attributes, to "Show pity to the humbled soul, And crush the sons of pride." And therefore, as the plan of this work we have undertaken requires, and as occasion offers, we must speak also of the earthly city, which, though it be mistress of the nations, is itself ruled by its lust of rule. . . .

Accordingly, two cities have been formed by two loves: the earthly by the love of self, even to the contempt of God; the heavenly by the love of God, even to the contempt of self. The former, in a word, glories in itself, the latter in the Lord. For the one seeks glory from men; but the greatest glory of the other is God, the witness of conscience. The one lifts up its head in its own glory; the other says to its God, "Thou art my glory, and the lifter up of mine head." In the one, the princes and the nations it subdues are ruled by the love of ruling; in the other, the princes and the subjects serve one another in love, the latter obeying, while the former take thought for all. The one delights in its own strength, represented in the persons of its rulers; the other says to its God, "I will love Thee, O Lord, my strength." And therefore the wise men of the one city, living according to man, have sought for profit to their own bodies or souls, or both, and those who have known God "glorified Him not as God, neither were thankful, but became vain in their imaginations, and their foolish heart was darkened; professing themselves to be wise," — that is, glorying in their own wisdom, and being possessed by pride, — "they became fools, and changed the glory of the incorruptible God into an image made like to corruptible man, and to birds, and four-footed beasts, and creeping things." For they were either leaders or followers of the people in adoring images, "and worshipped and served the creature more than the Creator, who is blessed for ever." But in the other city there is no human wisdom, but only godliness, which offers due worship to the true God, and looks for its reward in the society of the saints, of holy angels as well as holy men, "that God may be all in all."

READING AND DISCUSSION QUESTIONS

1.   What are the two cities? Where are they located?
2.   How does Augustine describe each city?
3.   Which city is more important? Does it matter what happens in the less important city?

DOCUMENT 7-4

GREGORY OF TOURS

The History of the Franks

594

The Frankish people converted to Christianity through the missionary work of a Roman soldier now known as Saint Martin of Tours. Martin established the foundations of an organized Christian church, and his name was associated with the French monarchy for centuries. In the sixth century, Gregory (ca. 538–594), the bishop of Tours, decided to write a history of the Franks. His work not only shows us how Christianity adapted to the Franks in Gaul, but it is also a source of evidence for many aspects of Frankish culture.

A great many things keep happening, some of them good, some of them bad. The inhabitants of different countries keep quarrelling fiercely with each other and kings go on losing their temper in the most furious way. Our churches are attacked by the heretics and then protected by the Catholics; the faith of Christ burns bright in many men, but it remains lukewarm in others; no sooner are the church-buildings endowed by the faithful than they are stripped bare again by those who have no faith. However, no writer has come to the fore who has been sufficiently skilled in setting things down in an orderly fashion to be able to describe these events in prose or in verse. In fact in the towns of Gaul the writing of literature has declined to the point where it has virtually disappeared altogether. Many people have complained about this, not once but time and time again. "What a poor period this is!" they have been heard to say. "If among all our people there is not one man to be found who can write a book about what is happening today, the pursuit of letters really is dead in us!"

I have often thought about these complaints and others like them. I have written this work to keep alive the memory of those dead and gone, and to bring them to the notice of future generations. . . .

From Gregory of Tours, *The History of the Franks*, trans. Lewis Thorpe (Baltimore: Penguin Books, 1974), pp. 63, 97–98, 219.

In the second year of the rule of Arcadius and Honorius,[5] Saint Martin, Bishop of Tours, who had done so many good deeds for the sick, who was so holy and had performed so many miracles, died at Candes, a village in his own diocese, in the eighty-first year of his age and the twenty-sixth year of his episcopate, and so went happily to meet Christ. He died at midnight on a Sunday. . . . As soon as this holy man was taken ill in the village of Candes, as I have said already, the people of Poitiers and Tours began to assemble at his death-bed. When he was dead, a great altercation arose between the two groups. The men of Poitiers said: "As a monk he is ours. He became an abbot in our town. We entrusted him to you, but we demand him back. It is sufficient for you that, while he was a Bishop on this earth, you enjoyed his company, you shared his table, you were strengthened by his blessing and above all you were cheered by his miracles. Let all these things suffice for you, and permit us at least to carry away his dead body." To this the men of Tours replied: "If you say that we should be satisfied with the miracles which he performed for us, then admit that while he was with you he did more than in our town. If all his other miracles are left out of the count, he raised two dead men for you and only one for us; and, as he himself used often to say, his miraculous power was greater before he was made Bishop than it was afterwards. It is therefore necessary that what he did not achieve with us when he was alive he should complete now that he is dead. God took him away from you, but only so that He might give him to us. If the custom established by the men of old is observed, then by God's will he shall be buried in the town where he was consecrated. If you propose to claim him because you have his monastery, then you must know this, that his first monastery was in Milan." They went on with their argument until the sun went down and night began to fall. The body was placed in the middle of the room, the doors were locked and he was watched over by the two groups. The men of Poitiers planned to carry off the body as soon as morning came, but Almighty God would not allow the town of Tours to be deprived of its patron. In the end all the men of Poitiers fell asleep in the middle of the night, and there was not one who remained on guard. When the men of Tours saw that all the Poitevins had fallen asleep, they took the mortal clay of that most holy body and some passed it out through the window while others stood outside to receive it. They

---

[5] **Arcadius and Honorius**: Brothers and Roman emperors. Arcadius ruled the Eastern Roman Empire, while Honorius ruled the Western half. The second year of their rule would have been 397.

placed it in a boat and all those present rowed down the River Vienne. As soon as they reached the River Loire, they set their course for the city of Tours, praising God and chanting psalms. The men of Poitiers were awakened by their voices and they went back home in great confusion, taking nothing of the treasure which they were supposed to be guarding. . . .

King Charibert married a woman called Ingoberg. He had by her a daughter who eventually married a man from Kent and went to live there. At that time Ingoberg had among her servants two young women who were the daughters of a poor man. The first of these, who wore the habits of a religious,[6] was called Marcovefa, and the other Merofled. The King fell violently in love with the two of them. As I implied, they were the daughters of a wool-worker. Ingoberg was jealous because of the love that the King bore them. She made a secret plan to set their father to work, in the hope that when Charibert saw this he would come to despise the two girls. When the man was working away Ingoberg summoned the King. Charibert came, hoping to see something interesting, and, without approaching too near, watched the man preparing wool for the royal household. He was so angry at what he saw that he dismissed Ingoberg and took Merofled in her place. He had another woman, the daughter of a shepherd who looked after his flocks. Her name was Theudechild and he is said to have had a son by her, but the child was buried immediately after his birth.

READING AND DISCUSSION QUESTIONS

1. Why does Gregory decide to write?
2. What does Gregory see changing in his lifetime?
3. Why do the people of Poitiers and Tours fight over the saint's body?
4. What does Gregory show about the relationship between kings and queens in Frankish culture?

---

[6] **habits of a religious**: She dressed like a nun.

VIEWPOINTS

The Character of an Emperor

DOCUMENT 7-5

EMPEROR JUSTINIAN

The Institutes of Justinian

529–533

Even though Justinian (r. 527–565) came from a peasant family, he was able to rise to imperial rank. His uncle Justin was a general in the imperial palace guard, and was chosen by Emperor Anastasius I to be his heir. Justin adopted his nephew, who was educated in Roman law. By the time Justinian became emperor, Roman law was a confused jumble of traditions dating back centuries. Justinian set his legal experts to work systematically organizing the various laws into one code. The influence of this work is seen even today in Western legal tradition. Before presenting the massive collection of individual laws, the code offers this statement of the principles behind the law.

The imperial majesty should be not only made glorious by arms, but also strengthened by laws, that, alike in time of peace and in time of war, the state may be well governed, and that the emperor may not only be victorious in the field of battle, but also may by every legal means repel the iniquities of men who abuse the laws, and may at once religiously uphold justice and triumph over his conquered enemies.

By our incessant labors and great care, with the blessing of God, we have attained this double end. The barbarian nations reduced under our yoke know our efforts in war; to which also Africa and very many other provinces bear witness, which, after so long an interval, have been restored to the dominion of Rome and our empire, by our victories gained through the favor of heaven. All nations moreover are governed by laws which we have already either promulgated or compiled.

From Thomas Collett Sandars, trans. and ed., *The Institutes of Justinian* (New York: Longman's, Green, and Co., 1917), pp. 1–7.

When we had arranged and brought into perfect harmony the hitherto confused mass of imperial constitutions, we then extended our care to the vast volumes of ancient law; and, sailing as it were across the mid-ocean, have now completed, through the favor of heaven, a work that once seemed beyond hope.

When by the blessing of God this task was accomplished, we summoned the most eminent . . . professors of law, all of whom have on many occasions proved to us their ability, legal knowledge, and obedience to our orders; and we have specially charged them to compose, under our authority and advice, Institutes, so that you may no more learn the first elements of law from old and erroneous sources, but apprehend them by the clear light of imperial wisdom; and that your minds and ears may receive nothing that is useless or misplaced, but only what obtains in actual practice. So that, whereas, formerly, the junior students could scarcely, after three years' study, read the imperial constitutions, you may now commence your studies by reading them, you who have been thought worthy of an honor and a happiness so great as that the first and last lessons in the knowledge of the law should issue for you from the mouth of the emperor. . . .

In these [Institutes] a brief exposition is given of the ancient laws, and of those also which, overshadowed by disuse, have been again brought to light by our imperial authority.

These four books of Institutes thus compiled, from all the Institutes left us by the ancients, and chiefly from the commentaries of our Gaius,[7] both in his Institutes, and in his work on daily affairs, and also from many other commentaries, were presented to us by the three learned men we have above named. We have read and examined them and have accorded to them all the force of our constitutions.

Receive, therefore, with eagerness, and study with cheerful diligence, these our laws, and show yourselves persons of such learning that you may conceive the flattering hope of yourselves being able, when your course of legal study is completed, to govern our empire in the different portions that may be entrusted to your care. . . .

The term *justice*, in its most extended sense, was taken by the Roman jurists to include all the commands laid upon men that they are bound to fulfill, both the commands of morality and of law. . . .

The maxims of law are these: to live honestly, to hurt no one, to give every one his due.

---

[7] **Gaius**: Gaius the Jurist (ca. 130–180), a Roman lawyer who wrote the *Institutes*, a textbook on Roman law.

READING AND DISCUSSION QUESTIONS

1. Why does Justinian want to see the laws put together in a systematic way?

2. How does a single, unified code of law benefit the people? How might it benefit the emperor?

3. Why is the concept of justice important to the law?

DOCUMENT 7-6

PROCOPIUS OF CAESAREA

The Secret History: *Justice for Sale*

ca. 550

Procopius of Caesarea was a scholar and advisor to a prominent Byzantine general. His learning and experience in this position enabled him to write the histories of Emperor Justinian's wars. He was also important enough to have had an opportunity to observe the workings of the court of Emperor Justinian and his wife, Empress Theodora. His Secret History is an extremely unflattering depiction of the couple, both as rulers and as human beings. The Secret History was published only after Procopius died.

Everything was done at the wrong time, and nothing that was established was allowed to continue. To prevent my narrative being interminable, I will merely mention a few instances, and pass over the remainder in silence. In the first place, Justinian neither possessed in himself the appearance of Imperial dignity, nor demanded that it should be respected by others, but imitated the barbarians in language, appearance, and ideas. When he had to issue an Imperial decree, he did not entrust it to the Quaestor[8] in the usual way, but for the most part delivered it himself by word of mouth, although he spoke his own language like a foreigner; or

---

From *Procopius, Literally and Completely Translated from the Greek for the First Time* (Athens: Athenian Society, 1896), pp. 116–121.

[8] **Quaestor**: An imperial official, usually in charge of finances.

else he left it in the hands of one of those by whom he was surrounded, so that those who had been injured by such resolutions did not know to whom to apply.

Those [secretaries] who . . . had from very ancient times fulfilled the duty of writing the secret dispatches of the Emperor, were no longer allowed to retain their privileges; for he himself wrote them nearly all, even the sentences of the municipal magistrates, no one throughout the Roman world being permitted to administer justice with a free hand. He took everything upon himself with unreasoning arrogance, and so managed cases that were to be decided, that, after he had heard one of the litigants, he immediately pronounced his verdict and obliged them to submit to it, acting in accordance with no law or principle of justice, but being evidently overpowered by shameful greed. For the Emperor was not ashamed to take bribes, since his avarice had deprived him of all feelings of shame. It frequently happened that the decrees of the Senate and the edicts of the Emperor were opposed to each other; for the Senate was as it were but an empty shadow, without the power of giving its vote or of keeping up its dignity; it was assembled merely for form's sake and in order to keep up an ancient custom, for none of its members were allowed to utter a single word. But the Emperor and his consort[9] took upon themselves the consideration of questions that were to be discussed, and whatever resolutions they came to between themselves prevailed. If he whose cause had been victorious had any doubt as to the legality of his success, all he had to do was to make a present of gold to the Emperor, who immediately promulgated a law contrary to all those formerly in force. If, again, anyone else desired the revival of the law that had been repealed, the autocrat did not disdain to revoke the existing order of things and to reestablish it. There was nothing stable in his authority, but the balance of justice inclined to one side or the other, according to the weight of gold in either scale. In the market-place there were buildings under the management of palace officials, where traffic was carried on, not only in judicial, but also in legislative decisions. The officers called "Referendars" (or mediators) found it difficult to present the requests of petitioners to the Emperor, and still more difficult to bring before the council in the usual manner the answer proper to be made to each of them; but, gathering together from all quarters worthless and false testimony, they deceived Justinian, who was naturally a fit subject for deception, by fallacious reports and misleading

---

[9] **consort**: Theodora.

statements. Then, immediately going out to the contending parties, without acquainting them with the conversation that had taken place, they extorted from them as much money as they required, without anyone venturing to oppose them.

Even the soldiers of the Praetorian guard,[10] whose duty it was to attend the judges in the court of the palace, forced from them whatsoever judgments they pleased. All, so to speak, abandoned their own sphere of duty, and followed the paths that pleased them, however difficult or untrodden they had previously been. Everything was out of gear; offices were degraded, not even their names being preserved. In a word, the Empire resembled a queen over boys at play. But I must pass over the rest, as I hinted at the commencement of this work.

I will now say something about the man who first taught the Emperor to traffic in the administration of justice. His name was Leo; he was a native of Cilicia, and passionately eager to enrich himself. He was the most utterly shameless of flatterers, and most apt in ingratiating himself with the ignorant, and with the Emperor, whose folly he made use of in order to ruin his subjects. It was this Leo who first persuaded Justinian to barter justice for money. When this man had once discovered these means of plunder, he never stopped. The evil spread and reached such a height that, if anyone desired to come off victorious in an unjust cause against an honest man, he immediately repaired to Leo, and, promising to give half of his claim to be divided between the latter and the Emperor, left the palace, having already gained his cause, contrary to all principles of right and justice. In this manner Leo acquired a vast fortune, and a great quantity of land, and became the chief cause of the ruin of the State. There was no longer any security in contracts, in law, in oaths, in written documents, in any penalty agreed upon, or in any other security, unless money had been previously given to Leo and the Emperor. Nor was even this method certain, for Justinian would accept bribes from both parties; and, after having drained the pockets of both of those who had put confidence in him, he was not ashamed to cheat one or other of them (no matter which), for, in his eyes, there was nothing disgraceful in playing a double part, provided only that it turned out profitable for him.

Such a man was Justinian.

---

[10] **Praetorian guard**: The soldiers assigned to protect the emperor and court officials.

READING AND DISCUSSION QUESTIONS

1. Just how bad a person does Procopius think Justinian is?

2. According to Procopius, how do Justinian's personal flaws influence the way he runs the empire?

3. What has happened to law and justice under Justinian?

COMPARATIVE QUESTIONS

1. How does the conversion of kings to Christianity affect the relationship between church and state?

2. Compare and contrast Augustine and Benedict. How do they think Christians should live? What does it mean to be Christian to them?

3. How does Justinian present himself, and why is it so radically different from how Procopius portrays him? How might you explain the difference?

4. Compare and contrast the Franks and the Byzantines. What do they have in common? What do their differences show about how the two parts of the Roman Empire are developing?

5. Compare and contrast the Franks as described by Gregory with the Germans as described by Tacitus (Document 6-2). How much do the Franks have in common with the earlier Germans, and how much have they adopted Roman civilization?

CHAPTER 8

Europe in the Early Middle Ages

600–1000

T he period between 600 and 1000 witnessed the emergence of powerful new empires, all of which were modeled on some aspect of Roman civilization. At the time of Muhammad's death in 632, Islam was largely confined to the Arabian peninsula, but the caliphs who followed him spread Islam throughout a vast empire, expanding into what was once part of the Roman Empire, In western Europe, conversion to Roman Catholicism helped spur the creation of new political entities. In the eighth and ninth centuries, Charlemagne, king of the Franks, led a revival of the Roman Empire (known to us as the Carolingian Renaissance), which included much of western and central Europe. Although a large part of this new empire was already Christian, Charlemagne forcibly converted pagans, most notably the Saxons, as he incorporated new territories. In 800, the pope crowned Charlemagne Holy Roman emperor. Following the reign of his son, Louis the Pious, the empire was split among Charlemagne's grandsons into three separate kingdoms. In Kievan Rus, the tenth-century conversion of the ruler Vladimir to the Eastern Orthodox Church laid the religious foundation for the eastern Slav states, which, many centuries later, would also claim to be the heirs to Rome.

DOCUMENT 8-1

IBN ABD-EL-HAKEM
The Conquest of Spain
ca. 870

Ibn Abd-el-Hakem, an Egyptian from a prominent family of legal scholars, wrote his history of the conquest of Spain more than a century after the actual events. As the oldest of the histories of the conquest written by an Islamic scholar, it was frequently cited by later Muslim historians. The events he describes are a combination of myth and fact. In the following excerpt, he describes both the violence and the cleverness of the Muslim invaders. After the conquest, the Muslims in Spain — the land they called al-Andalus — built a kingdom known as a center of culture and the arts that lasted for centuries.

The governor of the straits between this district [Tangiers] and Andalus was a foreigner called Ilyan, Lord of Septa. He was also the governor of a town called Alchadra, situated on the same side of the straits of Andalus as Tangiers. Ilyan was a subject of Roderic, the Lord of Andalus [i.e., king of Spain], who used to reside in Toledo. Tarik put himself in communication with Ilyan, and treated him kindly, until they made peace with each other. Ilyan had sent one of his daughters to Roderic, the Lord of Andalus, for her improvement and education; but she became pregnant by him. Ilyan having heard of this, said, I see for him no other punishment or recompense, than that I should bring the Arabs against him. He sent to Tarik, saying, I will bring you to Andalus. . . . But Tarik said I cannot trust you until you send me a hostage. So he sent his two daughters, having no other children. Tarik allowed them to remain in Tlemsen, guarding them closely. After that Tarik went to Ilyan who was in Septa on the straits. The latter rejoicing at his coming, said, I will bring you to Andalus. But there was a mountain called the mountain of Tarik between the two landing-places, that is, between Septa and Andalus. When the evening came, Ilyan brought him the vessels, in which he made him embark for that landing-place, where he concealed himself during the day, and in the evening sent back the vessels to bring over the rest of his companions. So they embarked for the

From Ibn Abd-el-Hakem, *History of the Conquest of Spain*, trans. John Harris Jones (Goettingen: Dietrich, 1858), pp. 18–20. Text modernized by Amy R. Caldwell.

landing-place, none of them being left behind: whereas the people of Andalus did not observe them, thinking that the vessels crossing and recrossing were similar to the trading vessels which for their benefit plied backwards and forwards. Tarik was in the last division which went across. He proceeded to his companions, Ilyan together with the merchants that were with him being left behind in Alchadra, in order that he might the better encourage his companions and countrymen. The news of Tarik and of those who were with him, as well as of the place where they were, reached the people of Andalus. Tarik, going along with his companions, marched over a bridge of mountains to a town called Cartagena. . . .

When the Muslims settled [on an island near Andalus], they found no other inhabitants there, than vinedressers.[1] They made them prisoners. After that they took one of the vinedressers, slaughtered him, cut him in pieces, and boiled him, while the rest of his companions looked on. They had also boiled meat in other cauldrons. When the meat was cooked, they threw away the flesh of that man which they had boiled; no one knowing that it was thrown away: and they ate the meat which they had boiled, while the rest of the vinedressers were spectators. These did not doubt but that the Muslims ate the flesh of their companion; the rest being afterwards sent away informed the people of Andalus that the Muslims feed on human flesh, acquainting them with what had been done to the vinedresser.

When Tarik landed, soldiers from Cordova came to meet him; and seeing the small number of his companions they despised him on that account. They then fought. The battle with Tarik was severe. They were routed, and he did not cease from the slaughter of them till they reached the town of Cordova. When Roderic heard of this, he came to their rescue from Toledo. . . . They fought a severe battle; but God, mighty and great, killed Roderic and his companions.

READING AND DISCUSSION QUESTIONS

1. What provokes the invasion of Roderic's kingdom?
2. What nonmilitary factors helped Tarik defeat Roderic?
3. Why did the Muslims pretend to eat the vinedresser?
4. What role does religion, both Christianity and Islam, play in these events?

---

[1] **vinedressers**: People who cultivate grapevines.

WILLIBALD

Saint Boniface Destroys the Oak of Thor

ca. 750

Saint Boniface (680–754) is known as the apostle of the Germans. He was born in England, which was already a center of Christianity, and was commissioned by Pope Gregory II to spread the gospel and reorganize the church in what is now Germany. Boniface's relative, Willibald (ca. 700–787), also a monk, recounts that as the missionary prepared to chop down the sacred oak, he challenged the pagan god Thor to strike him down. Boniface's survival was proof enough to convert many of the locals. When Boniface destroyed the oak, he was consciously imitating the prophet Elijah from the Hebrew Bible, who had challenged the worship of the god Baal.

Many of the people of Hesse were converted [by Boniface] to the Catholic faith and confirmed by the grace of the spirit: and they received the laying on of hands. But some there were, not yet strong of soul, who refused to accept wholly the teachings of the true faith. Some men sacrificed secretly, some even openly, to trees and springs. Some secretly practiced divining, soothsaying, and incantations, and some openly. But others, who were of sounder mind, cast aside all heathen profanation and did none of these things; and it was with the advice and consent of these men that Boniface sought to fell a certain tree of great size, at Geismar, and called, in the ancient speech of the region, the oak of Jove [i.e., Thor].

The man of God was surrounded by the servants of God. When he would cut down the tree, behold a great throng of pagans who were there cursed him bitterly among themselves because he was the enemy of their gods. And when he had cut into the trunk a little way, a breeze sent by God stirred overhead, and suddenly the branching top of the tree was broken off, and the oak in all its huge bulk fell to the ground. And it was broken into four parts, as if by the divine will, so that the trunk was divided into four huge sections without any effort of the brethren who stood by. When

From James Harvey Robinson, ed., *Readings in European History*, 2 vols. (Boston: Ginn, 1904), 1:106–107.

the pagans who had cursed did see this, they left off cursing and, believing, blessed God. Then the most holy priest took counsel with the brethren: and he built from the wood of the tree an oratory, and dedicated it to the holy apostle Peter.

READING AND DISCUSSION QUESTIONS

1. How fully did the people of Hesse accept Christianity?
2. What first inspires Saint Boniface to cut down the oak?
3. How does this passage illustrate what people of the time considered to be a miracle?

VIEWPOINTS
Religion and Empire

DOCUMENT 8-3

EINHARD
Life of Charlemagne
ca. 835

Although Einhard (ca. 775–840) came from a humble family, he was educated at the monastery at Fulda, which was one of the centers of learning in Frankish lands. Brought to the court to serve Charlemagne as a courtier, Einhard came to know the emperor well. After Charlemagne's death, Einhard became the private secretary of Charlemagne's son, Louis the Pious. It was Louis who asked Einhard to write the Life of Charlemagne, *which in a sense became an official biography. Einhard modeled his work on the* Life of Augustus *by the Roman historian Suetonius.*

From Einhard, "Life of Charlemagne," in James Harvey Robinson, ed., *Readings in European History*, abridged ed. (Boston: Ginn, 1906), pp. 65–71.

Charles[2] was large and robust, of commanding stature and excellent proportions, for it appears that he measured in height seven times the length of his own foot. The top of his head was round, his eyes large and animated, his nose somewhat long. He had a fine head of gray hair, and his face was bright and pleasant; so that, whether standing or sitting, he showed great presence and dignity. Although his neck was thick and rather short, and his belly too prominent, still the good proportions of his limbs concealed these defects. His walk was firm, and the whole carriage of his body was manly. His voice was clear, but not so strong as his frame would have led one to expect. . . .

He took constant exercise in riding and hunting, which was natural for a Frank,[3] since scarcely any nation can be found to equal them in these pursuits. . . .

He wore the dress of his native country, that is, the Frankish; [and] he thoroughly disliked the dress of foreigners, however fine; and he never put it on except at Rome. . . .

In his eating and drinking he was temperate; more particularly so in his drinking, for he had the greatest abhorrence of drunkenness in anybody, but more especially in himself and his companions. He was unable to abstain from food for any length of time, and often complained that fasting was injurious to him. On the other hand, he very rarely feasted, only on great festive occasions, when there were very large gatherings. The daily service of his table consisted of only four dishes in addition to the roast meat, which the hunters used to bring in on spits, and of which he partook more freely than of any other food.

While he was dining he listened to music or reading. History and the deeds of men of old were most often read. He derived much pleasure from the works of St. Augustine, especially from his book called *The City of God*. . . .

While he was dressing and binding on his sandals, he would receive his friends; and also, if the count of the palace announced that there was any case which could only be settled by his decision, the suitors were immediately ordered into his presence, and he heard the case and gave judgment as if sitting in court. And this was not the only business that he used to arrange at that time, for he also gave orders for whatever had to be done on that day by any officer or servant.

---

[2] **Charles**: Charlemagne's given name. He was later known as Charles the Great — Carolus Magnus in Latin and Charlemagne in French.
[3] **Frank**: Person of western Germanic origin or descent.

He was ready and fluent in speaking, and able to express himself with great clearness. He did not confine himself to his native tongue,[4] but took pains to learn foreign languages, acquiring such knowledge of Latin that he could make an address in that language as well as in his own. Greek he could better understand than speak. Indeed, he was so polished in speech that he might have passed for a learned man.

He was an ardent admirer of the liberal arts, and greatly revered their professors, whom he promoted to high honors. In order to learn grammar, he attended the lectures of the aged Peter of Pisa, a deacon; and for other branches he chose as his preceptor Albinus, otherwise called Alcuin, also a deacon, — a Saxon by race, from Britain, the most learned man of the day, with whom the king spent much time in learning rhetoric and logic, and more especially astronomy. He learned the art of determining the dates upon which the movable festivals of the Church fall, and with deep thought and skill most carefully calculated the courses of the planets.

Charles also tried to learn to write, and used to keep his tablets and writing book under the pillow of his couch, that when he had leisure he might practice his hand in forming letters; but he made little progress in this task, too long deferred and begun too late in life.

As Pope Leo [III] was riding from the Lateran[5] in Rome to service in the church of St. Lawrence, called "the Gridiron," he fell into an ambush which the Romans had set for him in the neighborhood of this church. He was dragged from off his horse and [his attackers tried to have] his eyes put out, his tongue cut off, and he was then left lying in the street, naked and half dead. Afterward the instigators of this deed ordered that he should be taken into the monastery of the holy martyr Erasmus to be cared for. His chamberlain Albinus succeeded, however, in letting him down over the wall at night, whereupon Duke Winigis of Spoleto, who had hurried to Rome on hearing of this deed of sacrilege, took him into his charge and carried him to Spoleto.

When the king [Charlemagne] received news of this occurrence, he gave orders that the Roman pope, the successor of St. Peter, should be brought to him, with all due honor. He did not, however, give up on this account the expedition into Saxony which he had undertaken. . . .

[*Charlemagne deals with several matters in his kingdom before heading to Rome.*]

---

[4] **his native tongue:** Scholars debate exactly which language Charlemagne would have spoken. It was probably a dialect of Old Frankish, from which the modern Dutch and German languages are descended.

[5] **Lateran:** Papal residence, at this time outside of Rome.

On the very day of his arrival Pope Leo went to meet him at Nomentum. He received the pope with great reverence, and they dined together. Then he remained behind while the pope returned to the city in order that he might be waiting to receive him the next morning on the steps of St. Peter's, together with the bishops and all the clergy.

When he appeared and dismounted from his horse, the pope received him with gratitude and thanksgiving and conducted him into the church, while all the people glorified God in hymns of praise. This was on the 24th day of November. Seven days later, the king publicly proclaimed, in an assembly which he had called together, all the reasons why he had come to Rome, and thenceforth he labored daily to carry out all that he had come to do.

He began with the most serious and difficult matter, namely, the investigation into the offenses of which the pope had been accused. But since no one could be found who was willing to substantiate the charges, the pope, carrying the Gospels in his hand, mounted the pulpit in St. Peter's and before all the people, and in the name of the Holy Trinity, took an oath to clear himself from the crimes imputed to him. . . .

On the most holy day of the birth of our Lord, the king went to mass at St. Peter's, and as he knelt in prayer before the altar Pope Leo set a crown upon his head, while all the Roman populace cried aloud, "Long life and victory to the mighty Charles, the great and pacific Emperor of the Romans, crowned of God!" After he had been thus acclaimed, the pope did homage to him, as had been the custom with the early rulers, and henceforth he dropped the title of Patrician and was called Emperor and Augustus.

READING AND DISCUSSION QUESTIONS

1. Why do you think Einhard describes Charlemagne's appearance at such great length? What does this description reveal about contemporary attitudes and about Einhard himself?

2. Charlemagne was a Frankish ruler. To what degree had the Franks assimilated the customs and practices of other people?

3. What is significant about the fact that Charlemagne, while dressing, would receive his friends and sometimes even hear cases?

4. What title does Charlemagne take after being crowned? What is significant about the pope's role in these events?

DOCUMENT 8-4

A Russian Chronicle of Religious Competition in Kievan Rus

ca. 1100

Vladimir the Great (r. 980–1015) became the ruler of Kievan Rus after a series of fratricidal wars. Originally, Vladimir had been a pious pagan, and some historians have argued that he had tried to reform Slavic religious beliefs by worshipping Perun, the god of thunder, as the ruler of the gods. In 987, after consulting with his nobles, Vladimir sent emissaries to learn about other religions. Vladimir was also intent on establishing an alliance with the Byzantine Empire. His marriage to Anna, the sister of the Byzantine emperor Basil II, marked the first time that an imperial princess had married a barbarian.

987 [c.e.] . . . Vladimir summoned together his vassals and the city elders, and said to them: "Behold, the Bulgarians came before me urging me to accept their religion. Then came the Germans and praised their own faith; and after them came the Jews. Finally the Greeks appeared, criticizing all other faiths but commending their own, and they spoke at length, telling the history of the whole world from its beginning. Their words were artful, and it was wondrous to listen and pleasant to hear them. They preach the existence of another world. 'Whoever adopts our religion and then dies shall arise and live forever. But whosoever embraces another faith, shall be consumed with fire in the next world.' What is your opinion on this subject, and what do you answer?" The vassals and the elders replied: "You know, O Prince, that no man condemns his own possessions, but praises them instead. If you desire to make certain, you have servants at your disposal. Send them to inquire about the ritual of each and how he worships God."

Their counsel pleased the prince and all the people, so that they chose good and wise men to the number of ten, and directed them to go first among the Bulgarians [i.e., the Turkic Volga Bulgars] and inspect their faith. The emissaries went their way, and when they arrived at their

From Serge A. Zenkovsky, ed., *Medieval Russia's Epics, Chronicles and Tales* (New York: Dutton, 1963), pp. 66–72.

destination they beheld the disgraceful actions of the Bulgarians and their worship in the mosque; then they returned to their own country. Vladimir then instructed them to go likewise among the Germans, and examine their faith, and finally to visit the Greeks. They thus went into Germany, and after viewing the German ceremonial, they proceeded to Constantinople where they appeared before the emperor. He inquired on what mission they had come, and they reported to him all that had occurred. When the emperor heard their words, he rejoiced, and did them great honor on that very day.

On the morrow, the emperor sent a message to the patriarch to inform him that a Russian delegation had arrived to examine the Greek faith, and directed him to prepare the church and the clergy, and to array himself in his sacerdotal robes,[6] so that the Russians might behold the glory of the God of the Greeks. When the patriarch received these commands, he bade the clergy assemble, and they performed the customary rites. They burned incense, and the choirs sang hymns. The emperor accompanied the Russians to the church, and placed them in a wide space, calling their attention to the beauty of the edifice, the chanting, and the offices of the archpriest and the ministry of the deacons, while he explained to them the worship of his God. The Russians were astonished, and in their wonder praised the Greek ceremonial. Then the Emperors Basil and Constantine invited the envoys to their presence, and said, "Go hence to your native country," and thus dismissed them with valuable presents and great honor.

Thus they returned to their own country, and the prince called together his vassals and the elders. Vladimir then announced the return of the envoys who had been sent out, and suggested that their report be heard. He thus commanded them to speak out before his vassals. The envoys reported: "When we journeyed among the Bulgarians, we beheld how they worship in their temple, called a mosque, while they stand ungirt.[7] The Bulgarian bows, sits down, looks hither and thither like one possessed, and there is no happiness among them, but instead only sorrow and a dreadful stench. Their religion is not good. Then we went among the Germans, and saw them performing many ceremonies in their temples; but we beheld no glory there. Then we went on to Greece, and the Greeks led us to the edifices where they worship their God, and we knew not whether we were in heaven or on earth. For on earth there is no such splendor or such beauty, and we are at a loss how to describe it. We know only that God dwells there among men, and their service is fairer than the

---

[6] **sacerdotal robes**: Clothing worn by a priest while performing religious ceremonies.
[7] **ungirt**: With belt loosened; rather sloppily.

ceremonies of other nations. For we cannot forget that beauty. Every man, after tasting something sweet, is afterward unwilling to accept that which is bitter, and therefore we cannot dwell longer here." Then the vassals spoke and said, "If the Greek faith were evil, it would not have been adopted by your grandmother Olga,[8] who was wiser than all other men." Vladimir then inquired where they should all accept baptism, and they replied that the decision rested with him.

[*However, Vladimir was not yet ready for baptism. He captured the Greek city of Kherson in the Crimea and demanded that the Byzantine emperor give him his daughter in marriage. The emperor refused unless Vladimir became a Christian. He gave his promise and the princess was dispatched to Russia, but still he refused to go through with the ceremony.*]

By divine agency, Vladimir was suffering at that moment from a disease of the eyes, and could see nothing, being in great distress. The princess declared to him that if he desired to be relieved of this disease, he should be baptized with all speed, otherwise it could not be cured. When Vladimir heard her message, he said, "If this proves true, then of a surety is the God of the Christians great," and gave order that he should be baptized. The Bishop of Kherson, together with the princess's priests, after announcing the tidings, baptized Vladimir, and as the bishop laid his hand upon him, he straightway received his sight. Upon experiencing this miraculous cure, Vladimir glorified God, saying, "I have now perceived the one true God." When his followers beheld this miracle, many of them were also baptized.

READING AND DISCUSSION QUESTIONS

1. What does it reveal about Kievan Rus that its ruler would send out emissaries to learn about the faiths of other peoples?

2. What did the emissaries have to say about the various faiths they encountered?

3. What impressed the emissaries most about Greek Orthodoxy?

4. Why did Vladimir finally convert?

---

[8] **Olga**: Saint Olga of Kiev, grandmother of Vladimir the Great, who ruled Kievan Rus (ca. 945–963) as a regent following her husband's death. She was the first Russian ruler to convert to Christianity.

DOCUMENT 8-5

The Song of Roland

ca. 1100–1300

The oldest example of French literature is The Song of Roland, *which tells the story of the death of one of Charlemagne's knights, his nephew Roland. The poem is based on a real battle fought by Charlemagne's army, but most of the details are far from factual. Epic poems like this one emerged from the songs that were sung to commemorate great battles. Over time, the precise details of the events were lost or distorted. For example, Charlemagne fought the Basques, not the Muslims. Despite its basis in legend, the poem still provides insight into the world of Charlemagne. The selection that follows shows that Charlemagne may have been the new Roman emperor, but that old Roman ideas had changed significantly.*

Charles, King of France,[9] the mighty, the Nations' Overlord,
Through seven full years hath tarried in the land of Spain, hath warred,
Till even down to the sea's lip he hath conquered the mountain-land,
Till not one castle remaineth whose towers against him stand,
Till never a city nor rampart abideth not cast down,
Save Saragossa, the fortress throned on a mountain's crown,
Yet holden of King Marsila: our God doth he abhor;
He is servant unto Mahomet,[10] and Apollo[11] doth he adore:
But he shall not avert God's sentence thus, and the doom in store.

So there in Saragossa the King Marsila stayed;
And he passed on a day 'neath an olive, he rested under its shade.
On a slab of the sea-blue marble layeth him down the King,
And he smiteth his hands together for the griefs that inly sting:
There warriors twenty thousand, yea, more, stood round in a ring.
And he cried to his great war-captains, to his earls he bemoaned him thus:

From Arthur S. Way, trans., *The Song of Roland, Translated into English Verse* (Cambridge: University Press, 1913), pp. 1–2, 7–9, 135–137, 140, 142.

[9] **Charles, King of France**: Charlemagne.
[10] **Mahomet**: Muhammad (ca. 570–632), Arab prophet and the founder of Islam.
[11] **Apollo**: Greek god of the sun.

"O ye my war-lords, hearken what evils encompass us!
Charles, Overlord of Nations, and goodly France's King,
Hath come into this our country for our discomfiting.
Ever he draweth nearer; I know how nigh is the fight;
Yet hosts have I none of prowess to shatter his iron might.
As beseemeth the wise and prudent, counsel me therefore ye,
And so from death redeem me, and save from infamy."
He spake; but of all those paynims [pagans] was none that answered
        a word,
Till spake at the last Blancandrin, Castel-Valfunda's lord.

Wise mid the wisest paynims Blancandrin was, and white
Was the hair whose silver ripples with his beard were mingled, a knight
Full knightly: for help of his liege-lord was he full of cunning sleight.
"King, be not dismayed," he answered, "but to Charles the haughty,
        the proud,
Send proffer of loyal service, and be utter friendship vowed.
Bears do thou send him, and lions, and hounds, as the gifts of a friend;
Let many a goodly war-steed and palfrey thy mission commend:
Seven hundred camels, and moulted falcons a thousand send.
Four hundred strong mules laden with gold and with silver prepare,
And money so much as fifty treasure-wains [carts] may bear,
Such glittering store of bezants[12] of fine gold tried in the fire
That thereof he may fully render to his men of war their hire.
And say: "O King, thou hast tarried so long in the land of Spain,
That well mayest thou turn backward to France and to Aix[13] again.
At Saint Michael's Feast[14] will I follow thee thither, thy proselyte,[15]
And receive the faith of the Christians by holy baptismal rite;
And thy man will I be, with my substance and love to serve my chief,
And will hold all Spain, thy vassal, henceforth of thee in fief.
Yea, hostages shalt thou send him, if this he require of my lord,
Be it ten, be it twenty, that credence be given so to thy word,
Yea, the sons of our noblest ladies; even thine thou shalt not spare:
Mine own son will I surrender to die, if it must be, there.
Rather it were to be chosen that the heads should fall of these,

---

[12] **bezants**: Coins made in Byzantium.
[13] **Aix**: Aachen in modern Germany.
[14] **Saint Michael's Feast**: September 29; also called Michaelmas.
[15] **proselyte**: Recent religious convert.

Than that we should be stripped, a nation, of our lands and our
      seignories,
And that begging our bread we should wander in misery of want."
Then low the paynims murmured, "Yea, all this well may we grant."

[*King Marsilla takes Blancandrin's advice and sends him as an ambassador
to Charlemagne. Charlemagne listens to the message, then consults with his
lords.*]

Spake Charles the emperor: "Barons, give ear unto me, my lords.
In council speak for my profit, yea, for your own, your words.
Messengers King Marsila hath sent, be it known unto you:
He is fain of his royal possessions to give rich gifts not a few:
Bears hath he sent, and lions, and hounds leashed two and two;
Horses of price, fleet-footed war-steeds goodly to see;
Seven hundred camels, a thousand mewed falcons[16] sendeth he;
Four hundred strong mules laden with gold of Araby,
And bezants so much as fifty treasure-wains may bear.
But — but he maketh conditions, that back unto France I fare:
Thereafter to Aix, to my palace, will he follow me, he saith,
And receive by the rite baptismal salvation through our faith,
And be made a Christian: his marches in fief shall he hold of me;
And, so long as life endureth, my servant shall he be.
Hostages ten, yea, twenty, for surety proffereth he.
Howbeit, what purpose he hideth within him, nowise I know."
"We must needs be exceeding wary!" the Frank lords murmured low.

So made he an end of speaking. To his feet Count Roland sprang.
He abhorred that counsel: clashing against it his voice outrang:
"O righteous lord, all trusting in the word of Marsila were vain!
Full seven years have passed over since we entered the land of Spain.
I have won for thee Morinda and Nobles by this right hand:
I have taken the burg Valterra, have given thee Pina's land:
Balgherra hath fallen, Tudela is thine, and royal Seville;
Aulert on the Spanish marches, and Pont on its castled hill.
But for this Marsila — a traitor he was, and is traitor still.
Unto thee of his infidel liars sent he not once fifteen,
Each man in his false hand bearing a bough of the olive green?[17]

---

[16] **mewed falcons**: Falcons trained to hunt.

[17] **a bough of the olive green**: Olive branch; a sign of peace.

And the selfsame words did they bring thee: a council didst thou call
Of thy Franks; and pitiful counsel they gave thee — fools were they all!
And so of thine earls thou sentest twain [two] — for the paynim to slay!
Basàn fared forth at thy bidding to his death with Basile that day;
For he shore their heads from their shoulders under the walls of Haltaye!
Now nay, let the war speed forward whereto thou hast set thine hand.
To the fortress Saragossa lead thou thy warrior-band;
Besiege it — yea, though the leaguer [siege] should last thine whole life
    through —
Until thou hast gotten vengeance for those whom the felon slew."

There with bowed head unmoving Charles sat, perplexèd sore:
At his beard he plucked, and the knightly fringe of his lips he tore,
The while to his nephew he answered no word of bad or good.
And all the Franks kept silence, till Ganelon forth stood;
For he sprang to his feet, forth striding he came before the King,
And his mien was exceeding haughty, and loud did the scorn of him ring:
"To give ear to a fool in his folly," he cried, "right ill were it done —
Be it I or another — take counsel of thine own profit alone.
Seeing that King Marsila his promise to thee hath sent
To become thy vassal, with claspèd hands at thy footstool bent,
And to hold all Spain by tenure of fief, his liege-lord thou,
And unto our faith to seal him by holy baptismal vow —
Now therefore, whoso adviseth that we thrust such proffer by,
My lord King, little he recketh by what deaths all we die!
Let counsels of pride with their glamour no longer delude our eyes.
Leave we the fools to their folly; henceforth let us hold by the wise."

[*Charlemagne decides he will offer to let Marsilla keep half of Spain if he
coverts to Christianity. The other half would go to Roland. At Roland's sug-
gestion, Ganelon is chosen to return with Blancandrin to deliver the message to Marsilla. Ganelon, believing that he was chosen because Roland
thinks Marsilla will kill him, plots with Blancandrin to arrange Roland's
death. Marsilla takes Ganelon's advice to refuse Charlemagne. They set up
a plan to leave Roland isolated in battle. The war begins, and Roland with
a small number of men face overwhelming odds. Roland dies heroically, and
Ganelon's plot is revealed.*]

In the ancient chronicle's record fair written doth it stand
How Charles sent forth his summons unto vassals of many a land
To gather in full assembly at Aix his chapel-hall:

And the set time was a high-day, a holy festival —
There be that affirm that the Saint's Day of Silvester the noble[18] it was.
That day began the judgment and the trial of the cause
Of Ganelon, whose devising had that great treason wrought.
Now the Emperor giveth commandment that before him he be brought.

"Lords of the land and barons," King Charles said, "hearken ye!"
This day judge righteous judgment 'twixt Ganelon and me.
He fared with me in mine army unto the land of Spain,
And by his contriving were Frenchmen twice ten thousand slain.
He hath reft from me my nephew, whom never more shall I see,
And Oliver the valiant, the flower of chivalry;
And the Twelve Peers[19] also for lucre [money] did he betray to their
     death."
Spake Ganelon: "Be I accursèd if aught I deny that he saith!
But this same Roland had wronged me as touching my gold and my land;
And for this I sought his destruction, for this his death I planned.
But for treason — I allow not that herein treason is!"
"Now take we heedful counsel," said the Franks, "as touching this."

Lo ye, in the Emperor's presence standeth Ganelon there:
His frame is goodly-shapen, his visage's favor is fair.
Had he been but a loyal vassal, he had seemed a noble knight.
He looked on the Franks, on the doomsmen appointed to judge the right,
On his thirty noble kinsmen who had gathered to his side:
With a great voice far-ringing unto them all he cried:
"For the love of God, ye barons, fair hearing to me accord!
I was indeed in the army of the Emperor my Lord,
And I served him at all seasons in love and in loyalty.
Howbeit his nephew Roland had a lodged hate unto me,
And to death did he adjudge me, to a death of shameful pain,
For through him was I forced to be herald unto King Marsila in Spain;
And, save by my wit and my wisdom, I had not escaped the snare.
For the doughty fighter Roland, I defied him then and there:
Yea, Oliver his comrade and the Twelve Peers I defied:
Herein must Charles and his barons bear witness on my side.
This therefore is private vengeance, but of treason not a whit."
"We will take heedful counsel," said the Franks, "as touching it." . . .

---

[18] **Saint's Day of Silvester the noble**: December 31.
[19] **the Twelve Peers**: Charlemagne's advisors and finest knights, led by Roland.

* * *

Unto Charlemagne his barons returned, and they said to the King:
"Sire, we beseech thee to pardon Count Ganelon in this thing;
So shall he serve thee hereafter in love and in loyalty.
Let him live, we beseech thee; valiant and gently born is he.
Lo, Roland is dead, and never his face again shall we see;
Never by all earth's treasures may we bring him back from the dead."
"Unto me have ye all turned traitors!" the King in his hot wrath said. . . .

[*Two knights propose that the judgment be determined with a trial by combat. One represented Charlemagne, the other Ganelon. Part of the trial involved leaving hostages to ensure the good behavior of the combatants.*]

Scarce have the two knights fallen ere again on their feet they stand;
Pinabel [Ganelon's knight] is right stalwart, lithe, swift of foot and hand;
Each rusheth to close with other — no war-steeds now have they —
And with great swords golden-hilted smiting hard they essay
To hew asunder the helmets: such giant blows they deal
That a marvel it is that unshattered abideth the morion's [helmet's]
    steel.
Thrilling with hope and with terror looked on each Frankish knight.
"Ah God," King Charlemagne murmured, "make manifest the
    right!" . . .

[*Ganelon's knight Pinabel loses the trial by combat.*]

Now Counts and Dukes are summoned to the presence of their Lord:
"What think ye," he saith, "of the kinsmen whom I have kept in ward?
To plead the cause of the traitor Ganelon came they all,
And for Pinabel were they sureties, with him to stand or fall."
And the Franks with one voice answered: "Let there not live of them
    one!"
Then gave the King commandment to his headsman [executioner], the
    grim Barbrun:
"Go thou, hang all those traitors upon the accursed tree!
And by this my beard and its hoary hairs I swear unto thee,
That thy life, if but one escape thee, for the life of him shall be."
"What task for mine hand were better than this?" did the man reply.
With a hundred serjeants he haled them to their doom all ruthlessly,
And on that tree evil-fruited did he hang them, knights thrice ten.
So is it — a traitor destroyeth with himself his fellow-men.

* * *

. . . above all other for this did the Frank lords cry —
That by strangest, fearfullest torment Ganelon should die.
Then four great battle-horses to the midst of the field brought they;
To his feet and his hands they bound them; that outstretched in the midst
    he lay.
High-mettled and swift are the chargers, four serjeants lash them to speed
Unto where for each stands waiting a filly afar on the mead [meadow].
Ah, now is the traitor delivered to a death of hideous pain!
The joints of his limbs and his sinews on a living rack they strain,
Till suddenly all his body is to fearful fragments rent,
And with crimson streams down-rushing is all the grass besprent.
Ganelon dies as the traitor should die, as the dastard should die!
Shall a traitor live — to triumph, to boast of his felony?

READING AND DISCUSSION QUESTIONS

1. Why does Ganelon want to kill Roland?

2. In this poem, the author calls Blancandrin "wise." What makes him wise, and what does that reveal about how the author views Muslims?

3. What is Ganelon's defense? Why does he think he is innocent? Why do the French lords think he's innocent?

COMPARATIVE QUESTIONS

1. Compare the miracle of Saint Boniface with that of Vladimir of Kievan Rus. What similarities do these two events share? What are the differences?

2. Compare and contrast *The Conquest of Spain* with *The Song of Roland*. Even though the authors are from different religious backgrounds, what similarities are there between these civilizations?

3. Compare and contrast the courts of Charlemagne and of the Byzantine emperors that Vladimir's envoy studied.

4. How does the idea of justice in *The Song of Roland* compare with Emperor Justinian's definition of justice in Document 7-5?

CHAPTER 9

State and Church in the High Middle Ages

1000–1300

I n the High Middle Ages, European monarchs began to consolidate their political authority and expand their influence, building upon the feudal system and expanding state and legal institutions. William I of England ordered a thorough survey of his developing state in order to identify its resources. In the twelfth century, William's great-grandson Henry II reformed the legal system and laid the foundations of English common law. As royal power grew, the great barons of the realm sought to define and protect their rights, resulting in the Magna Carta of 1215. During this period, however, the Roman church was also gaining power and implementing reform. The eleventh-century controversy over lay investiture — the appointment of church officials by secular rulers — created a power struggle between Pope Gregory VII and the Holy Roman emperor Henry IV. Papal claims to authority over Christians reached its pinnacle with the call for the Crusades, during which the Roman church sought to regain Christian holy lands that had been controlled by Muslims for centuries. In eastern Europe, the Orthodox church of Byzantium developed separately from the Roman church and, accordingly, had different ways of handling the relationship between church and state.

VIEWPOINTS

Imperial Representations

DOCUMENT 9-1

Otto III of the Holy Roman Empire

ca. 1000

Otto III (980–1002) was made king of Germany at the age of three upon the death of his father. He was crowned Holy Roman emperor at the age of sixteen. Growing up as a monarch, Otto conceived the idea that he should model himself on Constantine and Charlemagne. As Charlemagne protected the pope, so too did Otto intend to protect the papacy from the Italian noble families who sought to control it. He ran the Holy Roman Empire from Rome in order to prevent the nobles from overthrowing the pope.

READING AND DISCUSSION QUESTIONS

1. Who are the people on the emperor's right? On his left?
2. What does he hold in each hand? What do you think they mean?
3. If Otto were to stand, how would his height compare to those of the other figures? Why is he drawn this way?

Bildarchiv Preussischer Kulturbesitz/Art Resource, N.Y.

DOCUMENT 9-2

Otto IV and Innocent III

ca. 1209

Otto IV (1175–1218) was a troubled Holy Roman emperor. Born into the royal families of Bavaria and England, he was chosen to rule when Pope

akg–images/ullsteinbild.

Innocent III and the German nobles became dissatisfied with the current emperor, Philip of Swabia. Innocent, with the support of many German nobles, arranged to have Otto crowned in 1209, believing that Otto would follow his instructions. Once Otto was emperor, however, he began to act independently of the pope and invaded Italy. Since he crowned Otto, Innocent decided he could depose him, too, and did so in 1215.

DOCUMENT 9-3

Anglo-Saxon Chronicle:
William the Conqueror and the Domesday Book
1086

In 1066, William, duke of Normandy, conquered England, claiming to be the legitimate heir to the throne. Twenty years later, in December 1085, William ordered a complete survey of the entire kingdom. He wanted to ascertain how much of England consisted of crown land and to describe the country in enough detail to be able to tax it properly. The survey, assembled into what became known as the Domesday Book, *was remarkably thorough and stands as a testament to the Norman talent for administration. This description of how it came about is from the* Anglo-Saxon Chronicle, *a historical record begun in the ninth century and maintained by monastic scribes.*

At Midwinter the king was at Gloucester with his "witan" [advisors], and there held his court five days; and afterwards the archbishop and clergy had a synod [ecclesiastical assembly] three days. There was Maurice chosen bishop of London, and William, of Norfolk, and Robert, of Cheshire. They were all the king's clerks. After this the king had a great council, and

---

From James Harvey Robinson, ed., *Readings in European History*, 2 vols. (Boston: Ginn, 1904), 1:229–31.

very deep speech with his "witan" about this land, how it was peopled, or by what men; then he sent his men over all England, into every shire, and caused to be ascertained how many hundred hides were in the shire, or what land the king himself had, and cattle within the land, or what dues he ought to have, in twelve months, from the shire. Also he caused to be written how much land his archbishops had, and his suffragan bishops,[1] and his abbots, and his earls: and — though I may narrate somewhat pro-lixly[2] — what or how much each man had who was a landholder in England, in land, or in cattle, and how much money it might be worth. So very narrowly he caused it to be traced out, that there was not one single hide, nor one yard of land, nor even — it is shame to tell, though it seemed to him no shame to do — an ox, nor a cow, nor a swine, left that was not set down in his writ.

King William, about whom we speak, was a very wise man, and very powerful, more dignified and strong than any of his predecessors were. He was mild to the good men who loved God, and beyond all measure severe to the men who gainsaid his will. . . . He was also very dignified; thrice every year he wore his crown, as oft as he was in England. At Easter he wore it in Winchester; at Pentecost, in Westminster; at Midwinter, in Gloucester. And then were with him all the great men over all England, archbishops and suffragan bishops, abbots and earls, thanes[3] and knights.

So also was he a very rigid and cruel man, so that no one durst do anything against his will. He had earls in bonds who had acted against his will; bishops he cast from their bishoprics, and abbots from their abbacies, and thanes into prison; and at last he spared not his own brother, named Odo: he was a very rich bishop in Normandy; at Bayeux was his episcopal see;[4] and he was the foremost man besides the king; and he had an earl-dom in England, and when the king was in Normandy, then was he the most powerful in this land: and him the king put in prison.

Among other good things is not to be forgotten the good peace that he made in this land; so that a man who had any confidence in himself might go over his realm, with his bosom full of gold, unhurt. Nor durst any man slay another man had he done ever so great evil to the other. He reigned over England, and by his sagacity so thoroughly surveyed it that there was

---

[1] **suffragan bishop**: Assistant to an archbishop whose territory might be too large for one person to administer effectively.

[2] **prolixly**: Wordy, verbose, tiresome.

[3] **thane**: Low-ranking feudal lord.

[4] **episcopal see**: Bishop's official headquarters.

not a hide of land within England that he knew not who had it, or what it was worth, and afterwards set it in his writ.

Brytland [Wales] was in his power, and therein he built castles, and completely ruled over that race of men. In like manner he also subjected Scotland to him by his great strength. The land of Normandy was naturally his, and over the country which is called Le Maine he reigned; and if he might yet have lived two years he would, by his valor, have won Ireland, and without any weapons.

Certainly in his time men had great hardship and very many injuries. Castles he caused to be made, and poor men to be greatly oppressed. The king was very rigid, and took from his subjects many a mark of gold, and more hundred pounds of silver, all which he took, by right and with great unright, from his people, for little need. He had fallen into covetousness, and altogether loved greediness.

He planted a great preserve for deer, and he laid down laws therewith, that whosoever should slay hart[5] or hind[6] should be blinded. He forbade the harts and also the boars to be killed. As greatly did he love the tall deer as if he were their father. He also ordained concerning the hares that they should go free. His great men bewailed it, and the poor men murmured thereat; but he was so obdurate that he recked not of the hatred of them all; but they must wholly follow the king's will if they would live, or have land, or property, or even his peace. Alas that any man should be so proud, so raise himself up, and account himself above all men! May the Almighty God show mercy to his soul, and grant him forgiveness of his sins!

READING AND DISCUSSION QUESTIONS

1. The chronicler describes William as a "wise man" but also says that he was "very rigid and cruel." What does this reveal about what the chronicler seems to have expected from a king?

2. What were William's principal faults and virtues? How did they support or detract from one another?

3. How well had William established peace after conquering England? Give specific examples to support your position.

---

[5] **hart**: Male red deer.
[6] **hind**: Female red deer.

DOCUMENT 9-4

KING JOHN OF ENGLAND
From *Magna Carta: The Great Charter of Liberties*
1215

The English kings had extensive possessions in France and spent much of their resources trying to defend or expand these holdings. By 1215, King John — through a series of military defeats and poorly conducted alliances — had lost many of these French lands. To make up for his losses, John levied, to the point of abuse, the feudal payments that his vassals owed him. He also harshly enforced other traditional feudal rights, such as the laws governing the forests. In 1215, his nobles forced him to issue a charter that would clearly define both royal rights and the rights of subjects.

John, by the grace of God, king of England, lord of Ireland, duke of Normandy and Aquitaine, and count of Anjou, to the archbishops, bishops, abbots, earls, barons . . . [and] subjects, greeting. . . .

We have also granted to all free men of our kingdom, for us and our heirs forever, all the underwritten liberties, to be had and held by them and their heirs, of us and our heirs forever. . . .

No widow shall be compelled to marry, so long as she prefers to live without a husband, provided always that she gives security not to marry without our consent, if she holds [a fief] of us, or without the consent of her lord of whom she holds, if she holds of another. . . .

No scutage[7] or aid shall be imposed on our kingdom, unless by common counsel of our kingdom, except for ransoming our person, for making our eldest son a knight, and for once marrying our eldest daughter; and for these there shall not be levied more than a reasonable aid. . . .

Neither we nor our bailiffs shall take, for castles or for any other work of ours, wood which is not ours, against the will of the owner of that wood. . . .

From William Sharp McKechnie, *Magna Carta: A Commentary on the Great Charter of King John* (New York: Burt Franklin, 1914), pp.186, 191, 220, 232, 336–37, 375, 395, 399, 431, 466–67.

[7]**scutage:** Payment in lieu of performing military service.

We will not retain beyond one year and one day, the lands of those who have been convicted of felony, and the lands shall thereafter be handed over to the lords of the fiefs. . . .

No freeman shall be taken or [and] imprisoned or disseised [dispossessed] or exiled or in any way destroyed, nor will we [attack] him nor send [people to attack] him, except by the lawful judgment of his peers or [and] by the law of the land.

To no one will we sell, to no one will we refuse or delay, right or justice.

All merchants shall have safe and secure exit from England, and entry to England, with the right to tarry there and to move about as well by land as by water. . . .

We will appoint justices, constables, sheriffs, or bailiffs only such as know the law of the kingdom and mean to observe it well. . . .

Since, moreover, for God and the amendment of our kingdom and for the better allaying of the quarrel that has arisen between us and our barons, we have granted all these concessions, desirous that they should enjoy them incomplete and firm endurance for ever, we give and grant to them the underwritten security, namely, that the barons choose five-and-twenty barons of the kingdom, whomsoever they will, who shall be bound with all their might, to observe and hold, and cause to be observed, the peace and liberties we have granted and confirmed to them by this our present Charter.

READING AND DISCUSSION QUESTIONS

1. In what ways does the Magna Carta limit how the king can raise money?

2. Discuss how the Magna Carta seeks to reform the administration of justice.

3. Judging from these sections of the charter, who in the kingdom seemed to have the strongest grievances against the king? Use examples to support your claim.

DOCUMENT 9-5

POPE GREGORY VII AND EMPEROR HENRY IV
Mutual Recriminations: The Investiture Controversy Begins

1076

The investiture controversy centered on who had the right to appoint the officials of the Roman Catholic Church. In addition to being servants of the church, bishops and abbots were often great landowners. Because the clergy were the most extensive literate class, many royal or imperial officials were drawn from their ranks, and secular rulers sought to appoint men who were loyal to them. Those who were trying to reform the church from within, like Pope Gregory VII, argued that reform would be impossible if church officials owed their positions to secular rulers. Henry VI responded to the following admonition from Gregory with two letters. He sent a brief reply to Gregory himself. He circulated the inflammatory version that follows throughout Germany in hopes of gaining the support of the people.

[Pope Gregory VII to Emperor Henry IV]

Gregory, bishop, servant of God's servants, to King Henry, greeting and the apostolic benediction — but with the understanding that he obeys the Apostolic See[8] as becomes a Christian king.

Considering and weighing carefully to how strict a judge we must render any account of the stewardship committed to us by St. Peter, prince of the Apostles, we have hesitated to send you the apostolic benediction, since you are reported to be in voluntary communication with men who are under the censure of the Apostolic See. . . . If this be true, you yourself know that you cannot receive the favor of God nor the apostolic blessing unless you shall first put away those excommunicated persons and force them to do penance and shall yourself obtain absolution and forgiveness for your sin by due repentance and satisfaction. Wherefore we counsel

---

From Maureen C. Miller, *Power and the Holy in the Age of the Investiture Conflict: A Brief History with Documents* (Boston and New York: Bedford/St. Martin's, 2005), pp. 84–90.

[8] **Apostolic See**: The papacy.

Your Excellency, if you feel yourself guilty in this matter, to make your confession at once to some pious bishop who, with our sanction, may impose upon you a penance suited to the offense, may absolve you and with your consent in writing may be free to send us a true report of the manner of your penance.

We marvel exceedingly that you have sent us so many devoted letters and displayed such humility by the spoken words of your legates, calling yourself a son of our Holy Mother Church and subject to us in the faith, singular in affection, a leader in devotion, commending yourself with every expression of gentleness and reverence, and yet in action showing yourself most bitterly hostile to the canons and apostolic decrees in those duties especially required by loyalty to the Church. . . . And now, heaping wounds upon wounds, you have handed over the sees of Fermo and Spoleto — if indeed a church may be given over by any human power — to persons entirely unknown to us, whereas it is not lawful to consecrate anyone except after probation and with due knowledge.

It would have been becoming to you, since you confess yourself to be a son of the Church, to give more respectful attention to the master of the Church, that is, to Peter, prince of the Apostles. To him, if you are of the Lord's flock, you have been committed for your pasture, since Christ said to him: "Peter, feed my sheep" (John 21:17), and again: "to thee are given the keys of Heaven, and whatsoever thou shalt bind on earth shall be bound in Heaven, and whatsoever thou shalt loose on earth shall be loosed in Heaven" (Matt. 16:9). Now, while we, unworthy sinner that we are, stand in his place of power, still whatever you send to us, whether in writing or by word of mouth, he himself receives, and while we read what is written or hear the voice of those who speak, he discerns with subtle insight from what spirit the message comes. Wherefore Your Highness should beware lest any defect of will toward the Apostolic See be found in your words or in your messages. . . .

A synod[9] held at Rome during the current year, and over which Divine Providence willed us to preside, several of your subjects being present, we saw that the order of the Christian religion had long been greatly disturbed and its chief and proper function, the redemption of souls, had fallen low and through the wiles of the Devil had been trodden under foot. Startled by this danger and by the manifest ruin of the Lord's flock we returned to the teaching of the holy fathers, declaring no novelties nor any inventions of our own. . . .

---

[9] **synod**: Council of church officials.

Nevertheless, in order that these demands may not seem to you too burdensome or unfair we have sent word by your own liegemen not to be troubled by this reform of an evil practice but to send us prudent and pious [ambassadors] from your own people. If these can show in any reasonable way how we can moderate the decision of the holy fathers saving the honor of the eternal king and without peril to our own soul, we will condescend to hear their counsel. It would in fact have been the fair thing for you, even if you had not been so graciously admonished, to make reasonable inquiry of us in what respect we had offended you or assailed your honor, before you proceeded to violate the apostolic decrees. But how little you cared for our warnings or for doing right was shown by your later actions.

However, since the long-enduring patience of God summons you to improvement, we hope that with increase of understanding your heart and mind may be turned to obey the commands of God. We warn you with a father's love that you accept the rule of Christ, that you consider the peril of preferring your own honor to his, that you do not hamper by your actions the freedom of that church which he deigned to bind to himself as a bride by a divine union, but, that she may increase as greatly as possible, you will begin to lend to Almighty God and to St. Peter, by whom also your own glory may merit increase, the aid of your valor by faithful devotion.

[EMPEROR HENRY IV TO POPE GREGORY VII]

Henry, King not by usurpation, but by the pious ordination of God, to Hildebrand, now not Pope, but false monk:

You have deserved such a salutation as this because of the confusion you have wrought; for you left untouched no order of the Church which you could make a sharer of confusion instead of honor, of malediction instead of benediction.

For to discuss a few outstanding points among many: Not only have you dared to touch the rectors of the holy Church — the archbishops, the bishops, and the priests, anointed of the Lord as they are — but you have trodden them under foot like slaves who know not what their lord may do. In crushing them you have gained for yourself acclaim from the mouth of the rabble. You have judged that all these know nothing, while you alone know everything. In any case, you have sedulously[10] used this knowledge not for edification, but for destruction, so greatly that we may believe Saint Gregory, whose name you have arrogated to yourself, rightly made this prophesy of you when he said: "From the abundance of his subjects, the

---

[10] **sedulously**: With great care and effort.

mind of the prelate is often exalted, and he thinks that he has more knowledge than anyone else, since he sees that he has more power than anyone
else."

And we, indeed, bore with all these abuses, since we were eager to
preserve the honor of the Apostolic See. But you construed our humility as
fear, and so you were emboldened to rise up even against the royal power
itself, granted to us by God. You dared to threaten to take the kingship away
from us — as though we had received the kingship from you, as though
kingship and empire were in your hand and not in the hand of God.

Our Lord, Jesus Christ, has called us to kingship, but has not called
you to the priesthood. For you have risen by these steps: namely, by cunning, which the monastic profession abhors, to money; by money to favor;
by favor to the sword. By the sword you have come to the throne of peace,
and from the throne of peace you have destroyed the peace. You have
armed subjects against their prelates; you who have not been called by
God have taught that our bishops who have been called by God are to
be spurned; you have usurped for laymen the bishops' ministry over the
priests, with the result that these laymen depose and condemn the very
men whom the laymen themselves received as teachers from the hand of
God, through the imposition of the hands of bishops.

You have also touched me, one who, though unworthy, has been
anointed to kingship among the anointed. This wrong you have done to
me, although as the tradition of the holy Fathers has taught, I am to be
judged by God alone and am not to be deposed for any crime unless —
may it never happen — I should deviate from the Faith. For the prudence
of the holy bishops entrusted the judgment and the deposition even of [the
late Roman emperor] Julian the Apostate[11] not to themselves, but to God
alone. The true pope Saint Peter also exclaims, "Fear God, honor the
king." You, however, since you do not fear God, dishonor me, ordained
of Him.

Wherefore, when Saint Paul gave no quarter to an angel from heaven
if the angel should preach heterodoxy, he did not except you who are now
teaching heterodoxy throughout the earth. For he says, "If anyone, either I
or an angel from heaven, preach any other gospel unto you than that
which we have preached unto you, let him be accursed." Descend, therefore, condemned by this anathema and by the common judgment of all
our bishops and of ourself. Relinquish the Apostolic See which you have

---

[11] **Julian the Apostate**: Last pagan Roman emperor (r. ca. 355–363), known for
unsuccessfully trying to thwart the spread of Christianity within the empire.

arrogated. Let another mount the throne of Saint Peter, another who will not cloak violence with religion but who will teach the pure doctrine of Saint Peter.

I, Henry, King by the grace of God, together with all our bishops say to you: Descend! Descend!

READING AND DISCUSSION QUESTIONS

1. On what basis does Gregory claim the right to appoint church officials?
2. What authority does he claim to have over an emperor?
3. In what ways does the emperor claim that the pope was attacking both the church and imperial power?
4. How does Henry use both political and religious traditions to defend himself?

DOCUMENT 9-6

ROBERT THE MONK OF RHEIMS
Urban II at the Council of Clermont: A Call for Crusade
ca. 1120

By the late eleventh century, Christians were pushing back Muslim forces in many parts of the Mediterranean world. The Normans conquered Sicily in 1091, and the Christian kingdoms in Spain were expanding at the expense of their Muslim neighbors. The Byzantine emperor had appealed for mercenaries to fight against the Seljuk Turks, but Pope Urban II broadened this goal. He wanted to liberate Christians living under Muslim rule and to recapture the Holy Land — especially Jerusalem. The Crusaders captured the city in 1099 and established the Kingdom of Jerusalem and other Crusader

From James Harvey Robinson, ed., *Readings in European History*, 2 vols. (Boston: Ginn, 1904), 1:312–15.

states. In fewer than two hundred years, however, the Holy Land was once more under Muslim control. Little is known about the monk who wrote this account over twenty years after the council took place, though he may have attended the Council of Clermont in person.

"Oh, race of Franks, race from across the mountains, race beloved and chosen by God, — as is clear from many of your works, — set apart from all other nations by the situation of your country as well as by your Catholic faith and the honor which you render to the holy Church: to you our discourse is addressed, and for you our exhortations are intended. We wish you to know what a grievous cause has led us to your country, for it is the imminent peril threatening you and all the faithful which has brought us hither.

From the confines of Jerusalem and from the city of Constantinople a grievous report has gone forth and has repeatedly been brought to our ears; namely, that a race from the kingdom of the Persians, an accursed race, a race wholly alienated from God, 'a generation that set not their heart aright, and whose spirit was not steadfast with God,' has violently invaded the lands of those Christians and has depopulated them by pillage and fire. They have led away a part of the captives into their own country, and a part they have killed by cruel tortures. They have either destroyed the churches of God or appropriated them for the rites of their own religion. They destroy the altars, after having defiled them with their uncleanness. . . . The kingdom of the Greeks is now dismembered by them and has been deprived of territory so vast in extent that it could not be traversed in two months' time.

On whom, therefore, is the labor of avenging these wrongs and of recovering this territory incumbent, if not upon you, — you, upon whom, above all other nations, God has conferred remarkable glory in arms, great courage, bodily activity, and strength to humble the heads of those who resist you? Let the deeds of your ancestors encourage you and incite your minds to manly achievements: — the glory and greatness of King Charlemagne, and of his son Louis, and of your other monarchs, who have destroyed the kingdoms of the Turks and have extended the sway of the holy Church over lands previously pagan. Let the holy sepulcher of our Lord and Savior, which is possessed by the unclean nations, especially arouse you, and the holy places which are now treated with ignominy and irreverently polluted with the filth of the unclean. Oh, most valiant soldiers and descendants of invincible ancestors, do not degenerate, but recall the valor of your progenitors.

But if you are hindered by love of children, parents, or wife, remember what the Lord says in the Gospel, 'He that loveth father or mother more than me is not worthy of me.' 'Every one that hath forsaken houses, or brethren, or sisters, or father, or mother, or wife, or children, or lands, for my name's sake, shall receive an hundredfold, and shall inherit everlasting life.' Let none of your possessions retain you, nor solicitude for your family affairs. For this land which you inhabit, shut in on all sides by the seas and surrounded by the mountain peaks, is too narrow for your large population; nor does it abound in wealth; and it furnishes scarcely food enough for its cultivators. Hence it is that you murder and devour one another, that you wage war, and that very many among you perish in intestine strife.

Let hatred therefore depart from among you, let your quarrels end, let wars cease, and let all dissensions and controversies slumber. Enter upon the road to the Holy Sepulcher; wrest that land from the wicked race, and subject it to yourselves. That land which, as the Scripture says, 'floweth with milk and honey' was given by God into the power of the children of Israel. Jerusalem is the center of the earth; the land is fruitful above all others, like another paradise of delights. This spot the Redeemer of mankind has made illustrious by his advent, has beautified by his sojourn, has consecrated by his passion, has redeemed by his death, has glorified by his burial.

This royal city, however, situated at the center of the earth, is now held captive by the enemies of Christ and is subjected, by those who do not know God, to the worship of the heathen. She seeks, therefore, and desires to be liberated and ceases not to implore you to come to her aid. From you especially she asks succor, because, as we have already said, God has conferred upon you above all other nations great glory in arms. Accordingly, undertake this journey eagerly for the remission of your sins, with the assurance of the reward of imperishable glory in the kingdom of heaven."

When Pope Urban had urbanely said these and very many similar things, he so centered in one purpose the desires of all who were present that all cried out, "It is the will of God! It is the will of God!" When the venerable Roman pontiff heard that, with eyes uplifted to heaven, he gave thanks to God and, commanding silence with his hand, said:

"Most beloved brethren, to-day is manifest in you what the Lord says in the Gospel, 'Where two or three are gathered together in my name, there am I in the midst of them'; for unless God had been present in your spirits, all of you would not have uttered the same cry; since, although the cry issued from numerous mouths, yet the origin of the cry was one. Therefore I say to you that God, who implanted this in your breasts, has drawn it forth from you. Let that then be your war cry in combats, because it is given to you by God. When an armed attack is made upon the enemy, let this one cry be raised by all the soldiers of God: 'It is the will of God! It is the will of God!' [*Deus vult! Deus vult!*]"

READING AND DISCUSSION QUESTIONS

1. Why would Urban II's claim that the land of the Franks was "too nar-row for [its] large population" have been an important issue for the Crusaders?

2. In what ways were the Crusades examples of international cooper-ation?

3. What specific grievances does Urban II direct at the Muslims?

DOCUMENT 9-7

ANNA COMNENA
The Alexiad: *The Heresy of the Bogomils*
ca. 1148

Anna Comnena, daughter of Byzantine emperor Alexius, was trained to be a scholar and married a historian. She is one of the first female historians in Western history. In her fifties, she decided to write the history of her father's rule. Not only does her work serve as a crucial source of information about the Byzantine world, but it also shows how the relationship between church and state developed differently in the Eastern Roman Empire. By the time her father was emperor, the Eastern Orthodox churches and Western Roman Catholic churches had split over the pope's claim to authority over the lead-ers of the Eastern Orthodox church, as well as theological differences.

From Anna Comnena, *The Alexiad*, trans. E. R. A. Sewter (Middlesex, UK: Penguin, 1969), pp. 496–500.

Later, in . . . Alexius' reign there arose an extraordinary 'cloud of heretics,' a new, hostile group, hitherto unknown to the Church. . . . Apparently it was in existence before my father's time, but was unperceived (for the Bogomil sect is most adept at feigning virtue). No worldly hairstyles are to be seen among Bogomils: their wickedness is hidden beneath cloak and cowl. Your Bogomil wears a somber look; muffled up to the nose, he walks with a stoop, quietly muttering to himself — but inside he's a ravening wolf. This unpleasant race, like a serpent lurking in its hole, was brought to light and lured out by my father. . . . (For he was in everything superior to all his contemporaries: as a teacher he surpassed the educational experts, as a soldier and a general he excelled the professionals who were most admired.) The fame of the Bogomils had by now spread to all parts, for the impious sect was controlled with great cunning by a certain monk named Basil. He had twelve followers whom he called "apostles" and also dragged along with him certain female disciples, women of bad character, utterly depraved. In all quarters he made his wicked influence felt and when the evil, like some consuming fire, devoured many souls, the emperor could no longer bear it. He instituted a thorough inquiry into the heresy. Some of the Bogomils were brought to the palace; without exception they denounced their master . . . Basil. One of these, Diblatius, was imprisoned. Since under interrogation he was unwilling to confess, he was subjected to torture. He then admitted that Basil was the leader and he named the "apostles" whom Basil had chosen. Several men were accordingly given the task of finding him. Basil . . . was brought to light, dressed in monkish garb, austere of face, with a thin beard, very tall. At once the emperor, wishing to discover from him the man's innermost thoughts, tried compulsion, but with a show of persuasion: he invited him to the palace on some righteous pretext. He even rose from his seat when Basil came in, made him sit with him and share his own table. The whole line was run out for the catch, with all kinds of tempting bait on the hooks for this voracious monster to swallow; the monk, so practiced in villainy, was by every means urged to gulp down the whole treacherous offering. Alexius feigned a desire to become his disciple. . . . Alexius pretended to regard all his sayings as some divine oracle and gave way to every argument; his one hope, he said, was that the wretched Basil would effect his soul's salvation. "I, too, most reverend father," said he (for he smeared the cup's rim with honey-sweetness, so that the other in his lunacy might vomit forth his dark beliefs), "I too admire you for your virtue. I pray you make me understand in some degree the doctrines that Your Honor teaches, for those of our Church are all but worthless, in no way conducive to virtue." At first

Basil was coy, . . . and at the emperor's words shied away. Nevertheless he was filled with conceit by Alexius's praises — he had even invited Basil to share his meal. . . . Finally Basil did vomit forth the Bogomil doctrine. It happened thus: a curtain divided the women's quarters from the room where the brothers were, as this loathsome creature belched out and plainly declared all this heart's secrets; meanwhile, a secretary behind the curtain recorded what was said. The fool, to all appearances, was the teacher, while the emperor played the part of learner and the lesson was committed to writing by the secretary. The accursed fellow strung everything together, lawful and unlawful alike; no jot of his blasphemous doctrine was held back. . . . he even went so far as to call the holy churches the temples of demons. . . . Well, the emperor threw off his pretence and drew back the curtain. then a conference was summoned of all the senate, the chief army commanders, and the elders of the Church. The hateful teachings of the Bogomil were read aloud. The proof was incontestable. Indeed, the accused made no attempt to dispute the charge, promising that he was ready to undergo fire and scourgings, to die a thousand deaths. These misguided Bogomils are persuaded, you see, that they can endure any punishment without feeling pain, for angels (they think) will pluck them from the funeral pyre itself. And although all threatened him and reproached him for his irreverence — even those who had shared in his ruin — he was still the same Basil, inexorable, a true Bogomil. . . . He was sent to prison. Many times Alexius sent for him, many times called upon him to abjure his wickedness; but to all the emperor's pleadings he remained as deaf as ever. . . . Alexius sent for a monk named Zygabenus,[12] known to my grandmother on the maternal side and to all the clergy, who had a great reputation as a grammarian, was not unversed in rhetoric and had an unrivalled knowledge of dogma. Zygabenus was commanded to publish a list of all heresies, to deal with each separately and append in each case the refutation of it in the texts of the holy fathers. The Bogomil heresy was included, just as the impious Basil had interpreted it. This book Alexius named the *Dogmatic Panoply* and the volumes are so called to this day. . . . Alexius condemned the heretics out of hand: chorus and chorus-leader alike were to suffer death by burning.

---

[12] **Zygabenus**: Euthymius Zygabenus, a Byzantine scholar, about whom little is known.

READING AND DISCUSSION QUESTIONS

1. Who are the Bogomils? What is their leader like?

2. Who wants to see the Bogomils caught? Who takes the lead in investigating this heresy?

3. What role does the clergy play in investigating this heresy?

COMPARATIVE QUESTIONS

1. What is different about the way the two Ottos represent their relationship to the church? What do the images suggest changed between the time of Otto III (ca. 1000) and Otto IV (ca. 1209)?

2. Based on the descriptions in the *Domesday Book* story and Magna Carta, discuss how English kings might be able to abuse royal power.

3. Compare and contrast the arguments on both sides of the investiture controversy. Who has the better argument? Why?

4. What do both the investiture controversy and the call for the First Crusade reveal about the new powers of the church?

5. Compare and contrast the relationship between church and state in the Byzantine Empire with church and state in the western European kingdoms.

CHAPTER 10

The Life of the People in the High Middle Ages

1000–1300

By the year 1000, the strict social order of Christian society in Europe had begun to change, and social institutions along with it. Monasticism, which had long been an important part of European Christendom, experienced renewal and reform, especially with the founding of orders such as the Cistercians. Monasteries and convents offered basic schooling to boys. Even though the majority of people were illiterate, they learned of the Bible through spoken sermons and images depicting biblical stories. For many peasants, however, social life became more constricted. Various forms of unfree servitude, including serfdom, tied them to the soil. For those Europeans free to move as they wished, trade and the Crusades brought them into contact with people of other cultures and religion. While the more violent interactions among Christians, Jews, and Muslims often receive more attention from historians, it is important to note how these people interacted on a daily basis.

DOCUMENT 10-1

Manorial Records of Bernehorne

1307

In the High Middle Ages, agricultural production took place on manors. Serfs were bound to a specific manor and required to work its land, which was divided among the peasants and the lord. Peasants worked their assigned plot of land and shared part of their produce with him. They also had to

From James Harvey Robinson, ed., *Readings in European History*, abridged ed. (Boston: Ginn, 1906), pp. 181–184.

work the lord's share of the land and pay other fees and obligations. Mano-
rial court records kept track of how much peasants owed their lord. Medieval
English currency was based on a pound of silver, which was divided into
twenty shillings, abbreviated s., or 240 pence, abbreviated d.

Extent of the manor of Bernehorne, made on Wednesday following the
feast of St. Gregory the pope, in the thirty-fifth year of the reign of King
Edward, in the presence of Brother Thomas, keeper of Marley, John de la
More, and Adam de Thruhlegh, clerks, on the oath of William de Goce-
coumbe, Walter le Parker, Richard le Knyst, Richard the son of the latter,
Andrew of Estone, Stephen Morsprich, Thomas Brembel, William of
Swynham, John Pollard, Roger le Glede, John Syward, and John de
Lillingewist, who say that there are all the following holdings: . . .

John Pollard holds a half acre in Aldithewisse and owes 18d. at the
four terms, and owes for it relief and heriot.[1]

John Suthinton holds a house and 40 acres of land and owes 3s. 6d. at
Easter and Michaelmas.[2]

William of Swynham holds 1 acre of meadow in the thicket of Swynham and owes 1d. at the feast of Michaelmas.

Ralph of Leybourne holds a cottage and 1 acre of land in Pinden and
owes 3s. at Easter and Michaelmas, and attendance at the court in the
manor every three weeks, also relief and heriot.

Richard Knyst of Swynham holds 2 acres and a half of land and owes
yearly 4s.

William of Knelle holds 2 acres of land in Aldithewisse and owes
yearly 4s. . . .

They say, moreover, that John of Cayworth holds a house and 30 acres
of land, and owes yearly 2s. at Easter and Michaelmas; and he owes a cock
and two hens at Christmas of the value of 4d.

And he ought to harrow for 2 days at the Lenten sowing with one
man and his own horse and his own harrow, the value of the work being
4d.; and he is to receive from the lord on each day 3 meals, of the value
of 5d., and then the lord will be at a loss of 1d. Thus his harrowing is of
no value to the service of the lord.

---

[1] **relief and heriot**: Payments owed to the lord when a serf died.

[2] **Michaelmas**: Feast honoring the Archangel Michael; celebrated on September 29.

And he ought to carry the manure of the lord for 2 days with 1 cart, with his own 2 oxen, the value of the work being 8d.; and he is to receive from the lord each day 3 meals as above. And thus the service is worth 3d.

And he shall find one man for 2 days, for mowing the meadow of the lord, who can mow, by estimation, 1 acre and a half, the value of the mowing of an acre being 6d.: the sum is therefore 9d. And he is to receive each day 3 meals of the value given above. And thus that mowing is worth 4d. . . .

And he ought to carry wood from the woods of the lord as far as the manor, for two days in summer, with a cart and 3 animals of his own, the value of the work being 9d. And he shall receive from the lord each day 3 meals of the price given above. And thus the work is worth 4d.

William of Cayworth holds a house and 30 acres of land and owes at Easter and Michaelmas 2s. rent. And he shall do all customs just as the aforesaid John of Cayworth.

William atte Grene holds a house and 30 acres of land and owes in all things the same as the said John. . . .

And it is to be noted that none of the above-named villeins[3] can give their daughters in marriage, nor cause their sons to be tonsured,[4] nor can they cut down timber growing on the lands they hold, without license of the bailiff or sergeant of the lord, and then for building purposes and not otherwise. And after the death of any one of the aforesaid villeins, the lord shall have as a heriot his best animal, if he had any; if, however, he have no living beast, the lord shall have no heriot, as they say. The sons or daughters of the aforesaid villeins shall give, for entrance into the holding after the death of their predecessors, as much as they give of rent per year.

READING AND DISCUSSION QUESTIONS

1. For what things does a peasant owe a lord?
2. What does a peasant use to pay his lord?

---

[3] **villeins:** Serfs.

[4] **cause their sons to be tonsured:** Have their sons become monks.

On Laborers: A Dialogue Between Teacher and Student

ca. 1000

The following document was likely used to teach students Latin. It also provides a short explanation of social relations — information that would be useful for students who would later keep records or supervise workers. By 1000, especially in the countryside, various forms of unfree status had been imposed, although outright slavery was one of the less common forms. Serfs, for instance, could not be bought and sold as individuals, but they also could not leave their land, and their duties to their masters were care- fully prescribed. When the land they worked passed to another owner, they acquired a new master.

TEACHER: What do your companions know?

STUDENT: They are plowmen, shepherds, oxherds, huntsmen, fishermen, falconers, merchants, cobblers, salt-makers, and bakers.

TEACHER: What sayest thou plowman? How do you do your work?

PLOWMAN: O my lord, I work very hard: I go out at dawn, driving the cattle to the field, and I yoke them to the plow. Nor is the weather so bad in winter that I dare to stay at home, for fear of my lord: but when the oxen are yoked, and the plowshare and coulter attached to the plow, I must plow one whole field a day, or more.

TEACHER: Have you any assistant?

PLOWMAN: I have a boy to drive the oxen with a goad, and he too is hoarse with cold and shouting.

TEACHER: What more do you do in a day?

PLOWMAN: Certainly I do more. I must fill the manger of the oxen with hay, and water them and carry out the dung.

From Thomas Wright, ed., *Anglo-Saxon and Old English Vocabularies*, vol. 1 (London: Trubner, 1884), p. 88, reprinted in Roy C. Cave & Herbert H. Coulson, *A Source Book for Medieval Economic History* (New York: The Bruce Publishing Co., 1936; reprinted., New York: Biblo & Tannen, 1965), pp. 46–48. The text has been modernized by Jerome S. Arkenberg, California State University–Fullerton.

TEACHER: Indeed, that is a great labor.

PLOWMAN: Even so, it is a great labor for I am not free.

TEACHER: What have you to say shepherd? Have you heavy work too?

SHEPHERD: I have indeed. In the grey dawn I drive my sheep to the pasture and I stand watch over them, in heat and cold, with my dogs, lest the wolves devour them. And I bring them back to the fold and milk them twice a day. And I move their fold; and I make cheese and butter, and I am faithful to my lord.

TEACHER: Oxherd, what work do you do?

OXHERD: O my lord, I work hard. When the plowman unyokes the oxen I lead them to the pasture and I stand all night guarding them against thieves. Then in the morning I hand them over to the plowman well fed and watered.

TEACHER: What is your craft?

FISHERMAN: I am a fisherman.

TEACHER: What do you obtain from your work?

FISHERMAN: Food and clothing and money.

TEACHER: How do you take the fish?

FISHERMAN: I get into a boat, and place my nets in the water, and I throw out my hook and lines, and whatever they take I keep.

TEACHER: What if the fish should be unclean?

FISHERMAN: I throw out the unclean fish and use the clean as food.

TEACHER: Where do you sell your fish?

FISHERMAN: In the town.

TEACHER: Who buys them?

FISHERMAN: The citizens. I cannot catch as much as I can sell.

TEACHER: What fish do you take?

FISHERMAN: Herring, salmon, porpoises, sturgeon, oysters, crabs, mussels, periwinkles, cockles, plaice, sole, lobsters, and the like.

TEACHER: Do you wish to capture a whale?

FISHERMAN: No.

TEACHER: Why?

FISHERMAN: Because it is a dangerous thing to capture a whale. It is safer for me to go to the river with my boat than to go with many ships hunting whales.

TEACHER: Why so?

FISHERMAN: Because I prefer to take a fish that I can kill rather than one which with a single blow can sink or kill not only me but also my companions.

TEACHER: Yet many people do capture whales and escape the danger, and they obtain a great price for what they do.

FISHERMAN: You speak the truth, but I do not dare because of my cowardice.

READING AND DISCUSSION QUESTIONS

1. What can you deduce about the social status of the various speakers?
2. What are the duties of the plowman's helper?
3. In what ways does the social status of the fisherman differ from that of other speakers?

VIEWPOINTS
Christians, Muslims, and Jews in Contact

> DOCUMENT 10-3

FULCHER OF CHARTRES
Christians Far from Home
ca. 1100

Fulcher of Chartres (SHAHR-truh) was a priest who followed the call to crusade in 1096. While in service to Baldwin, king of Jerusalem, Fulcher began to write his history of the Crusades. He explained the political and military events that took place, but also included his observations about interactions among Crusaders from western Europe and people of different cultures in the Byzantine Empire.

From August Charles Krey, *The First Crusade: The Accounts of Eye-Witnesses and Participants* (Princeton, N.J.: Princeton University Press, 1921), pp. 280–281.

Consider, I pray, and reflect how in our time God has transferred the West into the East. For we who were Occidentals now have been made Orientals. He who was a Roman or a Frank is now a Galilaean, or an inhabitant of Palestine. One who was a citizen of Rheims or of Chartres now has been made a citizen of Tyre or of Antioch. We have already forgotten the places of our birth; already they have become unknown to many of us, or, at least, are unmentioned. Some already possess here homes and servants which they have received through inheritance. Some have taken wives not merely of their own people, but Syrians, or Armenians, or even Saracens who have received the grace of baptism. Some have with them father-in-law, or daughter-in-law, or son-in-law, or step-son, or step-father. There are here, too, grandchildren and great-grandchildren. One cultivates vines, another the fields. The one and the other use mutually the speech and the idioms of the different languages. Different languages, now made common, become known to both races, and faith unites those whose forefathers were strangers. As it is written, "The lion and the ox shall eat straw together." Those who were strangers are now natives; and he who was a sojourner now has become a resident. Our parents and relatives from day to day come to join us, abandoning, even though reluctantly, all that they possess. For those who were poor there, here God makes rich. Those who had few coins, here possess countless bezants; and those who had not had a villa, here, by the gift of God, already possess a city. Therefore, why should one who has found the East so favorable return to the West? God does not wish those to suffer want who, carrying their crosses, have vowed to follow Him, nay even unto the end. You see, therefore, that this is a great miracle, and one which must greatly astonish the whole world. Who has ever heard anything like it? Therefore, God wishes to enrich us all and to draw us to Himself as His most dear friends. And because He wishes it, we also freely desire the same; and what is pleasing to Him we do with a loving and submissive heart, that with Him we may reign happily throughout eternity.

READING AND DISCUSSION QUESTIONS

1. How do the Crusaders change once they have been in the East for some time?

2. What does Fulcher mean by "the lion and the ox shall eat straw together?"

DOCUMENT 10-4

USĀMAH IBN MUNQIDH
Observations on the Franks
ca. 1175

Usāmah ibn Munqidh (OO-sah-mah IH-buhn MUHN-kihth, 1095–1188) was a soldier, diplomat, and poet whose family ruled the fortress of Shaizar in Syria. He was exiled from Shaizar after a falling out with his uncle, the sultan, and subsequently took service as a soldier with other Muslim rulers, fighting against the Frankish Crusaders. He spent many years in the cities of Cairo, Damascus, and Jerusalem, where he had extensive contact with the Europeans who had moved there during the Crusades.

In the army of King Fulk,[5] son of Fulk, was a Frankish reverend knight who had just arrived from their land in order to make the holy pilgrimage and then return home. He was of my intimate fellowship and kept such constant company with me that he began to call me "my brother." Between us were mutual bonds of amity and friendship. When he resolved to return by sea to his homeland, he said to me:

"My brother, I am leaving for my country and I want you to send with me thy son (my son, who was then fourteen years old, was at that time in my company) to our country, where he can see the knights and learn wisdom and chivalry. When he returns, be will be like a wise man."

Thus there fell upon my ears words which would never come out of the head of a sensible man; for even if my son were to be taken captive, his captivity could not bring him a worse misfortune than carrying him into the lands of the Franks. However, I said to the man:

"By thy life, this has exactly been my idea. But the only thing that prevented me from carrying it out was the fact that his grandmother, my mother, is so fond of him and did not this time let him come out with me until she exacted an oath from me to the effect that I would return him to her."

From Usāmah ibn Munqidh, *An Arab-Syrian Gentleman and Warrior in the Period of the Crusades*, trans. Philip K. Hitti (New York: Columbia University Press, 2000), pp. 161, 163–164. ALCS Humanities E-Book Database.

[5] **King Fulk**: Frankish king of Jerusalem (r. 1131–1143).

Thereupon he asked, "Is thy mother still alive?" "Yes." I replied. "Well," said he, "disobey her not."

Everyone who is a fresh emigrant from the Frankish lands is ruder in character than those who have become acclimatized and have held long association with the Muslims. Here is an illustration of their rude character:

Whenever I visited Jerusalem I always entered the Aqsa Mosque,[6] beside which stood a small mosque which the Franks had converted into a church. When I used to enter the Aqsa Mosque, which was occupied by the Templars[7] . . . who were my friends, the Templars would evacuate the little adjoining mosque so that I might pray in it. One day, I entered this mosque, repeated the first formula, "Allah is great," and stood up in the act of praying, upon which one of the Franks rushed on me, got hold of me and turned my face eastward[8] saying, "This is the way you should pray!" A group of Templars hastened to him, seized him, and repelled him from me. I resumed my prayer. The same man, while the others were otherwise busy, rushed once more on me and turned my face eastward, saying, "This is the way you should pray!" The Templars again came in to him and expelled him. They apologized to me, saying, "This is a stranger who has only recently arrived from the land of the Franks and he has never before seen anyone praying except eastward." Thereupon I said to myself, "I have had enough prayer." So I went out and have ever been surprised at the conduct of this devil of a man, at the change in the color of his face, his trembling and his sentiment at the sight of one praying towards the qiblah.[9]

I saw one of the Franks come to al-Amīr Mu'in-al-Dīn (may Allah's mercy rest upon his soul!) when he was in the Dome of the Rock,[10] and say to him, "Do you want to see God as a child?" Mu'in-al-Dīn said, "Yes." The Frank walked ahead of us until he showed us the picture of Mary with Christ (may peace be upon him!) as an infant in her lap. He then said, "This is God as a child." But Allah is exalted far above what the infidels say about him!

---

[6] **Aqsa Mosque**: Most important mosque in Jerusalem and the third holiest site in Islam.

[7] **Templars**: Members of the Order of the Temple, a Christian order of warrior monks who fought during the Crusades.

[8] **eastward**: Medieval churches were traditionally built so to direct prayer toward the east. Muslims pray in the direction of Mecca, which is south of Jerusalem.

[9] **qiblah**: Direction for prayer in Islam.

[10] **Dome of the Rock**: Islamic shrine in Jerusalem, built on the remains of the Jewish temple.

READING AND DISCUSSION QUESTIONS

1. How many Christians does the author call friend in this passage?

2. How well does he seem to understand his Frankish friends? How well do they understand him?

3. What is said about Jesus in this document? Why would a Muslim say that?

DOCUMENT 10-5

BENJAMIN OF TUDELA
A Jewish Travel Journal

ca. 1173

Benjamin of Tudela, from the kingdom of Navarre in northern Spain, traveled on a pilgrimage to Jerusalem from 1165–1173. His journey took him across the Mediterranean, around the Arabian peninsula, and through Persia. Along the way, he recorded his observations and adventures in a travel journal, often noting the prominent Jewish inhabitants of a place. His journal was published as The Travels of Benjamin, *and was used by Jewish and Christian scholars for centuries as a guide to the peoples and geography of the Mediterranean region.*

From Marseilles one can take ship and in four days reach Genoa, which is also upon the sea. Here live two Jews, R. Samuel, son of Salim, and his brother, from the city of Ceuta, both of them good men. The city is surrounded by a wall, and the inhabitants are not governed by any king, but by judges whom they appoint at their pleasure. Each householder has a tower to his house, and at times of strife they fight from the tops of the towers with each other. They have command of the sea. They build ships which they call galleys, and make predatory attacks upon Edom and Ishmael and the land of Greece as far as Sicily, and they bring back to Genoa

From Benjamin of Tudela, *The Itinerary of Benjamin of Tudela: Critical Text, Translation, and Commentary*, trans. and ed. Marcus Nathan Adler (London: Henry Frowde/Oxford University Press, 1907), pp. 5–6, 22–23.

spoils from all these places. They are constantly at war with the men of Pisa. Between them and the Pisans there is a distance of two days' journey. . . .

Rome is the head of the kingdoms of Christendom, and contains about 200 Jews, who occupy an honorable position and pay no tribute, and amongst them are officials of the Pope Alexander, the spiritual head of all Christendom. Great scholars reside here, at the head of them being R. Daniel, the chief rabbi, and R. Jechiel, an official of the Pope. He is a handsome young man of intelligence and wisdom, and he has the entry of the Pope's palace; for he is the steward of his house and of all that he has. He is a grandson of E. Nathan, who composed the Aruch[11] and its commentaries. Other scholars are R. Joab, son of the chief rabbi R. Solomon, R. Menachem, head of the academy, R. Jechiel, who lives in Trastevere, and R. Benjamin, son of R. Shabbethai of blessed memory. . . .

[Jerusalem is] a small city, fortified by three walls. It is full of people whom the [Muslims] call Jacobites, Syrians, Greeks, Georgians and Franks, and of people of all tongues. It contains a dyeing-house, for which the Jews pay a small rent annually to the king, on condition that beside the Jews no other dyers be allowed in Jerusalem. There are about 200 Jews who dwell under the Tower of David in one corner of the city. The lower portion of the wall of the Tower of David, to the extent of about ten cubits, is part of the ancient foundation set up by our ancestors, the remaining portion having been built by the [Muslims]. There is no structure in the whole city stronger than the Tower of David. The city also contains two buildings, from one of which — the hospital — there issue forth four hundred knights; and therein all the sick who come thither are lodged and cared for in life and in death. The other building is called the Temple of Solomon; it is the palace built by Solomon the king of Israel. Three hundred knights are quartered there, and issue therefrom every day for military exercise, besides those who come from the land of the Franks and the other parts of Christendom, having taken upon themselves to serve there a year or two until their vow is fulfilled. In Jerusalem is the great church called the Sepulchre, and here is the burial-place of Jesus, unto which the Christians make pilgrimages. . . .

In Jerusalem, attached to the palace which belonged to Solomon, are the stables built by him, forming a very substantial structure, composed of large stones, and the like of it is not to be seen anywhere in the world. There is also visible up to this day the pool used by the priests before

---

[11]**Aruch**: A dictionary of Jewish law, compiled around 1101 A.D. in Rome.

offering their sacrifices, and the Jews coming thither write their names upon the wall. The gate of Jehoshaphat leads to the valley of Jehoshaphat, which is the gathering-place of nations. Here is the pillar called Absalom's Hand,[12] and the sepulchre of King Uzziah.[13]

In the neighborhood is also a great spring, called the Waters of Siloam, connected with the brook of Kidron. Over the spring is a large structure dating from the time of our ancestors, but little water is found, and the people of Jerusalem for the most part drink the rain-water, which they collect in cisterns in their houses.

READING AND DISCUSSION QUESTIONS

1. What kinds of details catch Benjamin's eye as he travels?

2. Who hires Jews in Rome? What kinds of occupations do Jews hold?

3. What interests Benjamin about Christians?

DOCUMENT 10-6

DUKE WILLIAM OF AQUITAINE
On the Foundation of Cluny
909

Cluny, founded in 909 by Duke William of Aquitaine (also known as William the Pious), became one of the leading abbeys in Europe and a model for monasteries in need of reform. According to the terms of its foundation, Cluny was subordinate only to the pope himself. This meant that the institution enjoyed a great deal of independence from local bishops and lords. In

From E. F. Henderson, *Select Historical Documents of the Middle Ages* (London: 1892), pp. 329–333.

[12] **Absalom**: Son of King David.
[13] **King Uzziah**: King of Judah, 792–750 B.C.E.

addition, Cluny became the "motherhouse" to other monasteries throughout Europe, and these subordinate houses came to enjoy the same privileges as Cluny itself. Cluny amassed such wealth that the monks eventually hired others to do the daily work of running the monastery and occupied themselves in almost constant prayer.

To all right thinkers it is clear that the providence of God has so provided for certain rich men that, by means of their transitory possessions, if they use them well, they may be able to merit everlasting rewards. As to which . . . I, William, count and duke by the grace of God, diligently pondering this, and desiring to provide for my own safety while I am still able, have considered it advisable — nay, most necessary, that from the temporal goods which have been conferred upon me I should give some little portion for the gain of my soul. I do this, indeed, in order that I who have thus increased in wealth, may not, perchance, at the last be accused of having spent all in caring for my body, but rather may rejoice, when fate at last shall snatch all things away, in having reserved something for myself. Which end, indeed, seems attainable by no more suitable means than that . . . I should support at my own expense a congregation of monks. And this is my trust, this my hope, indeed, that although I myself am unable to despise all things, nevertheless, by receiving despisers of the world, whom I believe to be righteous, I may receive the reward of the righteous. Therefore be it known to all . . . that, for the love of God and of our Savior Jesus Christ, I hand over from my own rule to the holy apostles, Peter, namely, and Paul, the possessions over which I hold sway, the town of Cluny, namely, with the court and demesne manor,[14] and the church in honor of St. Mary the mother of God and of St. Peter the prince of the apostles, together with all the things pertaining to it, the villas, indeed, the chapels, the serfs of both sexes, the vines, the fields, the meadows, the woods, the waters and their outlets, the mills, the incomes and revenues, what is cultivated and what is not, all in their entirety. Which things are situated in or about the country of Macon, each one surrounded by its own bounds. I give, moreover, all these things to the aforesaid apostles — I, William, and my wife Ingelberga — first for the love of God; then for soul of my lord king Odo, of my father and my mother; for myself and my wife — for the salvation, namely, of our souls and bodies; — and not least for that of Ava[15]

---

[14] **demesne manor**: Manor house and the estate land surrounding it.
[15] **Ava**: William's sister.

who left me these things in her will; for the souls also of our brothers and sisters and nephews, and of all our relatives of both sexes; for our faithful ones who adhere to our service; for the advancement, also, and integrity of the catholic religion. Finally, since all of us Christians are held together by one bond of love and faith, let this donation be for all, — for the orthodox, namely, of past, present, or future times. I give these things, moreover, with this understanding, that in Cluny a regular monastery shall be constructed in honor of the holy apostles Peter and Paul, and that there the monks shall congregate and live according to the rule of St. Benedict, and that they shall possess, hold, have and order these same things unto all time. . . . [The monks are to be under the protection of the pope, and no one — not even the pope — is to dare to violate Cluny's rights.]

If any one — which Heaven forbid, and which, through the mercy of God and the protection of the apostles I do not think will happen, — whether he be a neighbor or a stranger, no matter what his condition or power, should, through any kind of wile, attempt to do any act of violence contrary to this deed of gift which we have ordered to be drawn up for love of almighty God and for reverence of the chief apostles Peter and Paul: first, indeed, let him incur the wrath of almighty God, and let God remove him from the land of the living and wipe out his name from the book of life, and let his portion be with those who said to the Lord God: Depart from us; and, with Dathan and Abiron[16] whom the earth, opening its jaws, swallowed up, and hell absorbed while still alive, let him incur everlasting damnation. And being made a companion of Judas let him be kept thrust down there with eternal tortures, and, lest it seem to human eyes that he pass through the present world with impunity, let him experience in his own body, indeed, the torments of future damnation, sharing the double disaster with Heliodorus and Antiochus,[17] of whom one being coerced with sharp blows scarcely escaped alive; and the other struck down by the divine will, his members putrefying and swarming with vermin, perished most miserably. . . .

---

[16] **Dathan and Abiron:** Brothers who, as recounted in the Old Testament, tried to sabotage Moses during the exodus from Egypt. The earth swallowed them whole.
[17] **Heliodorus and Antiochus:** Heliodorus was the Seleucid minister sent by the emperor to take the treasures from the Jewish temple in Jerusalem. He failed in his task when God expelled him from the temple three times. Antiochus (175–164 B.C.E.) was the king of the Seleucid dynasty known for the actions that led to the Maccabee revolt (see Document 4-6).

I, William, commanded this act to be made and drawn up, and confirmed it with my own hand.

(Signed by Ingelberga and a number of bishops and nobles.)

READING AND DISCUSSION QUESTIONS

1. What is Duke William's stated motive for founding the abbey? What other motives could he have had?

2. Consider the following passage: "although I myself am unable to despise all things, nevertheless, by receiving despisers of the world, whom I believe to be righteous, I may receive the reward of the righteous." What does this reveal about William's religious beliefs?

3. Besides himself, who else does William expect will benefit from his gift? How does he expect they will benefit?

4. What specific punishments will befall anyone who defies the gift? Why is it significant that William includes these at the end of the document?

COMPARATIVE QUESTIONS

1. Compare and contrast the status of unfree persons as illustrated in the first two documents.

2. Compare and contrast the condition of serfs in the Middle Ages with the condition of slaves in the Roman Empire as evidenced in Document 5-3.

3. Compare the monastic reforms detailed by William of Aquitaine with those of Saint Benedict (Document 7-2).

4. How do Fulcher of Chartres, Usāmah ibn Munqidh, and Benjamin of Tudela view people from other religious groups? How would you characterize their interactions with these people?

CHAPTER 11

The Creativity and Challenges of Medieval Cities

1100–1300

The Roman Empire had been organized around great cities, but as the empire crumbled in the West, cities declined. Beginning around 1100, however, cities in western Europe were once again becoming important political, economic, and intellectual centers. On the Italian peninsula, commercial cities such as Florence, Venice, and Milan rose to prominence as intellectual and artistic hubs. At various times during the Middle Ages, they became, in effect, independent city-states, often governed by the guilds that represented merchants and artisans. France, too, witnessed an intellectual surge, often focused around the great cathedral schools such as Chartres and Laon. Most important was Paris, where the University of Paris became a center of theology and philosophy that drew students from all over western Europe. At the same time, the courts of the kings and the great nobles offered patronage to writers and artists. Growing alongside medieval cities were religious institutions and rituals, including new religious orders that ministered to city residents.

VIEWPOINTS

Living and Working in a Medieval City

DOCUMENT 11-1

The Charter of the Laon Commune

1328

As urban centers grew during the High Middle Ages, merchants began to look for ways to protect their livelihoods from local churchmen and nobles. In many cities across Europe, they banded together to protect each other from mutual threats. The communes sought guarantees from kings or great nobles that would guarantee certain rights for its members. In the twelfth century, merchants from the French town of Laon formed a commune to prevent their bishop from taxing them unjustly. The king granted them the rights of a commune, although for generations the bishops would have the commune's rights overturned, only to see the commune regain them.

1. Let no one arrest any freeman or serf for any offense without due process of law.
2. But if any one do injury to a clerk, soldier, or merchant, native or foreign, provided he who does the injury belongs to the same city as the injured person, let him, summoned after the fourth day, come for justice before the mayor and [judges].
7. If a thief is arrested, let him be brought to him on whose land he has been arrested; but if justice is not done by the lord, let it be done by the [judges].
12. We entirely abolish mortmain.[1]

From Frederic Austin Ogg, *A Source Book of Mediaeval History* (New York: American Book Company, 1908), pp. 327–328.

[1] **mortmain:** During the Middle Ages, property and land that had been acquired by the church that was rarely ever sold again.

18. The customary tallages[2] we have so reformed that every man owing such tallages, at the time when they are due, must pay four pence, and beyond that no more.

19. Let men of the peace not be compelled to resort to courts outside the city.

READING AND DISCUSSION QUESTIONS

1. What benefits do members of the commune have?

2. What judicial rights does the commune claim?

DOCUMENT 11-2

The Ordinances of London's Leatherworkers

1346

In urban areas, merchants working in similar kinds of trade formed merchant guilds, and those who specialized in producing the same kind of work formed craft guilds. These guilds determined who had the right to produce and sell in their city or town, and set quality standards for their craft. They also established standards for training new members of the profession. The document that follows is an example of how the guilds regulated themselves in ways other than just trade and production.

In honor of God, of Our Lady, and of all Saints, and for the nurture of tranquillity and peace among the good folks the Megucers, called "Whittawyers,"[3] the folks of the same trade have, by assent of Richard Lacer, Mayor, and of the Aldermen [of London], ordained the points under-written.

In the first place, they have ordained that they will find a wax candle, to burn before Our Lady in the Church of All Hallows near London Wall.

From Alfred Edward Bland, Philip Anthony Brown, and Richard Henry Tawney, eds., *English Economic History: Select Documents* (New York: Macmillan, 1919), pp. 136–138.

[2] **tallage**: Tax on land and property.
[3] **Megucers, called "Whittawyers"**: Leatherworkers who specialized in turning leather white.

Also, that each person of the said trade shall put in the box such sum as he shall think fit, in aid of maintaining the said candle.

Also, if by chance any one of the said trade shall fall into poverty, whether through old age, or because he cannot labor or work, and have nothing with which to help himself; he shall have every week from the said box 7*d.* for his support if he be a man of good repute. And after his decease, if he have a wife, a woman of good repute, she shall have weekly for her support 7*d.* from the said box, so long as she shall behave herself well, and keep single.

And that no stranger shall work in the said trade, or keep house [for the same] in the city, if he be not an apprentice, or a man admitted to the franchise of the said city.

And that no one shall take the serving man of another to work with him, during his term, unless it be with the permission of his master.

And if any one of the said trade shall have work in his house that he cannot complete, or if for want of assistance such work shall be in danger of being lost, those of the said trade shall aid him, that so the said work be not lost.

And if any one of the said trade shall depart this life, and have not wherewithal to be buried, he shall be buried at the expense of their common box; and when any one of the said trade shall die, all those of the said trade shall go to the Vigil, and make offering on the [next day].

And if any serving-man shall conduct himself in any other manner than properly towards his master, and act rebelliously towards him, no one of the said trade shall set him to work, until he shall have made amends before the Mayor and Aldermen. . . .

And that no one of the said trade shall behave himself the more thoughtlessly, in the way of speaking or acting amiss, by reason of the points aforesaid; and if any one shall do to the contrary thereof, he shall not follow the said trade until he shall have reasonably made amends.

And if any one of the said trade shall do to the contrary of any point of the Ordinances aforesaid, and be convicted thereof by good men of the said trade, he shall pay to the Chamber of the Guildhall of London, the first time 2*s.*, the second time 40*d.*, the third time half a mark, and the fourth time 10*s.*, and shall forswear the trade.

Also, that the good folks of the same trade shall once in the year be assembled in a certain place, convenient thereto, there to choose two men of the most loyal and befitting of the said trade, to be overseers of work and all other things touching the trade, for that year, which persons shall be presented to the Mayor and Aldermen for the time being, and sworn before them diligently to enquire and make search, and loyally to present to the said Mayor and Aldermen such defaults as they shall find touching the said trade without sparing any one for friendship or for hatred, or in any other manner. And if any one of the said trade shall be found rebellious against the said overseers, so as not to let them properly make their search and assay, as they ought to do; or if he shall absent himself from the meeting aforesaid, without reasonable cause, after due warning by the said overseers, he shall pay to the Chamber, upon the first default, 40d.; and on the second like default, half a mark; and on the third, one mark; and on the fourth, 20s. and shall forswear the trade for ever.

Also, that if the overseers shall be found lax and negligent about their duty, or partial to any person, . . . maintaining him, or voluntarily permitting him [to continue] in his default, and shall not present him to the Mayor and Aldermen, as before stated, they are to incur the penalty aforesaid.

Also, that each year, at such assemblies of the good folks of the said trade, there shall be chosen overseers, as before stated. And if it shall be found that through laxity or negligence of the said governors such assemblies are not held, each of the said overseers is to incur the said penalty.

Also, that all skins falsely and deceitfully wrought in their trade, which the said overseers shall find on sale in the hands of any person, citizen or foreigner, within the franchise, shall be forfeited to the said Chamber, and the worker thereof amerced in manner aforesaid.

Also, that no one who has not been an apprentice, and has not finished his term of apprenticeship in the said trade shall be made free of the same trade; unless it be attested by the overseers for the time being or by four persons of the said trade, that such person is able, and sufficiently skilled to be made free of the same.

Also, that no one of the said trade shall induce the servant of another to work with him in the same trade, until he has made a proper fine with his first master, at the discretion of the said overseers, or of four reputable men of the said trade. And if any one shall do to the contrary thereof, or receive the serving workman of another to work with him during his term, without leave of the trade, he is to incur the said penalty.

READING AND DISCUSSION QUESTIONS

1. What material benefits does the guild provide to members?
2. Other than standardizing the quality of work, what other things does the guild do to ensure the members produce good work?

3. What happens to those who break the rules of the guild?
4. What does the guild do for widows?

DOCUMENT 11-3

THE COMMUNE OF FLORENCE
A Sumptuary Law: Restrictions on Dress
1373

Sumptuary laws (laws regulating consumption) served a number of purposes — social, economic, and religious — and were most often associated with clothing. Sometimes religious or ethnic minorities, such as Jews at various times in European history, were required to wear distinctive clothing. In other cases, the hereditary aristocracy called for laws that forbade prosperous merchants or other members of the bourgeoisie from adopting aristocratic fashions. A ruler who was concerned that too much wealth was leaving the country might pass ordinances that forbade his subjects from wearing silks or precious stones that had to be imported.

It is well known to all that the worthy men, Benozzo di Francesco di Andrea . . . [and fifteen others] . . . have been selected to discover ways and means by which money will accrue to the Commune. . . . Considering the Commune's need for revenue to pay current expenses . . . they have enacted . . . the following:

First, all women and girls, whether married or not, whether betrothed or not, of whatever age, rank, and condition . . . who wear — or who wear in future — any gold, silver, pearls, precious stones, bells, ribbons of gold or silver, or cloth of silk brocade on their bodies or heads . . . for the ornamentation of their bodies . . . will be required to pay each year . . . the sum of 50 florins . . . to the treasurer of the gabelle[4] on contracts. . . . [The exceptions to this prohibition are] that every married woman may wear on her hand or hands as many as two rings. . . . And every married woman

---

From Gene Brucker, *The Society of Renaissance Florence* (New York: Harper & Row, 1971), pp. 46–47.

[4] **treasurer of the gabelle**: Officer in the Florentine government responsible for collecting taxes.

or girl who is betrothed may wear . . . a silver belt which does not exceed fourteen ounces in weight. . . .

So that the gabelle is not defrauded, and so that citizens — on account of clothing already made — are not forced to bear new expenditures, [the officials] have decreed that all dresses, gowns, coats, capes, and other items of clothing belonging to any women or girls above the age of ten years, which were made up to the present day and which are decorated in whatever manner, may be worn for ten years in the future without the payment of any gabelle.

READING AND DISCUSSION QUESTIONS

1. What was the principal reason for passing this sumptuary law?

2. In what ways did the sumptuary laws create a kind of income tax?

3. In what ways did the sumptuary laws make social divisions more rigid? Less rigid?

4. Identify the grandfather clause (a provision that exempts certain people from the law) in this document. Why was it included?

DOCUMENT 11-4

SAINT THOMAS AQUINAS
Summa Theologica: *Proof of the Existence of God*
1268

Thomas Aquinas (1225–1274) was one of the foremost theologians and philosophers of the Middle Ages. Although born in Sicily, he traveled widely, taught at great universities in France and Germany, and was an adviser to

---

From Oliver J. Thatcher, ed., *The Library of Original Sources*, vol. IV: *The Early Medieval World* (Milwaukee: University Research Extension Co., 1907), pp. 359–363.

popes and kings. Thomas and the other Scholastic thinkers adapted the teachings of Aristotle to Christian purposes. In some of his works, Thomas deals with the most abstract issues of philosophy and theology. Here he addresses a very basic religious topic: How does one know that a higher power exists?

ARTICLE II. WHETHER THE EXISTENCE OF GOD IS DEMONSTRABLE.

Let us proceed to the second point. It is objected (1) that the existence of God is not demonstrable: that God's existence is an article of faith, and that articles of faith are not demonstrable, because the office of demonstration is to prove, but faith pertains (only) to things that are not to be proven, as is evident from the Epistle to the Hebrews, 11. Hence that God's existence is not demonstrable.

Again, (2) that the subject matter of demonstration is that something exists, but in the case of God we cannot know what exists, but only what does not, as Damascenus[5] says (Of the Orthodox Faith, I., 4.) Hence that we cannot demonstrate God's existence.

Again, (3) that if God's existence is to be proved it must be from what He causes, and that what He effects is not sufficient for His supposed nature, since He is infinite, but the effects finite, and the finite is not proportional to the infinite. Since, therefore, a cause cannot be proved through an effect not proportional to itself, it is said that God's existence cannot be proved.

But against this argument the apostle says (Rom. I., 20), "The unseen things of God are visible through His manifest works." But this would not be so unless it were possible to demonstrate God's existence through His works. What ought to be understood concerning anything, is first of all, whether it exists.

Conclusion. It is possible to demonstrate God's existence, although not a priori (by pure reason), yet a posteriori[6] from some work of His more surely known to us.

In answer I must say that the proof is double. One is through the nature of a cause and is called *propter quid*: this is through the nature of preceding events simply. The other is through the nature of the effect, and is called *quia*, and is through the nature of preceding things as respects us.

---

[5] **Damascenus**: John of Damascus (ca. 676–749), a Christian theologian.

[6] **A priori . . . a posteriori**: A *priori* refers to knowledge gained through logic and reasoning. A *posteriori* is knowledge gained from facts and observation.

Since the effect is better known to us than the cause, we proceed from the effect to the knowledge of the cause. From any effect whatsoever it can be proved that a corresponding cause exists, if only the effects of it are sufficiently known to us, for since effects depend on causes, the effect being given, it is necessary that a preceding cause exists. Whence, that God exists, although this is not itself known to us, is provable through effects that are known to us.

To the first objection above, I reply, therefore, that God's existence, and those other things of this nature that can be known through natural reason concerning God, as is said in Rom. I., are not articles of faith, but preambles to these articles. So faith presupposes natural knowledge, so grace nature, and perfection a perfectible thing. Nothing prevents a thing that is in itself demonstrable and knowable, from being accepted as an article of faith by someone that does not accept the proof of it.

To the second objection, I reply that, since the cause is proven from the effect, one must use the effect in the place of a definition of the cause in demonstrating that the cause exists; and that this applies especially in the case of God, because for proving that anything exists, it is necessary to accept in this method what the name signifies, not however that anything exists, because the question *what it is* is secondary to the question *whether it exists at all*. The characteristics of God are drawn from His works as shall be shown hereafter, (Question XIII). Whence by proving that God exists through His works as shall be shown hereafter, (Question XIII). Whence by proving that God exists through His works, we are able by this very method to see what the name God signifies.

To the third objection, I reply that, although a perfect knowledge of the cause cannot be had from inadequate effects, yet that from any effect manifest to us it can be shown that a cause does exist, as has been said. And thus from the works of God His existence can be proved, although we cannot in this way know Him perfectly in accordance with His own essence.

ARTICLE III. WHETHER GOD EXISTS.

Let us proceed to the third article. It is objected (1) that God does not exist, because if one of two contradictory things is infinite, the other will be totally destroyed; that it is implied in the name God that there is a certain infinite goodness: if then God existed, no evil would be found. But evil is found in the world; therefore it is objected that God does not exist.

Again, that what can be accomplished through a less number of principles will not be accomplished through more. It is objected that all things that appear on the earth can be accounted for through other principles, without supposing that God exists, since what is natural can be traced to a natural principle, and what proceeds from a proposition can be traced to the human reason or will. Therefore that there is no necessity to suppose that God exists. But as against this note what is said of the person of God (Exod. III., 14) *I am that I am.*

Conclusion. There must be found in the nature of things one first immovable Being, a primary cause, necessarily existing, not created; existing the most widely, good, even the best possible; the first ruler through the intellect, and the ultimate end of all things, which is God.

I answer that it can be proved in five ways that God exists. The first and plainest is the method that proceeds from the point of view of motion. It is certain and in accord with experience, that things on earth undergo change. Now, everything that is moved is moved by something; nothing, indeed, is changed, except it is changed to something which it is in potentiality. Moreover, anything moves in accordance with something actually existing; change itself, is nothing else than to bring forth something from potentiality into actuality. Now, nothing can be brought from potentiality to actual existence except through something actually existing: thus heat in action, as fire, makes fire-wood, which is hot in potentiality, to be hot actually, and through this process, changes itself. The same thing cannot at the same time be actually and potentially the same thing, but only in regard to different things. What is actually hot cannot be at the same time potentially hot, but it is possible for it at the same time to be potentially cold. It is impossible, then, that anything should be both mover and the thing moved, in regard to the same thing and in the same way, or that it should move itself. Everything, therefore, is moved by something else. If, then, that by which it is moved, is also moved, this must be moved by something still different, and this, again, by something else. But this process cannot go on to infinity because there would not be any first mover, nor, because of this fact, anything else in motion, as the succeeding things would not move except because of what is moved by the first mover, just as a stick is not moved except through what is moved from the hand. Therefore it is necessary to go back to some first mover, which is itself moved by nothing — and this all men know as God.

The second proof is from the nature of the efficient cause. We find in our experience that there is a chain of causes: nor is it found possible for anything to be the efficient cause of itself, since it would have to exist before itself, which is impossible. Nor in the case of efficient causes can the chain go back indefinitely, because in all chains of efficient causes, the first is the cause of the middle, and these of the last, whether they be one or many. If the cause is removed, the effect is removed. Hence if there is not a first cause, there will not be a last, nor a middle. But if the chain were to go back infinitely, there would be no first cause, and thus no ultimate effect, nor middle causes, which is admittedly false. Hence we must presuppose some first efficient cause — which all call God.

The third proof is taken from the natures of the merely possible and necessary. We find that certain things either may or may not exist, since they are found to come into being and be destroyed, and in consequence potentially, either existent or non-existent. But it is impossible for all things that are of this character to exist eternally, because what *may* not exist, at length *will* not. If, then, all things were merely possible (mere accidents), eventually nothing among things would exist. If this is true, even now there would be nothing, because what does not exist, does not take its beginning except through something that does exist. If then nothing existed, it would be impossible for anything to begin, and there would now be nothing existing, which is admittedly false. Hence not all things are mere accidents, but there must be one necessarily existing being. Now every necessary thing either has a cause of its necessary existence, or has not. In the case of necessary things that have a cause for their necessary existence, the chain of causes cannot go back infinitely, just as not in the case of efficient causes, as proved. Hence there must be presupposed something necessarily existing through its own nature, not having a cause elsewhere but being itself the cause of the necessary existence of other things — which all call God.

The fourth proof arises from the degrees that are found in things. For there is found a greater and a less degree of goodness, truth, nobility, and the like. But more or less are terms spoken of various things as they approach in diverse ways toward something that is the greatest, just as in the case of hotter (more hot) which approaches nearer the greatest heat. There exists therefore something that is the truest, and best, and most noble, and in consequence, the greatest being. For what are the greatest truths are the greatest beings, as is said in the Metaphysics Bk. II. 2. What moreover is the greatest in its way, in another way is the cause of all things of its own kind (or genus); thus fire, which is the greatest heat, is the cause of all heat, as is said in the same book (cf. Plato and Aristotle). Therefore there exists something that is the cause of the existence of all things and of the goodness and of every perfection whatsoever — and this we call God.

The fifth proof arises from the ordering of things for we see that some things which lack reason, such as natural bodies, are operated in accordance with a plan. It appears from this that they are operated always or the more frequently in this same way the closer they follow what is the Highest; whence it is clear that they do not arrive at the result by chance but because of a purpose. The things, moreover, that do not have intelligence do not tend toward a result unless directed by some one knowing and intelligent; just as an arrow is sent by an archer. Therefore there is something intelligent by which all natural things are arranged in accordance with a plan — and this we call God.

In response to the first objection, then, I reply what Augustine says; that since God is entirely good, He would permit evil to exist in His works only if He were so good and omnipotent that He might bring forth good even from the evil. It therefore pertains to the infinite goodness of God that he permits evil to exist and from this brings forth good.

My reply to the second objection is that since nature is ordered in accordance with some defined purpose by the direction of some superior agent, those things that spring from nature must be dependent upon God, just as upon a first cause. Likewise, what springs from a proposition must be traceable to some higher cause which is not the human reason or will, because this is changeable and defective and everything changeable and liable to non-existence is dependent upon some unchangeable first principle that is necessarily self-existent as has been shown.

READING AND DISCUSSION QUESTIONS

1. What objections does Aquinas say one might have to the idea of the existence of God?

2. Summarize each of the five proofs in your own words.

3. Compare Aquinas with Aristotle (Document 3-6). What is similar about their work?

4. How many of the five proofs are religious, and how many are philosophical?

DOCUMENT 11-5

MARIE DE FRANCE
The Nightingale
ca. 1200

Music was a popular art form in the Middle Ages. Musicians entertained with songs of legendary heroes or of religious themes. In the High Middle Ages, the courtly love tradition was added to the European musical tradition. These songs featured romantic tales, like the stories of Lancelot and Guinevere from the Arthurian tales. Others are stories of average people. In general, it was the nobility that supported this art form, but the musicians, or troubadours, would also play their songs in the cities. Marie de France was one of the famous writers in this courtly love tradition.

In the country near St. Malo was a well-known village, in which two knights, whose bounty gave it fair name, had their homes and their parks.

The one was married to a lady who was wise, courteous and debonair; and marvellously he doted upon her, as often comes to pass in such a case.

The other was a bachelor who was known among his fellows for his prowess and his great courage. So eagerly did he seek honor that he was often at tournaments, spent freely, and gave largesse abundantly of what he had.

Now he came to love his neighbor's wife, and by dint of his entreaties and prayers brought it about that she loved him above all things. This was partly for his deserts,[7] partly because of the good which she heard said of him, and partly because he was ever at hand.

They loved each other well, yet wisely, so guarding their secret that they were not observed, nor discovered, nor even mistrusted. It was easy for them to do this, since their dwellings, both halls and donjons,[8] stood side by side, with no bar or barrier between them save a high wall of grey stone.

When the lady stood at the window of the chamber in which she slept, she could speak with her lover, and he from his side with her; and they could exchange gifts by throwing or by tossing.

From *Marie de France: Seven of Her Lays Done into English*, trans. Edith Rickert ([London:] David Nutt, 1901), pp. 87–91.

[7] **for his deserts**: Because he was worthy.
[8] **donjons**: Towers in a medieval castle.

They had nothing at all to grieve them; but were quite happy, except that they might not meet as they would, for the lady was straitly guarded when her lord was in the country. But at least none might hinder them from going to the window, either by day or by night, and there gazing upon each other and talking together.

A long time they were in love, until at length came summer, when wood and meadow were green once more, and copses were a-flower. The little birds right sweetly trilled their joy at the tips of the blossoms. 'Tis no marvel that he who has love-longing in his heart should give heed thereto; and so, I tell you truly, it was with this knight and this lady, both in words and in glances.

The nights when the moon shone clear, the lady rose from her husband's side, as he lay asleep, and wrapping herself in her mantle, went to stand at the window, for she knew that her lover would be there, since like herself he waked most of the night for love-longing. It was joy to them to see each other, since they might have no more.

So often she arose and stood there that at last her husband was vexed, and often asked her why she arose and whither she went.

"My lord," she answered," there is no joy in this world like that of hearing the nightingale sing, and this is why I come to stand here. So sweetly have I heard him trill at night, and such great pleasure has his song given me, that I long for it until I cannot close an eye in sleep!"

When her husband heard this, he laughed for sheer vexation and ill-humor; and bethought him that he would ensnare the nightingale.

Accordingly, there was no lad in his household who did not make trap or toil or net, to place in the copse. In every hazel and every chestnut they put net or lime, until at length they trapped and caught the bird, and brought it alive to their lord.

He, greatly pleased, took it into his wife's chamber, calling out:

"Wife, where are you? Come here and speak to us! I have limed the nightingale for which you have waked so often. Henceforth, you may lie in peace; he shall trouble you no more!"

When the lady heard this, she was both vexed and sorrowful, and demanded the bird of her husband. But he in his passion slew it, wringing its neck with his two hands — a churlish deed! — and flung the body at his wife, so that the front of her smock, a little above the breast, was stained with its blood. Thereupon he left the chamber.

The lady with bitter tears took up the little body, and cursed all who had devised traps and nets to ensnare the nightingale; for they had made an end of her great joy.

"Alas!" she said, " woe's me! Never again may I rise at night, and stand at the window to see my love. I know of a truth he will deem me false, and for this must I take counsel. I will send him the nightingale at once, and so tell him the whole story."

In a piece of gold-embroidered samite,[9] duly inscribed, she wrapped the little bird; and calling one of her pages, charged him with the message to her lover.

He went to the knight, and with greetings from his lady told all the message; and delivered to him the nightingale.

When the young lord had heard all the story, he grieved at the mischance; and being neither churlish nor slothful, he had a little casket fashioned, not of iron or steel, but all of fine gold set with rare and costly gems. Then he placed the nightingale within, and had a splendid cover sealed upon it; and everywhere that he went carried the casket about with him.

READING AND DISCUSSION QUESTIONS

1. What did the woman see in her lover?

2. Why does she grieve for the nightingale? What will happen to her love affair?

3. What does this document reveal about French attitudes toward sexual morality?

COMPARATIVE QUESTIONS

1. What do the first three documents in this chapter, considered together, reveal about social tensions in the Middle Ages?

2. Compare and contrast Aquinas with St. Augustine and St. Benedict of Nursia from Chapter 7. What do the universities add to the Christian intellectual traditions?

3. What makes Marie de France's storytelling different from that of Homer (Document 3-1) and from the Song of Roland (Document 8-5)?

---

[9] **samite**: An expensive silk fabric.

CHAPTER 12

The Crisis of the Later Middle Ages

1300–1450

B eginning around 1340, a series of disasters brought drastic change to western Europe. The Black Death (or Black Plague), beginning in 1347, killed an estimated 30 to 60 percent of western Europe's population. In the wake of the plague, peasant uprisings were frequent, and the urban poor periodically revolted against the wealthier guilds. In some cases those revolts brought about the end of serfdom or the expansion of political rights. Between 1337 and 1453, the Hundred Years' War — in actuality a series of wars and civil wars — wreaked havoc on France. Although these conflicts helped revolutionize warfare with new technologies, tactics, and strategies, the ideals of chivalry, which were derived from older military practices, remained as popular as ever. The papacy began to lose prestige and power — first during its exile to Avignon (ah-veen-YOHN), France, between 1309 and 1376. While dissent over the rightful holder of the papacy resulted in the Great Schism (1378–1417), and further weakened people's faith in the Church, new saints emerged to exert religious influence.

DOCUMENT 12-1

GIOVANNI BOCCACCIO

The Decameron: *The Plague Hits Florence*

ca. 1350

The first wave of the Black Death began in the late 1340s. The disease spread rapidly, and contemporaries understood very little about it, although they

From *The Decameron, or Ten Days' Entertainment of Boccaccio* (Chicago: Stewart & Kidd Company, 1920), pp. xix–xxii.

did associate it with rats. The only effective countermeasures were quar-
antine and isolation. The infection, which spread along trade routes from
Central Asia, killed some 75 million people. Even after the first incidence
receded, plague returned to Europe in many subsequent outbreaks until the
1700s, with varying mortality rates. In this document, excerpted from his
famous collection of novellas, the Italian writer Giovanni Boccaccio (JEE-
oh-VAH-nee buh-CAH-chee-oh) detailed the chaos unleashed in Florence as
a result of the plague.

In the year then of our Lord 1348, there happened at Florence, the finest
city in all Italy, a most terrible plague; which, whether owing to the influence of the planets, or that it was sent from God as a just punishment for
our sins, had broken out some years before in the Levant[1]; and after passing from place to place, and making incredible havoc all the way, had now
reached the west; where, in spite of all the means that art and human fore-
sight could suggest, such as keeping the city clear from filth, and excluding
all suspected persons, notwithstanding frequent consultations what else
was to be done; nor omitting prayers to God in frequent processions: in the
spring of the forgoing year, it began to show itself in a sad and wonderful[2]
manner; and, different from what it had been in the east, where bleeding
from the nose is the fatal prognostic, here there appeared certain tumors
in the groin, or under the armpits, some as big as a small apple, others as
an egg; and afterwards purple spots in most parts of the body; in some cases
large and but few in number, in others smaller and more numerous, both
sorts the usual messengers of death. . . .

These accidents, and others of the like sort, occasioned various fears
and devices amongst those people who survived, all tending to the same
uncharitable and cruel end; which was to avoid the sick, and everything
that had been near them, expecting by that means to save themselves. And
some holding it best to live temperately, and to avoid excesses of all kinds,
made parties, and shut themselves up from the rest of the world; eating
and drinking moderately of the best, and diverting themselves with music,
and such other entertainments as they might have within doors; never lis-
tening to anything from without, to make them uneasy. Others maintained
free living to be a better preservative, and would balk no passion or appetite they wished to gratify, drinking and revelling incessantly from tavern

---

[1] **the Levant**: The eastern Mediterranean.

[2] **wonderful**: Astonishing.

to tavern, or in private houses; which were frequently found deserted by the owners, and therefore common to every one, yet avoiding, with all this irregularity, to come near the infected. And such at that time was the public distress, that the laws, human and divine, were not regarded; for the officers, to put them in force, being either dead, sick, or in want of persons to assist them, every one did just as he pleased. A third sort of people chose a method between these two: not confining themselves to rules of diet like the former, and yet avoiding the intemperance of the latter; but eating and drinking what their appetites required, they walked everywhere with odors and nosegays³ to smell to; as holding it best to corroborate the brain: for they supposed the whole atmosphere to be tainted with the stink of dead bodies, arising partly from the distemper itself, and partly from the fermenting of the medicines within them. Others of a more cruel disposition, as perhaps the more safe to themselves, declared that the only remedy was to avoid it: persuaded, therefore, of this, and taking care for themselves only, men and women in great numbers left the city, their houses, relations, and effects, and fled into the country; as if the wrath of God had been restrained to visit those only within the walls of the city. . . . I pass over the little regard that citizens and relations showed to each other; for their terror was such that a brother even fled from his brother, a wife from her husband, and, what is more uncommon, a parent from its own child.

READING AND DISCUSSION QUESTIONS

1. According to this account, how did civil order break down during the plague?

2. How does the narrator try to explain why the plague happened?

3. What are some of the things people thought might save them from the plague?

---

³ **odors and nosegays:** Perfumes and small bunches of flowers.

The Anonimalle Chronicle:
The English Peasants' Revolt

1381

Agricultural labor was traditionally carried out by serfs (see Document 10-1), who were bound by tradition to fulfill their obligations to their lords. The high mortality rate of the plague, however, resulted in a labor shortage across Europe. Some peasants tried to act on this advantage and force the lords to end their serfdom. When their demands were not satisfied, peasants often rose up against their lords. In England in 1381, an unpopular tax on all adult males prompted thousands of peasants to revolt. The author of this document is unknown, but he was most likely a monk.

And on that Thursday, the said feast of Corpus Christi, the King, being in the Tower [of London] very sad and sorry, mounted up into a little turret towards St. Catherine's, where were lying a great number of the commons, and had proclamation made to them that they all should go peaceably to their homes, and he would pardon them all manner of their trespasses. But all cried with one voice that they would not go before they had captured the traitors who lay in the Tower, nor until they had got charters to free them from all manner of serfdom, and had got certain other points which they wished to demand. And the King benevolently granted all, and made a clerk write a bill in their presence in these terms: "Richard, King of England and France, gives great thanks to his good commons, for that they have so great a desire to see and to keep their king, and grants them pardon for all manner of trespasses and misprisions and felonies done up to this hour, and wills and commands that every one should now return to his own home, and wills and commands that each should put his grievances in writing, and have them sent to him; and he will provide, with the aid of his loyal lords and his good council, such remedy as shall be profitable both to him and to them, and to all the kingdom." On this document he sealed his signet in presence of them all, and sent out the said bill by the hands of two of his knights to the folks before St. Catherine's. And he

From Charles Oman, *The Great Revolt of 1381* (Oxford: Clarendon Press, 1906), pp. 196–203.

caused it to be read to them, and the knight who read it stood up on an old chair before the others so that all could hear. All this time the King was in the Tower in great distress of mind. And when the commons had heard the Bill, they said that this was nothing but trifles and mockery. Therefore they returned to London and had it cried around the City that all lawyers, and all the clerks of the Chancery and the Exchequer and every man who could write a brief or a letter should be beheaded, whenever they could be found. At this time they burnt several more houses in the City, and the King himself ascended to a high garret of the Tower and watched the fires. Then he came down again, and sent for the lords to have their counsel, but they knew not how they should counsel him, and all were wondrous abashed. . . .

And by seven o'clock the King [went to meet the peasants]. And when he was come the commons all knelt down to him, saying "Welcome our Lord King Richard, if it pleases you, and we will not have any other king but you." And Wat Tighler [Walter Tyler], their leader and chief, prayed in the name of the commons that he would suffer them to take and deal with all the traitors against him and the law, and the King granted that they should have at their disposition all who were traitors, and could be proved to be traitors by process of law. The said Walter and the commons were carrying two banners, and many pennons and pennoncels,[4] while they made their petition to the King. And they required that for the future no man should be in serfdom, nor make any manner of homage or suit to any lord, but should give a rent of 4d. an acre for his land. They asked also that no one should serve any man except by his own good will, and on terms of regular covenant.

And at this time the King made the commons draw themselves out in two lines, and proclaimed to them that he would confirm and grant it that they should be free, and generally should have their will, and that they might go through all the realm of England and catch all traitors and bring them to him in safety, and then he would deal with them as the law demanded.

[*Meanwhile, fighting between the nobles and peasants continued, and many lords lost their heads to the commoners.*]

And when he was summoned, . . . Wat Tighler of Maidstone, he came to the King with great confidence, mounted on a little horse, that the commons might see him. And he dismounted, holding in his hand a dagger

---

[4] **pennons and pennoncels**: Small banners attached to lances.

which he had taken from another man, and when he had dismounted he half bent his knee, and then took the King by the hand, and shook his arm forcibly and roughly, saying to him, "Brother, be of good comfort and joyful, for you shall have, in the fortnight that is to come, praise from the commons even more than you have yet had, and we shall be good companions." And the King said to Walter, "Why will you not go back to your own country?" But the other answered, with a great oath, that neither he nor his fellows would depart until they had got their charter such as they wished to have it, and had certain points rehearsed, and added to their charter which they wished to demand. And he said in a threatening fashion that the lords of the realm would rue it bitterly if these points were not settled to their pleasure. Then the King asked him what were the points which he wished to have revised, and he should have them freely, without contradiction, written out and sealed. Thereupon the said Walter rehearsed the points which were to be demanded; and he asked that . . . there should be equality among all people save only the King, and that the goods of Holy Church should not remain in the hands of the religious, nor of parsons and vicars, and other churchmen; but that clergy already in possession should have a sufficient sustenance from the endowments, and the rest of the goods should be divided among the people of the parish.

[*The King agreed to these terms, and after he left the Mayor of London captured Wat Tighler and killed him.*]

READING AND DISCUSSION QUESTIONS

1. What do the peasants demand?
2. Why does the king agree to their demands?
3. Why are the peasants willing to have a king, and instead direct their violence to the nobles?

DOCUMENT 12-3

PETRARCA-MEISTER

The Social Order

ca. 1515

This woodcut depicts the hierarchy of late medieval society. The artist has not been positively identified — he is simply known as the "Petrarch Master" in reference to the woodcuts he made for an edition of Remedies for Both Good and Bad Fortune *by Petrarch — but he may have been the Augsburg artist Hans Weiditz (VEE-dihtz). The pope and the emperor are in the highest branches; the bishops and nobles are below them, followed by craftsmen and merchants. The roots of the tree are peasants.*

READING AND DISCUSSION QUESTIONS

1. What is the overall structure of society in this picture?
2. Why do you think the artist chose a tree? Why are the peasants the roots?
3. Looking at this image, what do you think the peasant revolts accomplished?

DOCUMENT 12-4

JEAN FROISSART

The Sack of Limoges: On Warfare Without Chivalry

ca. 1400

The Hundred Years' War (1337–1453) broke out when Edward III of England claimed to be the legitimate heir to the French throne. Although there were extensive truces, France and England remained at war for most of this period. The war was also a civil war, in that large sections of France, especially Burgundy and Aquitaine, supported the English. Over the course of the conflict, both countries supported standing armies, which had not existed in western Europe since the end of the Roman Empire, and medieval warfare changed radically, as new weapons and tactics were introduced, However, some of these innovations — such as the one the English used to attack the French city of Limoges — offended those who still believed that the chivalric code should govern warfare. The author of this document, Jean Froissart (FROI-sahrt; ca. 1337–1405) was court poet to Philippa of Hainaut (HEY-no), the wife of King Edward III. Froissart traveled extensively with the queen in England, Wales, France, and Spain, and therefore was an eyewitness to many important events during the war.

The prince of Wales remained about a month, and not more, before the city of Limoges: he would not allow of any assaults or skirmishing, but kept his miners steadily at work. The knights in the town perceived what they were about, and made countermines to destroy them; but they failed in their attempt. When the miners of the prince (who, as they found themselves countermined, kept changing the line of direction of their own mine) had finished their business, they came to the prince, and said: "My lord, we are ready, and will throw down, whenever you please, a very large part of the wall into the ditch, through the breach of which you may enter the town at your ease and without danger." This news was very agreeable to the prince, who replied, "I wish then that you would prove your words

From Sir John Froissart, *The Chronicles of England, France, Spain, and the Adjoining Countries,* trans. Thomas Johnes (London: William Smith, 1848), 1:453–454.

to-morrow morning at six o'clock." The miners set fire to the combustibles in the mine; and on the morrow morning, as they had foretold the prince, they flung down a great piece of wall, which filled the ditches. The English saw this with pleasure, for they were all armed and prepared to enter the town. Those on foot did so, and ran to the gate, which they destroyed as well as the barriers, for there were no other defenses; and all this was done so suddenly that the inhabitants had not time to prevent it.

The prince, the duke of Lancaster, the earls of Cambridge and of Pembroke, sir Guiscard d'Angle and the others, with their men, rushed into the town. You would then have seen pillagers, active to do mischief, running through the town, slaying men, women, and children, according to their orders. It was a most melancholy business; for all ranks, ages, and sexes cast themselves on their knees before the prince, begging for mercy; but he was so inflamed with passion and revenge that he listened to none, but all were put to the sword, wherever they could be found, even those who were not guilty: for I know not why the poor were not spared, who could not have had any part in this treason; but they suffered for it, and indeed more than those who had been the leaders of the treachery. There was not that day in the city of Limoges any heart so hardened, or that had any sense of religion, who did not deeply bewail the unfortunate events passing before their eyes; for upwards of three thousand men, women, and children were put to death that day. God have mercy on their souls! for they were veritable martyrs.

READING AND DISCUSSION QUESTIONS

1. According to this document, how and why did the English troops destroy the town's fortifications?

2. Why is the scene with the bishop significant?

3. What does this passage reveal about the ideals of chivalry?

Women and Power

DOCUMENT 12-5

CATHERINE OF SIENA
Letter to Gregory XI
1372

In the early 1300s, the papacy moved its capital to Avignon, inside French territory. Because the pope was the bishop of Rome, it seemed wrong to move the head of the church away from his rightful home — and where he could be easily influenced by the French king. Many people blamed the Avignon papacy for the plague and warfare across Europe. Catherine of Siena, a Dominican nun and theologian, wrote several letters to Pope Gregory XI to persuade him to return to Rome. At the urging of Catherine as well as many others, he finally agreed, and the papacy left Avignon in 1377.

Alas, what confusion is this, to see those who ought to be a mirror of voluntary poverty, meek as lambs, distributing the possessions of Holy Church to the poor: and they appear in such luxury and state and pomp and worldly vanity, more than if they had turned them to the world a thousand times! Nay, many seculars put them to shame who live a good and holy life. . . . For ever since [the Church] has aimed more at temporal than at spiritual, things have gone from bad to worse. See therefore that God, in judgment, has allowed much persecution and tribulation to befall her. But comfort you, father, and fear not for anything that could happen, which God does to make her state perfect once more, in order that lambs may feed in that garden, and not wolves who devour the honor that should belong to God, which they steal and give to themselves. Comfort you in Christ sweet Jesus; for I hope that His aid will be near you, plenitude[5] of divine grace,

---

From Vida D. Scudder, trans. and ed., *Catherine of Siena as Seen in Her Lives and Letters* (London: J. M. Dent, 1906), pp. 131–132.

[5] **plenitude**: Full supply.

aid and support divine in the way that I said before. Out of war you will attain greatest peace; out of persecution, greatest unity; not by human power, but by holy virtue, you will discomfit those visible demons, wicked men, and those invisible demons who never sleep around us.

But reflect, sweet father, that you could not do this easily unless you accomplished the other two things which precede the completion of the other: that is, your return to Rome and uplifting of the standard of the most holy Cross. Let not your holy desire fail on account of any scandal or rebellion of cities which you might see or hear; nay, let the flame of holy desire be more kindled to wish to do swiftly. Do not delay, then, your coming.

READING AND DISCUSSION QUESTIONS

1. What does Catherine want the pope to do, and why does she want him to do it?
2. What happened to the church when the pope left Rome for Avignon?
3. What authority does Catherine have to make demands of the pope?

DOCUMENT 12-6

JOAN OF ARC
Letter to the English
1431

Joan of Arc (ca. 1412–1431), a peasant woman from eastern France, helped the French win important victories against the English in the Hundred Years' War. She claimed to have heard the voices of Saint Michael, Saint Catherine, and Saint Margaret commanding her to drive out the English and to take the crown prince to Reims (REEMS) for coronation. Some historians argue that Joan was more important as a symbol, inspiring French morale, while others argue that she was a skillful military strategist. She

From Ronald Sutherland Gower, *Joan of Arc* (New York: Charles Scribner's Sons, 1893), pp. 47–48. Project Gutenberg. Web. January 8, 2010.

wrote the letter that follows to encourage the English to withdraw from France. After her capture by Burgundian troops, the English put her on trial for heresy, and she was burned at the stake.

In the name of Jesus and Mary — You, King of England; and you, Duke of Bedford, who call yourself Regent of France; you, William de la Pole; you, Earl of Suffolk; you, John Lord Talbot; and you, Thomas Lord Scales, who call yourselves Lieutenants of the said Bedford, in the name of the King of Heaven, render the keys of all the good towns which you have taken and violated in France, to the Maid[6] sent hither by the King of Heaven. She is ready to make peace if you will consent to return and to pay for what you have taken. And all of you, soldiers, and archers, and men-at-arms, now before Orleans, return to your country, in God's name. If this is not done, King of England, I, as a leader in war, whenever I shall meet with your people in France, will oblige them to go whether they be willing or not; and if they go not, they will perish; but if they will depart I will pardon them. I have come from the King of Heaven to drive you out of France. And do not imagine that you will ever permanently hold France, for the true heir, King Charles, shall possess it, for it is God's wish that it should belong to him. And this has been revealed to him by the Maid, who will enter Paris. If you will not obey, we shall make such a stir as hath not happened these thousand years in France. The Maid and her soldiers will have the victory. Therefore the Maid is willing that you, Duke of Bedford, should not destroy yourself.

READING AND DISCUSSION QUESTIONS

1. What does Joan want the English to do?
2. What authority does she claim to have?
3. What will she do if the duke does not withdraw?

---

[6] **Maid**: Joan refers to herself as "the Maid."

COMPARATIVE QUESTIONS

1. Consider the account of the English Peasants' Revolt and *The Social Order*. In what ways is the old social order changing? What appears to have remained the same?

2. Compare and contrast the ideas of honor and chivalry in the documents in this chapter. What common themes or actions can you identify?

3. Tragedy and warfare served as a breeding ground for Christian idealism and religious martyrdom, but also spurred less admirable behavior. Provide examples from both the description of the plague in Florence and the recounting of the sack of Limoges. Could one be both righteous and violent?

4. What do Catherine and Joan have in common? What kind of power do they have, and how do they use it?

CHAPTER 13

European Society in the Age of the Renaissance

1350–1550

The Renaissance, a revival and flourishing of learning and art, began in the Italian cities of the fourteenth century and spread throughout Europe. Renaissance scholars, known as humanists, thought that the right form of education made people better human beings. Their educational program was an attempt to revive Greco-Roman culture through the liberal studies (the study of poetry, rhetoric, history, ethics, and grammar) and stressed the power of human reason over divine intervention. Many, though not all, of the Renaissance thinkers wrote in Latin, and successful authors such as Petrarch and Leonardo Bruni acquired international reputations. Although the Italian peninsula was a center of learning and commerce, it was not a unified country. City-states such as Venice, Milan, and Florence often conflicted with one another as well as with outside powers. Although nationalism was still in its earliest stages, modern nation-states were beginning to take shape in France, England, and Spain. Spanish rulers even attempted to impose uniformity of religion by expelling Jews and Muslims who resisted conversion to Christianity. In the context of these changes, many writers considered the role of the state and its leaders in creating a stable society.

DOCUMENT 13-1

PETRARCH
Letter to Livy
1350 C.E.

Francesco Petrarca, or Petrarch (1304–1374), an Italian scholar and poet, is generally considered the first literary humanist. He tried to revive Greco-Roman culture, which he considered the ideal, by imitating it. While the great works of the ancient world were known to medieval scholars, none of them sought to recreate the past as Petrarch did. He dismissed medieval scholarship and believed that studying the classics in Latin and Greek would result in a new era of intellectual and social enlightenment. Petrarch not only imitated the literary style of the ancients, but he wrote letters to them, including the one to Livy (see Document 5-1) that follows.

I should wish (if it were permitted from on high) either that I had been born in thine age or thou in ours; in the latter case our age itself, and in the former I personally should have been the better for it. I should surely have been one of those pilgrims who visited thee. For the sake of seeing thee I should have gone not merely to Rome, but indeed, from either Gaul or Spain I should have found my way to thee as far as India. . . . We know that thou didst write one hundred and forty-two books on Roman affairs. With what fervor, with what unflagging zeal must thou have labored; and of that entire number there are now extant scarcely thirty. . . . It is over these small remains that I toil whenever I wish to forget these regions, these times, and these customs. Often I am filled with bitter indignation against the morals of today, when men value nothing except gold and silver, and desire nothing except sensual, physical pleasures. If these are to be considered the goal of mankind, then not only the dumb beasts of the field, but even insensible and inert matter has a richer, a higher goal than that proposed to itself by thinking man. But of this elsewhere.

It is now fitter that I should render thee thanks, for many reasons indeed, but for this in especial: that thou didst so frequently cause me to forget the present evils, and transfer me to happier times. . . .

From Marco Emilio Cosenza, trans. *Petrarch's Letters to Classical Authors* (Chicago: University of Chicago Press, 1910), pp. 100–103.

Pray greet in my behalf thy predecessors Polybius and Quintus Claudius and Valerius Antias, and all those whose glory thine own greater light has dimmed; and of the later historians, give greeting to Pliny the Younger, of Verona, a neighbor of thine, and also to thy former rival Crispus Sallustius. . . . Farewell forever, thou matchless historian!

Written in the land of the living, in that part of Italy and in that city in which I am now living and where thou were once born and buried, . . . and in view of thy very tombstone; on the twenty-second of February, in the thirteen hundred and fiftieth year from the birth of Him whom thou wouldst have seen, or of whose birth thou couldst have heard, hadst thou lived a little longer.

READING AND DISCUSSION QUESTIONS

1. Why does Petrarch admire Livy?
2. Why does he wish he lived in Livy's day? Or, why would he like Livy to live in his own time?
3. What tone does Petrarch use while addressing Livy?

VIEWPOINTS

The Renaissance State

DOCUMENT 13-2

LEONARDO BRUNI

Panegyric to Florence

ca. 1403

Leonardo Bruni (1369–1444) served his native Florence as a statesman and government official. As a humanist, he was well acquainted with authors

From Benjamin G. Kohl and Ronald G. Witt, eds., *The Earthly Republic: Italian Humanists on Government and Society* (Philadelphia: University of Pennsylvania Press, 1978), pp. 151–152, 169, 173–175.

like Thucydides, Plato, and Livy, and their notions of the ideal state. His writings were modeled on the great Greek and Roman authors. The following is his praise for Florence, in which he uses the liberal studies to emphasize the virtues of republics and good citizenship. Bruni delivered this panegyric (a speech given to praise of something or someone) to commemorate the death of soldiers in Florence's war with Milan (1403–1404) and published it in the 1430s.

I think something has been true and is true in this city more than in any other; the men of Florence especially enjoy perfect freedom and are the greatest enemies of tyrants. So I believe that from its very founding Florence conceived such a hatred for the destroyers of the Roman state and underminers of the Roman Republic that it has never forgotten to this very day. Now this interest in republicanism is not new to the Florentine people, nor did it begin . . . only a short time since. Rather, this struggle against tyranny was begun a long time ago when certain evil men undertook the worst crime of all — the destruction of the liberty, honor, and dignity of the Roman people. At that time, fired by a desire for freedom, the Florentines adopted their penchant for fighting and their zeal for the republican side, and this attitude has persisted down to the present day. . . .

Now, first of all, great care is taken so that justice is held most sacred in the city, for without justice there can be no city, nor would Florence even be worthy to be called a city. Next there is provision for freedom, without which this great people would not even consider that life was worth living. These two principles are joined . . . to all the institutions and statutes that the Florentine government has created.

Indeed, the magistracies were created to carry out justice; they have been empowered to punish criminals and especially to ensure that there is no one in Florence who stands above the law. Thus, all conditions of men must submit to the decisions of these magistracies, a nod they must pay due respect to the symbols of these offices. In many ways care has been taken that these upholders of the law to whom great power has been entrusted do not come to imagine that, instead of the custodianship of the citizens, a tyrannical post has been given to them. Many provisions are made so that these magistrates do not lord it over others or undermine the great freedom of the Florentines. First of all, the chief magistracy that is commonly viewed as possessing the sovereignty of the state is controlled by a system of checks and balances. Hence there are nine magistrates instead of one, and their term is for two months, not for one year. This method of governing has been devised so that the Florentine state may be well governed, since a majority will correct any errors in judgment, and the short terms of office will curb any possible insolence. . . .

Therefore, under these magistracies this city has been governed with such diligence and competence that one could not find better discipline even in a household ruled by a solicitous father. . . . All classes of men can be brought to trial; laws are made prudently for the common good, and they are fashioned to help the citizens. There is no place on earth where there is greater justice open equally to everyone. Nowhere else does freedom grow so vigorously, and nowhere else are rich and poor alike treated with such equality. . . . The city has judged it consistent with its ideals of justice and prudence that those who have the most need should also be helped the most. Therefore, the different classes are treated according to a certain sense of equity; the upper class is protected by its wealth, the lower class by the state, and fear of punishment defends both. From this arises the saying that has been directed very often against the more powerful citizens when they have threatened the lower classes; in such a case the members of the lower class say: "'I also am a Florentine citizen.'" With this saying the poor mean to point out and to warn dearly that no one should malign them simply because they are weak, nor should anyone threaten them with harm simply because someone is powerful. Rather, everyone is of equal rank since the Florentine state itself has promised to protect the less powerful. . . .

Now what shall I say of the persuasiveness of their speech and the elegance of their discourse? Indeed, in this category the Florentines are the unquestioned leaders. . . . The study of literature — and I don't mean simply mercantile and vile writings but that which is especially worthy of free men — which always flourishes among every great people, grows in this city in full vigor. . . .

Florence has done and daily continues to do great deeds of honor and virtue both at home and abroad. . . . What more can a city desire? Nothing at all. What, therefore, should we say now? What remains to be done? Nothing other than to venerate God on account of His great beneficence and to offer our prayers to God.

READING AND DISCUSSION QUESTIONS

1. According to Bruni, what makes Florence great?

2. What is good about the Florentine system of government? How does it prevent tyranny?

3. What role do individual citizens play in making Florence a strong republic?

DOCUMENT 13-3

NICCOLÒ MACHIAVELLI

The Prince: *Power Politics During the Italian Renaissance*

1513

Niccolò Machiavelli (NEE-koh-loh mah-KEY-ah-vel-ee; 1469–1527) was a political philosopher and diplomat who had represented the Italian republic of Florence on numerous diplomatic missions. In 1512, when the powerful Medici family regained control of Florence, the anti-Medici Machiavelli was arrested and tortured. In 1513, he wrote The Prince, *a guide to gaining political power, and dedicated to Lorenzo de Medici, perhaps as a way to curry favor with the new rulers. Machiavelli claimed that he was simply drawing conclusions from his reading of history and from the example of successful contemporary rulers. The book circulated privately until after Machiavelli's death.*

Every one understands how praiseworthy it is in a prince to keep faith, and to live uprightly and not craftily. Nevertheless we see, from what has taken place in our own days, that princes who have set little store by their word, but have known how to overreach men by their cunning, have accomplished great things, and in the end got the better of those who trusted to honest dealing.

From Niccolò Machiavelli, *The Prince*, trans. N. H. Thomson, in James Harvey Robinson, ed., *Readings in European History*, 2 vols. (Boston: Ginn, 1906), 2:10–13.

Be it known, then, that there are two ways of contending, — one in accordance with the laws, the other by force; the first of which is proper to men, the second to beasts. But since the first method is often ineffectual, it becomes necessary to resort to the second. A prince should, therefore, understand how to use well both the man and the beast. . . . But inasmuch as a prince should know how to use the beast's nature wisely, he ought of beasts to choose both the lion and the fox; for the lion cannot guard himself from the toils, nor the fox from wolves. He must therefore be a fox to discern toils, and a lion to drive off wolves.

To rely wholly on the lion is unwise; and for this reason a prudent prince neither can nor ought to keep his word when to keep it is hurtful to him and the causes which led him to pledge it are removed. If all men were good, this would not be good advice, but since they are dishonest and do not keep faith with you, you in return need not keep faith with them; and no prince was ever at a loss for plausible reasons to cloak a breach of faith. Of this numberless recent instances could be given, and it might be shown how many solemn treaties and engagements have been rendered inoperative and idle through want of faith among princes, and that he who has best known how to play the fox has had the best success.

It is necessary, indeed, to put a good color on this nature, and to be skilled in simulating and dissembling. But men are so simple, and governed so absolutely by their present needs, that he who wishes to deceive will never fail in finding willing dupes. One recent example I will not omit. Pope Alexander VI had no care or thought but how to deceive, and always found material to work on. No man ever had a more effective manner or asseverating, or made promises with more solemn protestations, or observed them less. And yet, because he understood this side of human nature, his frauds always succeeded. . . .

In his efforts to aggrandize his son the duke [Cesare Borgia], Alexander VI had to face many difficulties, both immediate and remote. In the first place, he saw no way to make him ruler of any state which did not belong to the Church. Yet, if he sought to take for him a state of the Church, he knew that the duke of Milan and the Venetians would withhold their consent, Faenza and Rimini [towns in the province of Romagna] being already under the protection of the latter. Further, he saw that the forces of Italy, and those more especially of which he might have availed himself, were in the hands of men who had reason to fear his aggrandizement, — that is, of the Orsini, the Colonnesi [Roman noble families] and their followers. These, therefore, he could not trust. . . .

And since this part of his [Cesare Borgia's] conduct merits both attention and imitation, I shall not pass it over in silence. After the duke had taken Romagna, finding that it had been ruled by feeble lords, who thought more of plundering than of governing their subjects, — which gave them more cause for division than for union, so that the country was overrun with robbery, tumult, and every kind of outrage, — he judged it necessary, with a view to rendering it peaceful, and obedient to his authority, to provide it with a good government. Accordingly he set over it Messer Remiro d'Orco, a stern and prompt ruler, who, being entrusted with the fullest powers, in a very short time, and with much credit to himself, restored it to tranquility and order. But afterwards the duke, apprehending that such unlimited authority might become odious, decided that it was no longer needed, and established [at] the center of the province a civil tribunal, with an excellent president, in which every town was represented by its advocate. And knowing that past severities had generated ill feeling against himself, in order to purge the minds of the people and gain their good will, he sought to show them that any cruelty which had been done had not originated with him, but in the harsh disposition of this minister. Availing himself of the pretext which this afforded, he one morning caused Remiro to be beheaded, and exposed in the market place of Cesena with a block and bloody ax by his side. The barbarity of this spectacle at once astounded and satisfied the populace.

READING AND DISCUSSION QUESTIONS

1. Why must a prince be both a lion and a fox? What qualities do these animals represent?
2. Why does Machiavelli believe that sometimes a prince must break his word?
3. Explain why Machiavelli approves, or disapproves, of the execution of Remiro d'Orco.

DOCUMENT 13-4

BALDASSARE CASTIGLIONE

The Book of the Courtier: *The Ideal Courtier*

1528

Baldassare Castiglione (ball-duh-SAH-ree kahs-teel-YOH-nay; 1478–1529) was an Italian diplomat who spent many years traveling through the courts of Europe. Based on his experiences, he wrote The Book of the Courtier *as a manual on the proper education, manners, dress, and skills of a companion to and defender of royalty. The book was written in the form of a conversation among some of the leading nobility in Italy and was a best seller in its time.*

I wish then, that this Courtier of ours should be nobly born. I am of the opinion that the principal and true profession of the courtier ought to be that of arms;[1] which I would have him follow actively above all else, and be known among others as bold and strong, and loyal to whomsoever he serves. . . .

Therefore let the man we are seeking be very bold, stern, and always among the first, where the enemy are to be seen; and in every other place, gentle, modest, reserved, above all things avoiding ostentation and that impudent self-praise by which men ever excite hatred and disgust in all who hear him. . . .

And so I would have him well built and shapely of limb, and would have him show strength and lightness and suppleness, and know all bodily exercises that befit a man of war: whereof I think the first should be to handle every sort of weapon well on foot and on horse. . . .

There are also many other exercises, which although not immediately dependent upon arms, yet are closely connected therewith, and greatly foster manly sturdiness; and one of the chief among these seems to me to be the chase,[2] because it bears a certain likeness to war; and truly it is an

---

From Baldassare Castiglione, *The Book of the Courtier*, trans. Leonard Opdycke (New York: Charles Scribner's Sons, 1903), pp. 22, 26, 29, 31, 93–94.

[1] **arms**: Weaponry.
[2] **chase**: Hunting.

amusement for great lords and befitting a man at court, and furthermore it is seen to have been much cultivated among the ancients. It is fitting also to know how to swim, to leap, to run, to throw stones, for besides the use that may be made of this in war, a man often has occasion to show what he can do in such matters; whence good esteem is to be won, especially with the multitude, who must be taken into account withal. Another admirable exercise, and one fitting a man at court, is the game of tennis, in which are well shown the disposition of the body. . . .

I think that the conversation, which the Courtier ought most to try in every way to make acceptable, is that which he holds with his prince; and although this word "conversation" implies a certain equality that seems impossible between a lord and his inferior, yet we will call it so for the moment. Therefore, besides daily showing everyone that he possesses the worth we have already described, I would have the Courtier strive, with all the thoughts and forces of his mind, to love and almost adore the prince whom he serves, above every other thing, and mold his ways to his prince's liking. . . .

Moreover it is possible without flattery to obey and further the wishes of him we serve, for I am speaking of those wishes that are reasonable and right, or of those that in themselves are neither good not evil, such as would be a liking for a play or devotion to one kind of exercise above another. And I would have the Courtier bend himself to this even if he be by nature alien to it, so that on seeing him his lord shall always feel that he will have something agreeable to say. . . . He will not be an idle or untruthful tattler, nor a boaster not pointless flatterer, but modest and reserved, always and especially in public showing the reverence and respect which befit the servant towards the master.

READING AND DISCUSSION QUESTIONS

1. What is a good courtier like? What is the importance of the specific attributes Castiglione lists?
2. Does the courtier serve a prince or a government?
3. How should the courtier treat the people of his prince's state?

CHRISTINE DE PIZAN

The Book of the City of Ladies:
Against Those Men Who Claim It Is
Not Good for Women to Be Educated

1404

Christine de Pizan (ca. 1363–1434) may have been the first European woman to earn her living as a writer. After de Pizan's birth in Venice, her father became a physician and astrologer at the French court, where Christine studied languages and the classics. In 1390, when her husband died in an epidemic and left her with three children, Christine began her literary career. Her works were popular among the French nobility, and she even enjoyed the financial support of the French queen. Humanists were divided in their opinions on the education of women. Some thought women were simply not capable of learning. Others thought a limited form of education in good morals was sufficient. Christine challenged both these ideas, and some scholars now regard her as one of the first Western feminists.

I realize that women have accomplished many good things and that even if evil women have done evil, it seems to me, nevertheless, that the benefits accrued and still accruing because of good women — particularly the wise and literary ones and those educated in the natural sciences whom I mentioned above — outweigh the evil. Therefore, I am amazed by the opinion of some men who claim that they do not want their daughters, wives, or kinswomen to be educated because their mores would be ruined as a result.

Here you can clearly see that not all opinions of men are based on reason and that these men are wrong. For it must not be presumed that mores necessarily grow worse from knowing the moral sciences, which teach the virtues, indeed, there is not the slightest doubt that moral education amends and ennobles them. How could anyone think or believe that whoever follows good teaching or doctrine is the worse for it? Such an

From Christine de Pizan, *The Book of the City of Ladies*, trans. Earl Jeffrey Richards (New York: Persea Books, 1982), pp. 153–155.

opinion cannot be expressed or maintained. I do not mean that it would be good for a man or a woman to study the art of divination or those fields of learning which are forbidden — for the holy Church did not remove them from common use without good reason — but it should not be believed that women are the worse for knowing what is good.

Quintus Hortensius, a great rhetorician and consummately skilled orator in Rome, did not share this opinion. He had a daughter, named Hortensia, whom he greatly loved for the subtlety of her wit. He had her learn letters and study the science of rhetoric, which she mastered so thoroughly that she resembled her father Hortensius not only in wit and lively memory but also in her excellent delivery and order of speech — in fact, he surpassed her in nothing. . . . That is, during the time when Rome was governed by three men, this Hortensia began to support the cause of women and to undertake what no man dared to undertake. There was a question whether certain taxes should be levied on women and on their jewelry during a needy period in Rome. This woman's eloquence was so compelling that she was listened to, no less readily than her father would have been, and she won her case.

Similarly, to speak of more recent times, without searching for examples in ancient history, Giovanni Andrea, a solemn law professor in Bologna not quite sixty years ago, was not of the opinion that it was bad for women to be educated. He had a fair and good daughter, named Novella, who was educated in the law to such an advanced degree that when he was occupied by some task and not at leisure to present his lectures to his students, he would send Novella, his daughter, in his place to lecture to the students from his chair. And to prevent her beauty from distracting the concentration of her audience, she had a little curtain drawn in front of her. In this manner she could on occasion supplement and lighten her father's occupation. . . .

Thus, not all men (and especially the wisest) share the opinion that it is bad for women to be educated. But it is very true that many foolish men have claimed this because it displeased them that women knew more than they did. [My] father, who was a great scientist and philosopher, did not believe that women were worth less by knowing science; rather, as you know, he took great pleasure from seeing your inclination to learning.

READING AND DISCUSSION QUESTIONS

1. How does Christine defend a woman's ability to learn?

2. What examples of learned women does she provide?

3. According to Christine, why do some men not want to see women educated?

DOCUMENT 13-6

Account of an Italian Jew Expelled from Spain

1492

In 1492, the same year in which the last Islamic stronghold in Spain was overcome, Jews were given the choice of forcible conversion or expulsion. Even those who did convert endured persecution, because the authorities often believed that these conversos continued to practice their old religion in secret. One of the principal tasks of the Inquisition in Spain was to root out secret Jews. The Jews who were expelled scattered over vast areas of the Muslim and Christian world. Muhammad had ordained that Muslims allow Jews to practice their religion, but there was no similar instruction for Christians.

And in the year 1492, in the days of King Ferdinand [of Spain], the Lord visited the remnant of his people a second time and exiled them. After the King had captured the city of Granada from the Moors, . . . he ordered the expulsion of all the Jews in all parts of his kingdom — in the kingdoms of Castile, Catalonia, Aragon, Galicia, Majorca, Minorca, the Basque provinces, the islands of Sardinia and Sicily, and the kingdom of Valencia.

The King gave them three months' time in which to leave. . . .

About their number there is no agreement, but, after many inquiries, I found that the most generally accepted estimate is 50,000 families. . . .

They had houses, fields, vineyards, and cattle, and most of them were artisans. At that time there existed many academies in Spain, and at the head of the greatest of them were Rabbi Isaac Aboab in Guadalajara, Rabbi Isaac Veçudó in Leon, and Rabbi Jacob Habib in Salamanca. . . .

From Jacob Marcus, *The Jew in the Medieval World: A Sourcebook, 315–1791* (New York: JPS, 1938), pp. 51–55.

In the course of the three months' respite granted them they endeavored to effect an arrangement permitting them to stay on in the country, and they felt confident of success. Their representatives were the rabbi, Don Abraham Seneor, the leader of the Spanish congregations, who was attended by a retinue on thirty mules, and Rabbi Meïr Melamed, who was secretary to the King, and Don Isaac Abravanel, who had fled to Castile from the King of Portugal, and then occupied an equally prominent position at the Spanish royal court. He, too, was later expelled, went to Naples, and was highly esteemed by the King of Naples. . . .

The agreement permitting them to remain in the country on the payment of a large sum of money was almost completed when it was frustrated by the interference of a prior who was called the Prior of Santa Cruz. Then the Queen gave an answer to the representatives of the Jews, similar to the saying of King Solomon: "The king's heart is in the hand of the Lord, as the rivers of water. God turneth it withersoever He will." She said furthermore: "Do you believe that this comes upon you from us? The Lord hath put this thing into the heart of the king."

Then they saw that there was evil determined against them by the King, and they gave up the hope of remaining. But the time had become short, and they had to hasten their exodus from Spain. They sold their houses, their landed estates, and their cattle for very small prices, to save themselves. The King did not allow them to carry silver and gold out of his country, so that they were compelled to exchange their silver and gold for merchandise of cloths and skins and other things.

One hundred and twenty thousand of them went to Portugal, according to a compact which a prominent man, Don Vidal bar Benveniste del Cavalleria, had made with the King of Portugal, and they paid one ducat for every soul, and the fourth part of all the merchandise they had carried thither; and he allowed them to stay in his country six months. This King acted much worse toward them than the King of Spain, and after the six months had elapsed he made slaves of all those that remained in his country, and banished seven hundred children to a remote island to settle it, and all of them died. . . .

Many of the exiled Spaniards went to Mohammedan countries, to Fez, Tlemçen, and the Berber provinces, under the King of Tunis. On account of their large numbers the Moors did not allow them into their cities, and many of them died in the fields from hunger, thirst, and lack of everything. The lions and bears, which are numerous in this country, killed some of them while they lay starving outside of the cities. . . .

When the edict of expulsion became known in the other countries, vessels came from Genoa to the Spanish harbors to carry away the Jews. The crews of these vessels, too, acted maliciously and meanly toward the Jews, robbed them, and delivered some of them to the famous pirate of that time who was called the Corsair of Genoa. To those who escaped and arrived at Genoa the people of the city showed themselves merciless, and oppressed and robbed them, and the cruelty of their wicked hearts went so far that they took the infants from the mothers' breasts.

Many ships with Jews, especially from Sicily, went to the city of Naples on the coast. The King of this country was friendly to the Jews, received them all, and was merciful towards them, and he helped them with money. The Jews that were at Naples supplied them with food as much as they could, and sent around to the other parts of Italy to collect money to sustain them. The Marranos[3] in this city lent them money on pledges without interest; even the Dominican Brotherhood acted mercifully toward them. On account of their very large number, all this was not enough. Some of them died by famine, others sold their children to Christians to sustain their life. Finally, a plague broke out among them, spread to Naples, and very many of them died, so that the living wearied of burying the dead. . . .

He who said unto His world, Enough, may He also say Enough unto our sufferings, and may He look down upon our impotence. May He turn again, and have compassion upon us, and hasten out salvation. Thus may it be Thy will!

READING AND DISCUSSION QUESTIONS

1. Why did the negotiations that might have allowed Jews to remain in Spain fail?

2. Which countries treated Jewish refugees best? Worst? Explain your answer.

3. Jews suffered greatly even in countries where the rulers tried to act with some decency. What does this reveal about Europe's social and economic infrastructure?

4. How do you think contemporaries reacted to the outbreak of plague that accompanied the arrival of Jews and spread to Naples?

---

[3] **Marranos**: Secret Jews, living under the guise of Christianity.

COMPARATIVE QUESTIONS

1. How do Petrarch and Bruni show their admiration for classical Greco-Roman culture? What elements of those ancient civilizations do they want to see revived in their own time?

2. Compare and contrast Bruni's republic, Machiavelli's prince, and Castiglione's courtier. How does each one envision the Renaissance state? What does each one think is necessary for a government to function well?

3. Ferdinand of Aragon, who ordered the expulsion of Jews described in Document 13-6, was one of the contemporary princes that Machiavelli most admired. What would Machiavelli have found to admire in a prince like Ferdinand?

4. Compare and contrast Christine de Pizan with the other humanists in this chapter — Bruni, Petrarch, Machiavelli, and Castiglione. In what ways is her work similar to theirs? What makes her writings different?

5. The exodus of Jews from Spain was not the first Jewish exodus. Revisit Documents 2-2, 4-6, and 10-5. How have the Jews developed as a people since the days of the ancient Hebrews?

CHAPTER 14

Reformations and Religious Wars

1500–1600

E ven before Martin Luther posted his "Ninety-five Theses on the
Power of Indulgences," numerous Catholic practices had come
under widespread criticism. The specific political situation in the Holy
Roman Empire enabled Luther and other reformers to spread their ideas.
Strong local governments and high nobles, who exercised more power in
their territories than did the central government of the Holy Roman
Empire, welcomed Lutheran ideas and offered safe havens to the Protestants. Protestant reform extended to social thought as well — for example,
priests were no longer required to remain celibate in the Protestant tradition. Some reformers, including Michael Servetus, adopted beliefs that
were far more radical than the ideas of either Luther or other reformers,
and were condemned by Protestants and Catholics alike. The Catholic
Church developed its own plans for reform at this time, both to counter
the Protestant attacks and to revitalize the church.

DOCUMENT 14-1

MARTIN LUTHER

Ninety-five Theses on the Power of Indulgences

1517

*Martin Luther (1483–1546), the acknowledged initiator of the Protestant
Reformation, was a theologian, preacher, and pamphleteer. His German*

From Martin Luther, "Ninety-five Theses," in *Translations and Reprints from the
Original Sources of European History* (Philadelphia: University of Pennsylvania Press,
1898), 2/6:12–18.

*translation of the Bible was a shaping force in the development of the mod-
ern German language. Some historians argue that Luther had no intention
of breaking with the Catholic Church when he developed the Ninety-five
Theses — he had enclosed a copy in a letter to the archbishop of Mainz and
the form in which he cast his ideas (the theses) was a common way for scholars to invite others to debate.*

1. Our Lord and Master Jesus Christ in saying "Repent ye" etc.,
    intended that the whole life of believers should be penitence.

2. This word cannot be understood as sacramental penance, that is, of
    the confession and satisfaction which are performed under the min-
    istry of priests.

3. It does not, however, refer solely to inward penitence; nay such
    inward penitence is naught, unless it outwardly produces various
    mortifications of the flesh.

4. The penalty thus continues as long as the hatred of self (that is, true
    inward penitence); namely, till our entrance into the kingdom of
    heaven.

5. The pope has neither the will nor the power to remit any penalties
    except those which he has imposed by his own authority, or by that
    of the canons.

6. The pope has no power to remit any guilt, except by declaring and
    warranting it to have been remitted by God; or at most by remitting
    cases reserved for himself; in which cases, if his power were despised,
    guilt would certainly remain.

7. Certainly God remits no man's guilt without at the same time sub-
    jecting him, humbled in all things, to the authority of his represen-
    tative the priest. . . .

20. Therefore the pope, when he speaks of the plenary remission of all
    penalties, does not mean really of all, but only of those imposed by
    himself.

21. Thus those preachers of indulgences are in error who say that by
    the indulgences of the pope a man is freed and saved from all
    punishment.

22. For in fact he remits to souls in purgatory no penalty which they
    would have had to pay in this life according to the canons.

23. If any entire remission of all penalties can be granted to any one it
    is certain that it is granted to none but the most perfect, that is to
    very few.

24. Hence, the greater part of the people must needs be deceived by this indiscriminate and high-sounding promise of release from penalties. . . .

26. The pope acts most rightly in granting remission to souls not by the power of the keys (which is of no avail in this case) but by the way of intercession.[1]

27. They preach man who say that the soul flies out of Purgatory as soon as the money thrown into the chest rattles.[2]

28. It is certain that, when the money rattles in the chest, avarice and gain may be increased, but the effect of the intercession of the Church depends on the will of God alone. . . .

30. No man is sure of the reality of his own contrition, much less of the attainment of plenary remission. . . .

35. They preach no Christian doctrine who teach that contrition is not necessary for those who buy souls [out of purgatory] or buy confessional licenses.

36. Every Christian who feels true compunction has of right plenary remission of punishment and guilt even without letters of pardon.

37. Every true Christian, whether living or dead, has a share in all the benefits of Christ and of the Church, given him by God, even without letters of pardon. . . .

38. The remission, however, imparted by the pope is by no means to be despised, since it is, as I have said, a declaration of the divine remission.

39. It is a most difficult thing, even for the most learned theologians, to exalt at the same time in the eyes of the people the ample effect of pardons and the necessity of true contrition.

40. True contrition seeks and loves punishment; while the ampleness of pardons relaxes it, and causes men to hate it, or at least gives occasion for them to do so. . . .

43. Christians should be taught that he who gives to a poor man, or lends to a needy man, does better than if he bought pardons.

44. Because by works of charity, charity increases, and the man becomes better; while by means of pardons, he does not become better, but only freer from punishment.

---

[1] **intercession**: Prayer to God on another's behalf.

[2] **They preach . . . rattles**: This was the claim being made by the indulgence seller Tetzel in Luther's Saxony.

49. Christians should be taught that the pope's pardons are useful if they do not put their trust in them, but most hurtful if through them they lose the fear of God. . . .

54. Wrong is done to the Word of God when, in the same sermon, an equal or longer time is spent on pardons than on it.

55. The mind of the pope necessarily is that, if pardons, which are a very small matter, are celebrated with single bells, single processions, and single ceremonies, the Gospel, which is a very great matter, should be preached with a hundred bells, a hundred processions, and a hundred ceremonies.

56. The treasures of the Church, whence the pope grants indulgences, are neither sufficiently named nor known among the people of Christ.

57. It is clear that they are at least not temporal treasures, for these are not so readily lavished, but only accumulated, by many of the preachers. . . .

67. Those indulgences, which the preachers loudly proclaim to be the greatest graces, are seen to be truly such as regards the promotion of gain.

68. Yet they are in reality most insignificant when compared to the grace of God and the piety of the cross. . . .

75. To think that the papal pardons have such power that they could absolve a man even if — by an impossibility — he had violated the Mother of God, is madness.

76. We affirm on the contrary that papal pardons cannot take away even the least of venial sins, as regards its guilt. . . .

79. To say that the cross set up among the insignia of the papal arms is of equal power with the cross of Christ, is blasphemy.

80. Those bishops, priests, and theologians who allow such discourses to have currency among the people will have to render an account. . . .

82. As for instance: Why does not the pope empty purgatory for the sake of most holy charity and of the supreme necessity of souls — this being the most just of all reasons — if he redeems an infinite number of souls for the sake of that most fatal thing, money, to be spent on building a basilica — this being a very slight reason?

83. Again; why do funeral masses and anniversary masses for the deceased continue, and why does not the pope return, or permit the withdrawal of, the funds bequeathed for this purpose, since it is a wrong to pray for those who are already redeemed?

84. Again; what is this new kindness of God and the pope, in that, for money's sake, they permit an impious man and an enemy of God to redeem a pious soul which loves God, and yet do not redeem that same pious and beloved soul out of free charity on account of its own need?

85. Again; why is it that the penitential canons, long since abrogated and dead in themselves, in very fact and not only by usage, are yet still redeemed with money, through the granting of indulgences, as if they were full of life?

86. Again; why does not the pope, whose riches are at this day more ample than those of the wealthiest of the wealthy, build the single Basilica of St. Peter with his own money rather than with that of poor believers? . . .

89. Since it is the salvation of souls, rather than money, that the pope seeks by his pardons, why does he suspend the letters and pardons granted long ago, since they are equally efficacious? . . .

91. If all these pardons were preached according to the spirit and mind of the pope, all these questions would be resolved with ease; nay, would not exist.

READING AND DISCUSSION QUESTIONS

1. In Thesis 36, Luther writes, "Every Christian who feels true compunction has of right plenary remission of punishment and guilt even without letters of pardon." Why would many interpret this as an attack on the papacy?

2. Luther claims that in some cases, people who buy indulgences are actually purchasing the anger of God (see Thesis 45). What does this suggest about his notions of charity?

3. According to the theses, in what ways have the leaders of the church failed to teach true Christian doctrine?

4. Based on your reading of Theses 82–91, how would you classify the sorts of reform that Luther would like to see within the church?

DOCUMENT 14-2

HANS HOLBEIN THE YOUNGER
Luther as the German Hercules

ca. 1519

Two of Martin Luther's greatest assets were the printing press and several prominent German artists, such as Hans Holbein the Younger (1498–1543), who created this woodcut. Lutheran ideas spread rapidly through his writings, but the average person was illiterate. Those people often learned of the reformation through images such as this woodcut. Broadsheets — posters with images and words — like this one were widely distributed, and the literate would translate the simple texts for those who could not read. In this woodcut, Luther is depicted as the Greek hero Hercules, who killed the hydra, a beast with nine heads. The artist has replaced the hydra with nine churchmen, including the theologian Thomas Aquinas (see Document 11-4), monks, and priests. The strangled pope, identifiable by his triple crown, dangles from the rope in Luther's mouth.

READING AND DISCUSSION QUESTIONS

1. What impact do you think this image might have had on those who saw it? Does it communicate its message clearly?

2. How would you describe the way Luther is depicted here?

Women and Marriage

DOCUMENT 14-3

KATHARINA SCHÜTZ ZELL
Apologia for Master Matthew Zell:
Clerical Marriage
1524

Katharina Schütz Zell (1497–1562) was one of the first women to marry a priest during the Protestant Reformation. As a child she had decided to live the life of a nun, even though her parents could not afford to send her to a convent. She changed her mind after hearing the new Protestant ideas on marriage. To those who still believed in the Catholic idea of priestly celibacy, her 1521 marriage to Strasbourg priest Matthew Zell was not valid, meaning that Katharina was little better than a prostitute. In 1524, she wrote this defense (apologia) of her marriage, and continued to write pamphlets and hymns for the rest of her life.

Another reason they resist clerical marriage is that, should priests have (legal) wives, they would have to choose one and give up the others. They will not be able to behave as they do with the prostitutes: throwing out one, taking in another. For Paul says, "A bishop should be the husband of one wife" [1 Timothy 3:2]. Therefore they must each live honorably, and if having the same woman does not please the man, he may not exchange her. For in marriage the couple must have and bear many griefs with each other (on which account these priests do not wish to be bound by marriage). Still, one often suffers more from a harlot — he would not suffer half of that from an honest (legal) wife!

From Katharina Schütz Zell, *Church Mother: The Writings of a Protestant Reformer in Sixteenth-Century Germany*, trans. and ed. Elsie McKee (Chicago: University of Chicago Press, 2006), pp. 75, 77–78.

However, if they wanted to treat clerical marriage honorably, they would then need to punish adultery in the pulpit more strictly. Otherwise how can they punish it when they are mixed up in it? In such a case (when they are mixed up in it also) the going thing is a mutual blind eye: "If you overlook my fault, I will overlook yours." If, however, a priest had a (legal) wife and then did evil, one would know how to punish him. But this way the clergy always have an excuse to say nothing else than, "You worldly folk can talk about this easily; you have your wives. So I also am a man; how can I behave like an angel?" and so forth. And that is also true. Oh, then why not leave things the way God made them?! "Let each one have his wife, on account of harlotry" [1 Corinthians 7:2]. Does God not know better than the devil what is good? For the prohibition of marriage comes only from the devil and marriage comes from God, says the Holy Spirit Himself in the epistle to Timothy [1 Timothy 4:3]. . . .

With God's help I was also the first woman in Strasbourg who opened the way for clerical marriage, when I was then still not consenting or wishing to marry any man. However, since I saw the great fear and furious opposition to clerical marriage, and also the great harlotry of the clergy, I myself married a priest with the intention of encouraging and making a way for all Christians — as I hope has also happened. Therefore I also made a little book, in which I showed the foundation of my faith and reason for my marriage, because many people had been greatly amazed by my marriage. For no one had in any way been able to perceive in me, by word or deed, that I wanted to be married. . . .

These reasons also moved my husband (so far as I have experience of him and I can still neither find nor sense anything else in him). He began such a marriage because he wanted very much to raise up God's honor, his own salvation, and that of all his brothers. For I can perceive in him no dishonorableness, no inclination toward lust or other such thing — for I am not gifted with either overwhelming beauty or riches or other virtue that might move one to seek me in marriage! Because of his [Zell's] behavior in teaching and life, he has borne such envy from the godless that it is as if his body and life were given over to the birds in the air and the worms on the earth — to say nothing about what people have done. And so I come again to my beginning, that is, to justify him. Such envy of him is so deeply rooted in the hearts of the godless that if they cannot discredit him in body, soul, and life, they do it through such great devilish lies invented and spoken about him and spread in all lands.

READING AND DISCUSSION QUESTIONS

1. Why does Zell think the Catholic Church does not want to allow clerical marriage?
2. What benefit does Zell think there is in allowing clerical marriage?
3. What has been the reaction to her marriage?
4. Why does she make the point that she had never wanted to marry earlier in life?

DOCUMENT 14-4

JEANNE DE JUSSIE
The Short Chronicle: *Defending the Convent*
ca. 1530

Jeanne de Jussie (zhahn deh ZHOU-see; 1503–1561) was born in a small village outside Geneva. At age eighteen, she joined Geneva's Convent of Poor Clares, and remained a nun of that order until she died. Geneva was a city in religious upheaval in the 1530s. Catholic and Protestant factions each tried to take control of the city, resulting in periodic religious violence. Fearing that the Protestant faction in the city was too strong, the nuns left Geneva in 1535 and moved their convent to Annecy, in France.

The poor secluded ladies, the nuns of Madame Saint Clare, terribly frightened by those people [Genevan Protestants] and afraid they would hurt them, with the fury they were showing toward pious people, prayed tearfully night and day, and they gathered together in the chapter room to decide what to do about it. And they made a very humble plea to messieurs the syndics[3] and councilors written by myself in the following manner and substance:

From Jeanne de Jussie, *Short Chronicle: A Poor Clare's Account of the Reformation of Geneva*, ed. and trans. Carrie Klaus (Chicago: University of Chicago Press, 2006), pp. 46–47.

[3] **syndics**: Highest elected officials in Geneva.

"Our magnificent and most honored lords, fathers, and good protectors, we have heard of the arrival of God's enemies in your town and of the evil and disrespectful things they are doing in the church of God and to pious people, and we are very afraid. We therefore beg you very humbly, kneeling prostrate on the ground with our hands folded in honor of Our Redeemer and His sorrowful passion and of His Virgin Mother and of Monsieur Saint Peter, Monsieur Saint Francis, and Madame Saint Clare and of all the saints in paradise, please to keep us in your safeguard and protection so that those enemies of God do not violate or disturb us. For we do not want any innovation of religion or law or to turn away from divine service, but we are determined to live and die in our holy vocation here in your convent praying to Our Lord for the peace and preservation of your noble town, if you lords will agree to preserve and protect us all here as your ancestors have done; and if not, let us leave our convent and your town, to save ourselves and seek refuge elsewhere to observe divine service, and we will keep you, as our fathers, in our prayers there, and we ask you for your good will and for an answer."

The letter was presented on Thursday evening [October 6]. On Friday morning [October 7], three of the aldermen came to hear Mass at the convent, and after Mass they asked the father confessor and his associates to give the sisters their answer, saying, "Messieurs and the council have seen and considered the ladies' humble request, and they should not worry about anything because the city will take care of them and make sure that no harm comes to them, and they should also have no fear for their religion, for the city does not want to be Lutheran."

The sisters were a bit cheered and, in this hope, remained in their convent.

READING AND DISCUSSION QUESTIONS

1. What are the nuns afraid of?
2. What do the nuns mean when they say they do not want to be "turned away from divine service?"
3. What would they do if the city became Lutheran?

DOCUMENT 14-5

NICHOLAS DE LA FONTAINE

The Trial of Michael Servetus in Calvin's Geneva

1553

Michael Servetus (1511–1553) was a Spanish scientist, humanist, and theologian. Both Catholics and Protestants condemned his teachings, especially his rejection of both the doctrine of the Trinity and the practice of infant baptism. While fleeing from Catholic authorities in France, he passed through Geneva, which was then under the leadership of the Protestant reformer John Calvin. The author of this document, Nicholas de la Fontaine, took the most active role in the prosecution of Michael Servetus and drew up the list of charges. After being found guilty of heresy, Servetus was burned at the stake.

Nicholas de la Fontaine asserts that he has instituted proceedings against Michael Servetus, and on this account he has allowed himself to be held prisoner in criminal process.

1. In the first place that about twenty-four years ago the defendant commenced to annoy the churches of Germany with his errors and heresies, and was condemned and took to flight in order to escape the punishment prepared for him.
2. Item, that on or about this time he printed a wretched book,[4] which has infected many people.
3. Item, that since that time he has not ceased by all means in his power to scatter his poison, as much by his construction of biblical text, as by certain annotations which he has made upon Ptolemy.[5]

From Nicholas de la Fontaine, in *Translations and Reprints from the Original Sources of European History* (Philadelphia: University of Pennsylvania Press, 1898), 3/2:12–15.

[4] **wretched book**: *On the Errors of the Trinity*, published in 1531.

[5] **certain annotations . . . Ptolemy**: Servetus edited and updated the Roman-Egyptian's treatise *Geography*. Fontaine may be referring to Servetus's comment that the territory given to the Hebrews in the Bible was not good land, making God's gift of a "promised land" a poor gift.

4. Item, that since that time he has printed in secrecy another book containing endless blasphemies.

5. Item, that while detained in prison in the city of Vienne [in France], when he saw that they were willing to pardon him on condition of his recanting, he found means to escape from prison. Said Nicholas demands that said Servetus be examined upon all these points. And since he is able to evade the question by pretending that his blasphemies and heresies are nought else than good doctrine, said Nicholas proposes certain articles upon which he demands said heretic be examined.

6. To wit, whether he has not written and falsely taught and published that to believe that in a single essence of God there are three distinct persons, the Father, the Son, and the Holy Ghost, is to create four phantoms, which cannot and ought not to be imagined.

7. Item, that to put such distinction into the essence of God is to cause God to be divided into three parts, and that this is a three-headed devil, like to Cerberus, whom the ancient poets have called the dog of hell, a monster, and things equally injurious. . . .

9. Item, whether he does not say that our Lord Jesus Christ is not the Son of God, except in so much as he was conceived of the Holy Ghost in the womb of the virgin Mary.

10. Item, that those who believe Jesus Christ to have been the word of God the Father, engendered through all eternity, have a scheme of redemption which is fanciful and of the nature of sorcery.

11. Item, that Jesus Christ is God, insomuch as God has caused him to be such. . . .

27. Item, that the soul of man is mortal, and that the only thing which is immortal is an elementary breath, which is the substance that Jesus Christ now possesses in heaven and which is also the elementary and divine and incorruptible substance of the Holy Ghost. . . .

32. Item, that the baptism of little children is an invention of the Devil, an infernal falsehood tending to the destruction of all Christianity. . . .

37. Item, that in the person of M. Calvin, minister of the word of God in the Church of Geneva, he has defamed with printed book the doctrine which he preached, uttering all the injurious and blasphemous things which it is possible to invent.

READING AND DISCUSSION QUESTIONS

1. When had Michael Servetus come into conflict with religious author-
    ities on earlier occasions? Why are these earlier occasions mentioned
    in the present indictment?

2. Why is the charge that Michael Servetus argued that the human soul
    is mortal such an important part of the indictment? To what extent, if
    any, is this charge justified?

3. What are the major points on which Michael Servetus disagreed with
    orthodox Christian teachings?

> ### DOCUMENT 14-6

IGNATIUS OF LOYOLA
Rules for Right Thinking
1548

*While recovering from an injury, the Spanish soldier Ignatius (ig-NAY-shus)
of Loyola (1491–1556) had a religious experience that inspired him to found
a new monastic order unlike most others. This order, which became known
as the Society of Jesus, or the Jesuits, emphasized education as well as obedience to the church. Jesuits rejected isolation in a monastery and instead
served as teachers and missionaries. They were instrumental in bringing
Christianity to the new European colonies in the Americas and sent missionaries to Asian countries as well. They played an active role in trying to
convert Protestant lands back to Catholicism, especially in England and
Germany.*

First Rule. The first: All judgment laid aside, we ought to have our mind
ready and prompt to obey, in all, the true Spouse of Christ our Lord, which
is our holy Mother the Church. . . .

From Father Elder Mullen, S.J., trans., *The Spiritual Exercises of St. Ignatius of
Loyola* (New York: P. J. Kennedy & Sons, 1914), p. 39. Christian Classics Ethereal
Library. Web. February 24, 2010.

Fifth Rule. The fifth: To praise vows of Religion, of obedience, of poverty, of chastity, and of other perfections. . . .

Sixth Rule. To praise relics of the Saints, giving veneration to them and praying to the Saints; and to praise . . . pilgrimages, indulgences, . . . and candles lighted in the churches.

Eighth Rule. To praise the ornaments and the buildings of churches; likewise images, and to venerate them according to what they represent.

Ninth Rule. Finally, to praise all precepts of the Church, keeping the mind prompt to find reasons in their defense and in no manner against them.

Tenth Rule. We ought to be more prompt to find good and praise as well the . . . recommendations as the ways of our Superiors. Because, although some are not or have not been [upright], to speak against them, whether preaching in public or discoursing before the common people, would rather give rise to fault-finding and scandal than profit; and so the people would be incensed against their Superiors, whether temporal or spiritual. So that, as it does harm to speak evil to the common people of Superiors in their absence, so it can make profit to speak of the evil ways to the persons themselves who can remedy them.

Twelfth Rule. We ought to be on our guard in making comparison of those of us who are alive to the blessed passed away, because error is committed not a little in this; that is to say, in saying, this one knows more than St. Augustine; he is another, or greater than, St. Francis; he is another St. Paul in goodness, holiness, etc.

Thirteenth Rule. To be right in everything, we ought always to hold that the white which I see, is black, if the Church so decides it, believing that between Christ our Lord, . . . and the Church, . . . there is the same Spirit which governs and directs us for the salvation of our souls. Because by the same Spirit and our Lord Who gave the ten Commandments, our holy Mother the Church is directed and governed.

Fourteenth Rule. Although there is much truth in the assertion that no one can save himself without being predestined and without having faith and grace; we must be very cautious in the manner of speaking and communicating with others about all these things.

Fifteenth Rule. We ought not, by way of custom, to speak much of predestination; but if in some way and at some times one speaks, let him so speak that the common people may not come into any error, as sometimes happens, saying: Whether I have to be saved or condemned is already determined, and no other thing can now be, through my doing well or ill; and with this, growing lazy, they become negligent in the works which lead to the salvation and the spiritual.

Sixteenth Rule. In the same way, we must be on our guard that by talking much and with much insistence of faith, without any distinction and explanation, occasion be not given to the people to be lazy and slothful in works, whether before faith is formed in charity or after.

READING AND DISCUSSION QUESTIONS

1. What rules should the Jesuits follow in order to be faithful to the church?

2. What should a Jesuit do if he disagrees with the church?

3. What things should not be spoken of to the people? Why?

COMPARATIVE QUESTIONS

1. What impact did Luther's ideas have on others? Consider how the authors of other documents have added to Protestant ideas beyond the "Ninety-five Theses."

2. What impact did the Reformation have on women? Would Zell or de Jussie say it was positive or negative? Why?

3. Which thinker, Luther or Servetus, posed the more serious threat to traditional Christianity? Why? What would Ignatius say to someone like Servetus with similar disagreements on Christianity?

4. Compare and contrast the image of the pope in the woodcut (c. 1519) with what Luther said of him in his "Ninety-five Theses" (1517). What seems to have changed in the two years separating the documents?

CHAPTER 15

European Exploration and Conquest

1450–1650

I n the mid-1400s, western Europe faced a rapidly expanding Muslim power in the east. The Ottoman Empire captured Constantinople in 1453 and over time came to rule, directly or indirectly, much of eastern Europe. In the west, the Portuguese began exploring the west coast of Africa, eventually rounding the tip of Africa and reaching India. After the voyages of Columbus, the Spaniards and the Portuguese began to explore and conquer the Americas. The establishment of colonial empires in the Americas led to a new era of worldwide trade in African slaves. Through trade, travel, and missionary work, Europeans came into increasing contact with peoples of whom they had previously had little or no knowledge. Sometimes this contact led Europeans to question their own society, particularly in light of the religious wars dividing Europe.

DOCUMENT 15-1

DUCAS

Historia Turcobyzantia: *The Fall of Constantinople to the Ottomans*

ca. 1465

On May 29, 1453, Constantinople, the city that had been "the second Rome" — the capital of the eastern half of the Roman Empire — and a center of Christian learning throughout the Middle Ages, fell to the Ottoman Turks. In the years that followed Constantinople's fall, the Ottomans continued to

---

From Ducas, *Historia Turcobyzantia, 1341–1462,* in *Byzantium: Church, Society, and Civilization Seen Through Contemporary Eyes,* ed. Deno John Geanokoplos (Chicago: University of Chicago Press, 1984), p. 389.

advance into central Europe, seizing control of the Balkan Peninsula and even besieging Vienna, once in the sixteenth century and again in the seventeenth century. The author of this account was a descendant of the Ducas dynasty of Byzantine emperors who had ruled in the eleventh century.

And the entire City [its inhabitants and wealth] was to be seen in the tents of the [Turkish] camp, the city deserted, lying lifeless, naked, soundless, without either form or beauty. O City, City, head of all cities! O City, City, center of the four corners of the world! O City, City, pride of the Romans, civilizer of the barbarians! O City, second paradise planted toward the west, possessing all kinds of vegetation, laden with spiritual fruits! Where is your beauty, O paradise, where the beneficent strength of the charms of your spirit, soul, and body? Where are the bodies of the Apostles of my Lord, which were implanted long ago in the always-green paradise, having in their midst the purple cloak, the lance, the sponge, the reed, which, when we kissed them, made us believe that we were seeing him who was raised on the Cross? Where are the relics of the saints, those of the martyrs? Where the remains of Constantine the Great and the other emperors? Roads, courtyards, crossroads, fields, and vineyard enclosures, all teem with the relics of saints, with the bodies of nobles, of the chaste, and of male and female ascetics.[1] Oh what a loss! "The dead bodies of thy servants, O Lord, have they given to be meat unto the fowls of the heaven, the flesh of thy saints unto the beasts of the earth round about New Sion and there was none to bury them." [Psalm 78:2–3]

O temple [Hagia Sophia[2]]! O earthly heaven! O heavenly altar! O sacred and divine places! O magnificence of the churches! O holy books and words of God! O ancient and modern laws! O tablets inscribed by the finger of God! O Scriptures spoken by his mouth! O divine discourses of angels who bore flesh! O doctrines of men filled with the Holy Spirit! O teachings of semi-divine heroes! O commonwealth! O citizens! O army, formerly beyond number, now removed from sight like a ship sunk into the sea! O houses and palaces of every type! O sacred walls! Today I invoke you all, and as if incarnate beings I mourn with you, having Jeremiah[3] as [choral] leader of this lamentable tragedy!

---

[1] **ascetics**: Those who deny themselves material possessions and comforts.

[2] **Hagia Sophia**: At one time the largest Christian church in the world, it was built on the orders of Emperor Justinian in the sixth century. After the fall of Constantinople, it was converted to a mosque.

[3] **Jeremiah**: "Brokenhearted prophet" of the Hebrew Bible, who predicted the collapse of Assyria and the destruction of Jerusalem.

READING AND DISCUSSION QUESTIONS

1. This account was written more than ten years after the fall of Constantinople. How does this affect its value as an eyewitness account?

2. What does the reference to Psalm 78 at the end of the first paragraph tell you about both the siege and the author of this account?

3. How does Ducas describe the destruction of Constantinople, both physical and spiritual?

4. What does Ducas's account reveal about the place of Constantinople in the Christian world?

DOCUMENT 15-2

HERNANDO CORTÉS

Two Letters to Charles V: On the Conquest of the Aztecs

1521

In a number of letters to his sovereign, the Holy Roman emperor Charles V, who was also king of Spain, Hernando Cortés (1485–1547) described his conquest of the Aztec Empire of Mexico. While Cortés was surprised, even impressed by the advanced culture he encountered, his conquests were not without considerable violence. In one incident, one of his men ordered the massacre of thousands of unarmed members of the Aztec nobility who had assembled peaceably. Under examination, Cortés claimed that this act was done to instill fear and prevent future treachery. Some contemporaries speculated that Cortés embellished his accounts in order to retain the favor of the king.

[SECOND LETTER]

This great city of Tenochtitlan is built on the salt lake.... It has four approaches by means of artificial causeways.... The city is as large as Seville or Cordoba. Its streets ... are very broad and straight, some of these, and all the others, are one half land, and the other half water on

From *Letters of Cortés*, trans. Francis A. MacNutt (New York: 1908), 1:256–257, 2:244.

which they go about in canoes. . . . There are bridges, very large, strong, and well constructed, so that, over many, ten horsemen can ride abreast. . . . The city has many squares where markets are held. . . . There is one square, twice as large as that of Salamanca, all surrounded by arcades, where there are daily more than sixty thousand souls, buying and selling . . . in the service and manners of its people, their fashion of living was almost the same as in Spain, with just as much harmony and order; and considering that these people were barbarous, so cut off from the knowledge of God and other civilized peoples, it is admirable to see to what they attained in every respect.

[Fifth Letter]

It happened . . . that a Spaniard saw an Indian . . . eating a piece of flesh taken from the body of an Indian who had been killed. . . . I had the culprit burned, explaining that the cause was his having killed that Indian and eaten him which was prohibited by Your Majesty, and by me in Your Royal name. I further made the chief understand that all the people . . . must abstain from this custom. . . . I came . . . to protect their lives as well as their property, and to teach them that they were to adore but one God . . . that they must turn from their idols, and the rites they had practiced until then, for these were lies and deceptions which the devil . . . had invented. . . . I, likewise, had come to teach them that Your Majesty, by the will of Divine Providence, rules the universe, and that they also must submit themselves to the imperial yoke, and do all that we who are Your Majesty's ministers here might order them.

READING AND DISCUSSION QUESTIONS

1. Although Cortés describes the people of Tenochtitlán as "barbarous" and laments that they are "cut off from the knowledge of God and other civilized peoples," what positive qualities does he attribute to the city and its people?

2. Why do you think Cortés chooses to describe an act of cannibalism? What does his commentary on this incident reveal about his conception of his mission?

3. What different images of Mexico was Cortés trying to impress upon Charles?

VIEWPOINTS
The Slave Trade in Africa

DOCUMENT 15-3

ALVISE DA CA' DA MOSTO
Description of Capo Bianco and the Islands Nearest to It: Fifteenth-Century Slave Trade in West Africa

1455–1456

Alvise da Ca' da Mosto (ca. 1428–1483) was an Italian trader and explorer. After his father was banished from Venice, Ca' da Mosto took up service with Prince Henry of Portugal, who was promoting exploration of the West African coast. In 1455, he traveled to the Canary and Madeira Islands and sailed past Cape Verde to the Gambia River. During another voyage in 1456, Ca' da Mosto discovered islands off Cape Verde and sailed sixty miles up the Gambia River. In the excerpt that follows, Ca' da Mosto describes the African Muslims who serve as middlemen in the Atlantic slave trade.

You should also know that behind this Cauo Bianco[4] on the land, is a place called Hoden,[5] which is about six days inland by camel. This place is not walled, but is frequented by Arabs, and is a market where the caravans arrive from Tanbutu [Timbuktu], and from other places in the land of the Blacks, on their way to our nearer Barbary. The food of the peoples of this place is dates, and barley, of which there is sufficient, for they grow in some of these places, but not abundantly. They drink the milk of camels

---

From Alvise da Ca' da Mosto, "Description of Capo Bianco and the Islands Nearest to It," in *European Reconnaissance: Selected Documents*, ed. J. H. Parry (New York: Walker, 1968), pp. 59–61.

[4] **Cauo Bianco**: West African port.
[5] **Hoden**: Wadan, an important desert market about 350 miles east of Arguim. Later, in 1487, when the Portuguese sought to penetrate the interior, they attempted to establish a trading factory at Wadan that acted as a feeder to Arguim, tapping the northbound caravan traffic and diverting some of it to the west coast.

and other animals, for they have no wine. They also have cows and goats, but not many, for the land is dry. Their oxen and cows, compared with ours, are small.

They are Muhammadans, and very hostile to Christians. They never remain settled, but are always wandering over these deserts. These are the men who go to the land of the Blacks, and also to our nearer Barbary. They are very numerous, and have many camels on which they carry brass and silver from Barbary and other things to Tanbutu and to the land of the Blacks. Thence they carry away gold and pepper, which they bring hither. They are brown complexioned, and wear white cloaks edged with a red stripe: their women also dress thus, without shifts. On their heads the men wear turbans in the Moorish fashion, and they always go barefooted. In these sandy districts there are many lions, leopards, and ostriches, the eggs of which I have often eaten and found good.

You should know that the said Lord Infante of Portugal [the crown prince, Henry the Navigator] has leased this island of Argin to Christians [for ten years], so that no one can enter the bay to trade with the Arabs save those who hold the license. These have dwellings on the island and factories where they buy and sell with the said Arabs who come to the coast to trade for merchandise of various kinds, such as woollen cloths, cotton, silver, and "alchezeli," that is, cloaks, carpets, and similar articles and above all, corn, for they are always short of food. They give in exchange slaves whom the Arabs bring from the land of the Blacks, and gold tiber [gold dust]. The Lord Infante therefore caused a castle to be built on the island to protect this trade for ever. For this reason, Portuguese caravels are coming and going all the year to this island.

These Arabs also have many Berber horses, which they trade, and take to the land of the Blacks, exchanging them with the rulers for slaves. Ten or fifteen slaves are given for one of these horses, according to their quality. The Arabs likewise take articles of Moorish silk, made in Granata and in Tunis of Barbary, silver, and other goods, obtaining in exchange any number of these slaves, and some gold. These slaves are brought to the market and town of Hoden; there they are divided: some go to the mountains of Barcha, and thence to Sicily, [others to the said town of Tunis and to all the coasts of Barbary], and others again are taken to this place, Argin, and sold to the Portuguese leaseholders. As a result every year the Portuguese carry away from Argin a thousand slaves. Note that before this traffic was organized, the Portuguese caravels, sometimes four, sometimes more, were wont to come armed to the Golfo d'Argin, and descending on the land by night, would assail the fisher villages, and so ravage the land. Thus they took of these Arabs both men and women, and carried them to Portugal for sale: behaving in a like manner along all the rest of the coast, which stretches from Cauo Bianco to the Rio di Senega and even beyond.

READING AND DISCUSSION QUESTIONS

1. Why do you think Ca' da Mosto wrote this account?
2. Describe the principal patterns of commerce in northern Africa.
3. Describe the groups that were involved in the various facets of the slave trade.
4. In what ways did the Portuguese change slavery and the slave trade?

DOCUMENT 15-4

KING NZINGA MBEMBA AFFONSO OF CONGO
Letters on the Slave Trade
1526

In 1491, the Portuguese were allowed to send merchants and missionaries into the West African kingdom of Congo. The king of Congo converted to Christianity, and the trading relationship between Portugal and Congo created many lucrative opportunities for merchants from both countries. In 1526, however, King Affonso of Congo noted the negative impact that the slave trade was having on his kingdom. The following selection contains two letters from Affonso to the king of Portugal, written in July and October 1526.

[FIRST LETTER]

Sir, Your Highness should know how our Kingdom is being lost in so many ways that it is convenient to provide for the necessary remedy, since this is caused by the excessive freedom given by your agents and officials to the

From Basil Davidson, *The African Past: Chronicles from Antiquity to Modern Times* (Boston: Little, Brown and Company, 1964), pp. 191–193; reissued by Africa World Press in 1990 as *African Civilization Revisited: From Antiquity to Modern Times.*

men and merchants who are allowed to come to this Kingdom to set up shops with goods and many things which have been prohibited by us, and which they spread throughout our Kingdoms and Domains in such an abundance that many of our vassals, whom we had in obedience, do not comply because they have the things in greater abundance than we ourselves; and it was with these things that we had them content and subjected under our vassalage and jurisdiction, so it is doing a great harm not only to the service of God, but the security and peace of our Kingdoms and State as well.

And we cannot reckon how great the damage is, since the mentioned merchants are taking every day our natives, sons of the land and the sons of our noblemen and vassals and our relatives, because the thieves and men of bad conscience grab them wishing to have the things and wares of this Kingdom which they are ambitious of; they grab them and get them to be sold; and so great, Sir, is the corruption and licentiousness that our country is being completely depopulated, and Your Highness should not agree with this nor accept it as in your service. And to avoid it we need from those [your] Kingdoms no more than some priests and a few people to teach in schools, and no other goods except wine and flour for the holy sacrament. That is why we beg of Your Highness to help and assist us in this matter, commanding your factors that they should not send here either merchants or wares, because it is *our will that in these Kingdoms there should not be any trade of slaves nor outlet for them*. . . .

[Second Letter]

Moreover, Sir, in our Kingdoms there is another great inconvenience which is of little service to God, and this is that many of our people, keenly desirous as they are of the wares and things of your Kingdoms, which are brought here by your people, and in order to satisfy their voracious appetite, seize many of our people, freed and exempt men, and very often it happens that they kidnap even noblemen and the sons of noblemen, and our relatives, and take them to be sold to the white men who are in our Kingdoms; and for this purpose they have concealed them; and others are brought during the night so that they might not be recognized.

And as soon as they are taken by the white men they are immediately ironed and branded with fire, and when they are carried to be embarked, if they are caught by our guards' men the whites allege that they have bought them but they cannot say from whom, so that it is our duty to do justice and to restore to the freemen their freedom, but it cannot be done if your subjects feel offended, as they claim to be.

And to avoid such a great evil we passed a law so that any white man living in our Kingdoms and wanting to purchase goods in any way should first inform three of our noblemen and officials of our court whom we rely upon in this matter, and these are Dom Pedro Manipanza and Dom Manuel Manissaba, our chief usher, and Gonçalo Pires our chief freighter, who should investigate if the mentioned goods are captives or free men, and if cleared by them there will be no further doubt nor embargo for them to be taken and embarked. But if the white men do not comply with it they will lose the aforementioned goods. And if we do them this favor and concession it is for the part Your Highness has in it, since we know that it is in your service too that these goods are taken from our Kingdom, otherwise we should not consent to this.

READING AND DISCUSSION QUESTIONS

1. How is the slave trade affecting Congo economically, politically, and socially?

2. Who profits from the slave trade?

3. What does King Affonso propose to do about the slave trade in the first letter? In the second letter? Why do you think he changes his plan?

DOCUMENT 15-5

SAINT FRANCIS XAVIER
Missionaries in Japan
1552

The Society of Jesus (see Document 14-6) was founded in part to stop the spread of Protestant ideas and teach Catholic ideas in Europe. One of its

From Henry James Coleridge, ed., *The Life and Letters of St. Francis Xavier*, 3d ed. (London: Burns & Oates, 1876), 2:331–348.

other purposes was to spread Christianity around the world. Francis Xavier (1506–1552) was one of the first members of the Society of Jesus, and also one of the first Jesuits to travel across Asia as a missionary. His letters recount the activities of the missionaries as well as his observations of the peoples they encountered.

But to return to what we did in Japan. In the first place, we landed, as I told you, at Cagoxima,[6] Paul's[7] native place, where by his constant instructions he converted all his family to Jesus Christ, and where, but for the opposition of the bonzes,[8] he would easily have converted the whole town also. The bonzes persuaded the King, whose authority extends over a good part of the country, that, if he were to sanction the introduction of the divine law into his dominions, the result would infallibly be the ruin, not only of his entire kingdom, but also of the worship of the gods and of the institutions of his ancestors; and that he ought for the future to forbid any one becoming a Christian, on pain of death.

After the lapse of a year, seeing this prince openly opposed to the progress of the Gospel, we bade farewell to our [converts] at Cagoxima, and to Paul, in whose care we left them, and went on thence to a town in the kingdom of Amanguchi.[9] . . . I myself went on to . . . the capital of the kingdom, an immense city containing more than ten thousand houses. Here we preached the Gospel to the people in the public streets, to the princes and nobles in their own residences. Many heard us eagerly, others with reluctance. We did not always escape unhurt, having many insults offered us by the boys and the crowds in the streets. The King of the country summoned us to his presence, and, having asked the reason of our coming, invited us of his own accord to explain the law of God to him; he listened to us with deep attention for a whole hour while we spoke to him of religion. . . .

The king was made favorable to us by the letters and presents sent by the Bishop and the Governors from India and Malacca, and we obtained from him without difficulty the publication of edicts declaring his approval of the promulgation of the divine law in the cities of his dominions, and permitting such of his subjects as pleased to embrace it. When he had

---

[6] **Cagoxima**: Region in southwestern Japan.
[7] **Paul's**: A Japanese convert to Christianity.
[8] **bonzes**: Buddhist monks.
[9] **Amanguchi**: Yamaguchi, in southwestern Japan.

done us this favor he also assigned a monastery to us for a residence. Here by means of daily sermons and disputes with the bonzes, the sorcerers, and other such men, we converted to the religion of Jesus Christ a great number of persons, several of whom were nobles. Amongst them we found some able to inform us, and we made it our business to gain acquaintance with the various sects and opinions of Japan, and so know how to refute them by arguments and proofs prepared for the purpose.

READING AND DISCUSSION QUESTIONS

1. What is the Jesuits' goal in Japan?
2. How do the Japanese respond to the missionaries' preaching of Christianity?
3. Why is the king important to the Jesuits?

DOCUMENT 15-6

MICHEL DE MONTAIGNE
Of Cannibals
1580

Michel de Montaigne (duh mahn-TAYN) (1533–1592), a French lawyer and government official, wrote about his personal experiences and travels in his Essays of 1580. By reflecting on his personal experiences, Montaigne critiqued European assumptions of philosophy, religion, government, and society during an age of religious warfare at home and expanding contact with the world. The essay "Of Cannibals" was written during the French Wars of Religion (1562–1598), decades of intermittent warfare between the French Calvinists (known as Huguenots) and Catholic factions. Even though he was Catholic, Montaigne did not take sides during the wars. In the essay, Montaigne recounts what he has heard about the peoples of the Americas.

From *Essays of Montaigne*, trans. Charles Cotton, ed. William Carew Hazlitt (London: Reeves and Turner, 1902), I:237–252.

When King Pyrrhus[10] invaded Italy, having viewed and considered the order of the army the Romans sent out to meet him; "I know not," said he, "what kind of barbarians" (for so the Greeks called all other nations) "these may be; but the disposition of this army that I see has nothing of barbarism in it." . . . By which it appears how cautious men ought to be of taking things upon trust from vulgar opinion, and that we are to judge by the eye of reason, and not from common report.

I long had a man in my house that lived ten or twelve years in the New World, discovered in these latter days, and in that part of it where Ville-gaignon landed, which he called Antarctic France.[11] This discovery of so vast a country seems to be of very great consideration. I cannot be sure, that hereafter there may not be another, so many wiser men than we having been deceived in this. I am afraid our eyes are bigger than our bellies, and that we have more curiosity than capacity; for we grasp at all, but catch nothing but wind. . . .

This man that I had was a plain ignorant fellow, and therefore the more likely to tell truth: for your better-bred sort of men are much more curious in their observation; . . . they never represent things to you simply as they are, but rather as they appeared to them, or as they would have them appear to you. . . . I would have every one write what he knows, and as much as he knows, but no more; and that not in this only but in all other subjects. . . .

Now, to return to my subject, I find that there is nothing barbarous and savage in this nation, by anything that I can gather, excepting, that every one gives the title of barbarism to everything that is not in use in his own country. As, indeed, we have no other level of truth and reason than the example and idea of the opinions and customs of the place wherein we live: there is always the perfect religion, there the perfect government, there the most exact and accomplished usage of all things. . . .

These nations then seem to me to be so far barbarous, as having received but very little form and fashion from art and human invention, and consequently to be not much remote from their original simplicity. The laws of nature, however, govern them still, not as yet much [corrupted]

---

[10] **Pyrrhus**: Greek king of Sicily (319–272 B.C.E.) who attempted to prevent Roman armies from advancing into southern Italy.

[11] **and in that part . . . Antarctic France**: Nicolas Durand de Villegaignon (1510–1571) was an officer in the French navy who in 1555 captured the region surrounding what is now Rio de Janeiro, Brazil, from the Portuguese. In addition to creating new trading opportunities, his goal was to build a refuge for the French Calvinists to escape religious persecution in France. Portugal retook the colony in 1567.

with any mixture of ours: but 'tis in such purity, that I am sometimes troubled we were not sooner acquainted with these people, and that they were not discovered in those better times, when there were men much more able to judge of them than we are. . . . To my apprehension, what we now see in those nations, does not only surpass all the pictures with which the poets have adorned the golden age, and all their inventions in feigning a happy state of man, but, moreover, the fancy and even the wish and desire of philosophy itself; so native and so pure a simplicity, as we by experience see to be in them, could never enter into their imagination, nor could they ever believe that human society could have been maintained with so little artifice and human patchwork. I should tell Plato[12] that it is a nation wherein there is no manner of traffic, no knowledge of letters, no science of numbers, no name of magistrate or political superiority; no use of service, riches or poverty, no contracts, no successions, no dividends, no properties, no employments, but those of leisure, no respect of kindred, but common, no clothing, no agriculture, no metal, no use of corn or wine; the very words that signify lying, treachery, dissimulation, avarice, envy, detraction, pardon, never heard of. How much would he find his imaginary Republic short of his perfection? . . .

As to the rest, they live in a country very pleasant and temperate, so that, as my witnesses inform me, 'tis rare to hear of a sick person, and they moreover assure me, that they never saw any of the natives, either paralytic, bleary-eyed, toothless, or crooked with age. The situation of their country is along the sea-shore. . . . They have great store of fish and flesh that have no resemblance to those of ours: which they eat without any other cookery, than plain boiling, roasting, and broiling. The first that rode a horse thither, though in several other voyages he had contracted an acquaintance and familiarity with them, put them into so terrible a fright, with his centaur[13] appearance, that they killed him with their arrows before they could come to discover who he was. Their buildings are very long, and of capacity to hold two or three hundred people. . . . They have wood so hard, that they cut with it, and make their swords of it, and their grills of it to broil their meat. Their beds are of cotton, hung swinging from the roof, like our seamen's hammocks, every man his own, for the wives lie apart from their husbands. They rise with the sun, and so soon as they are up, eat for all day, for they have no more meals but that; they do not then drink, . . . but drink very often all day after, and sometimes to a rousing

---

[12] **Plato**: Greek philosopher (427–347 B.C.E.) and author of *The Republic*, who wrote about an ideal city in which people were ruled by philosophers (see Document 3-5).
[13] **centaur**: Half-human, half-horse creature from Greek mythology.

pitch. . . . The whole day is spent in dancing. Their young men go a-hunting after wild beasts with bows and arrows; one part of their women are employed in preparing their drink the while, which is their chief employment. One of their old men, in the morning before they fall to eating, preaches to the whole family, walking from the one end of the house to the other, and several times repeating the same sentence, till he has finished the round, for their houses are at least a hundred yards long. Valor towards their enemies and love towards their wives, are the two heads of his discourse. . . . They believe in the immortality of the soul, and that those who have merited well of the gods are lodged in that part of heaven where the sun rises, and the accursed in the west. . . .

They have continual war with the nations that live further within the mainland, beyond their mountains, to which they go naked, and without other arms than their bows and wooden swords, fashioned at one end like the head of our javelins. The obstinacy of their battles is wonderful, and they never end without great effusion of blood: for as to running away, they know not what it is. Every one for a trophy brings home the head of an enemy he has killed, which he fixes over the door of his house. After having a long time treated their prisoners very well, and given them all the regales they can think of, he to whom the prisoner belongs, invites a great assembly of his friends. They being come, he ties a rope to one of the arms of the prisoner, of which, at a distance, out of his reach, he holds the one end himself, and gives to the friend he loves best the other arm to hold after the same manner; which being done, they two, in the presence of all the assembly, dispatch him with their swords. After that, they roast him, eat him amongst them, and send some chops to their absent friends. They do not do this, as some think, for nourishment, . . . but as a representation of an extreme revenge; as will appear by this: that having observed the Portuguese, who were in league with their enemies, to inflict another sort of death upon any of them they took prisoners, which was . . . to shoot at [them] till [they were] stuck full of arrows, and then to hang them, they thought those people of the other world . . . did not exercise this sort of revenge without a meaning, and that it must needs be more painful than theirs, they began to leave their old way, and to follow this. I am not sorry that we should here take notice of the barbarous horror of so cruel an action, but that, seeing so clearly into their faults, we should be so blind to our own. I conceive there is more barbarity in eating a man alive, than when he is dead; in tearing a body limb from limb by racks and torments, that is yet in perfect sense; in roasting it by degrees; in causing it to be bitten and worried by dogs and swine (as we have not only read, but lately seen, not amongst inveterate and mortal enemies, but among neighbors and fellow-citizens, and, which is worse, under color of piety and religion), than to roast and eat him after he is dead. . . .

We may then call these people barbarous, in respect to the rules of reason: but not in respect to ourselves, who in all sorts of barbarity exceed them. Their wars are throughout noble and generous, and carry as much excuse and fair pretence, as that human malady is capable of; having with them no other foundation than the sole jealousy of valor. Their disputes are not for the conquest of new lands, for these they already possess are so fruitful by nature, as to supply them without labor or concern, with all things necessary, in such abundance that they have no need to enlarge their borders. And they are, moreover, happy in this, that they only covet so much as their natural necessities require: all beyond that is superfluous to them. . . . If their neighbors pass over the mountains to assault them, and obtain a victory, all the victors gain by it is glory only, and the advantage of having proved themselves the better in valor and virtue: for they never meddle with the goods of the conquered, but presently return into their own country, where they have no want of anything necessary, nor of this greatest of all goods, to know happily how to enjoy their condition and to be content. And those in turn do the same; they demand of their prisoners no other ransom, than acknowledgment that they are overcome. . . . There is not a man amongst them who had not rather be killed and eaten, than so much as to open his mouth to entreat he may not. They use them with all liberality and freedom, to the end their lives may be so much the dearer to them; but frequently entertain them with menaces of their approaching death, of the torments they are to suffer, of the preparations making in order to it, of the mangling of their limbs, and of the feast that is to be made, where their carcass is to be the only dish. All which they do, to no other end, but only to extort some gentle or submissive word from them, or to frighten them so as to make them run away, to obtain this advantage that they were terrified, and that their constancy was shaken; and indeed, if rightly taken, it is in this point only that a true victory consists. . . .

But to return to my story: these prisoners are so far from discovering the least weakness, for all the terrors that can be represented to them, that, on the contrary, during the two or three months they are kept, they always appear with a cheerful countenance; importune their masters to make haste to bring them to the test, defy, rail at them, and reproach them with cowardice, and the number of battles they have lost against those of their country. I have a song made by one of these prisoners, wherein he bids them "come all, and dine upon him, and welcome, for they shall withal eat their own fathers and grandfathers, whose flesh has served to feed and nourish him. These muscles," says he, "this flesh and these veins, are your own: poor silly souls as you are, you little think that the substance of your ancestors' limbs is here yet; notice what you eat, and you will find in it the taste of your own flesh:" in which song there is to be observed an invention that nothing relishes of the barbarian. Those that paint these people dying after this manner, represent the prisoner spitting in the faces of his executioners and making wry mouths at them. And 'tis most certain, that to the very last gasp, they never cease to brave and defy them both in word and gesture. In plain truth, these men are very savage in comparison of us; of necessity, they must either be absolutely so or else we are savages; for there is a vast difference betwixt their manners and ours.

READING AND DISCUSSION QUESTIONS

1. Why does Montaigne write that the words of a "plain ignorant fellow" are more reliable than the words of someone who has been educated? Why does he think it important that reason should be the guide to understanding?

2. How does Montaigne use the word *barbarian* in this essay? To him, what makes someone a barbarian, and why?

3. On what points does Montaigne compare and contrast this society with Portuguese society? In what ways does he find the Portuguese inferior to cannibals? Why?

COMPARATIVE QUESTIONS

1. Compare and contrast the fall of Constantinople as portrayed by Ducas and Cortés's capture of Tenochtitlán, taking into consideration the different perspective of each account.

2. Compare and contrast the two documents on the African slave trade. What tactics do the Portuguese use to operate the slave trade?

3. Based on your reading of these documents, which distinctions among peoples seem most important for Europeans of the fifteenth and sixteenth centuries? Do the Jesuits and Montaigne show similar or different attitudes to non-Europeans?

CHAPTER 16

Absolutism and Constitutionalism in Europe

ca. 1589–1725

Sixteenth- and seventeenth-century Europe witnessed a prolonged struggle between monarchs seeking to consolidate and extend their power, and social groups and institutions opposing those efforts. Many factors — political, social, and economic — influenced the course of this struggle, and the outcome varied from country to country. France's kings managed to suppress some of the opposition to royal power and thus are termed "absolutist" monarchs, although even the greatest of them, Louis XIV, lacked the power and authority to exert his unchallenged will over all of his subjects, in particular the great nobles. Eastern European rulers in Prussia, Austria, and Russia also augmented their power and authority, although there were significant differences from state to state, and none matched Louis XIV's achievement. Still, all experienced greater success in expanding royal authority than did their counterparts in the Netherlands and England. Two English kings, Charles I and James II, lost their thrones as a consequence of political revolutions, and the former was also tried and executed for crimes against his subjects.

DOCUMENT 16-1

HENRY IV

Edict of Nantes: *Limited Toleration for the Huguenots*

1598

Prince Henry of Navarre (1553–1610) was a Huguenot, or Protestant, in an overwhelmingly Roman Catholic country. He ascended to the French throne as Henry IV in 1589 in the midst of the French Wars of Religion. A pragmatist, Henry realized that the country's Catholic majority would never accept a Protestant as their legitimate ruler, so he converted to Catholicism. However, in order to protect the Huguenots against religiously motivated attacks, as well as to establish peace among the people he was determined to rule, he issued the Edict of Nantes. In so doing, Henry legally sanctioned a degree of religious tolerance in a Europe previously characterized by the formula "one king, one people, one faith."

Among the infinite benefits which it has pleased God to heap upon us, the most signal and precious is his granting us the strength and ability to withstand the fearful disorders and troubles which prevailed on our advent in this kingdom. The realm was so torn by innumerable factions and sects that the most legitimate of all the parties[1] was fewest in numbers. God has given us strength to stand out against this storm; we have finally surmounted the waves and made our port of safety, — peace for our state. For which his be the glory all in all, and ours a free recognition of his grace in making use of our instrumentality in the good work. . . . We implore and await from the Divine Goodness the same protection and favor which he has ever granted to this kingdom from the beginning. . . .

From King Henry of Navarre, "Edict of Nantes," in *Readings in European History*, ed. James Harvey Robinson, 2 vols. (Boston: Ginn, 1906), 2:183–185.

[1] **the most legitimate of all the parties**: Faction supporting Valois King Henry III (r. 1574–1589) during the French Wars of Religion (1561–1598). Henry's subsequent reference to "one party or the other" refers to the three factions, two of them Catholic, one of them Protestant, that struggled for control of the French throne.

We have, by this perpetual and irrevocable edict, established and proclaimed and do establish and proclaim:

I. First, that the recollection of everything done by one party or the other between March, 1585, and our accession to the crown, and during all the preceding period of troubles, remain obliterated and forgotten, as if no such things had ever happened. . . .

III. We ordain that the Catholic Apostolic and Roman religion shall be restored and reestablished in all places and localities of this our kingdom and countries subject to our sway, where the exercise of the same has been interrupted, in order that it may be peaceably and freely exercised, without any trouble or hindrance; forbidding very expressly all persons, of whatsoever estate, quality, or condition, from troubling, molesting, or disturbing ecclesiastics in the celebration of divine service, in the enjoyment or collection of tithes, fruits, or revenues of their benefices, and all other rights and dues belonging to them; and that all those who during the troubles have taken possession of churches, houses, goods, or revenues, belonging to the said ecclesiastics, shall surrender to them entire possession and peaceable enjoyment of such rights, liberties, and sureties as they had before they were deprived of them. . . .

VI. And in order to leave no occasion for troubles or differences between our subjects, we have permitted, and herewith permit, those of the said religion called Reformed [Protestant] to live and abide in all the cities and places of this our kingdom and countries of our sway, without being annoyed, molested, or compelled to do anything in the matter of religion contrary to their consciences, . . . upon conditions that they comport themselves in other respects according to that which is contained in this our present edict.

VII. It is permitted to all lords, gentlemen, and other persons making profession of the said religion called Reformed, holding the right of high justice [or a certain feudal tenure], to exercise the said religion in their houses. . . .

IX. We also permit those of the said religion to make and continue the exercise of the same in all villages and places of our dominion where it was established by them and publicly enjoyed several and divers times in the year 1597, up to the end of the month of August, notwithstanding all decrees and judgments to the contrary. . . .

XIII. We very expressly forbid to all those of the said religion its exercise, either in respect to ministry, regulation, discipline, or the public instruction of children, or otherwise, in this our kingdom and lands of our dominion, otherwise than in the places permitted and granted by the present edict.

XIV. It is forbidden as well to perform any function of the said religion on our court or retinue, or in our lands and territories beyond the mountains, or in our city of Paris, or within five leagues of the said city. . . .

XVIII. We also forbid all our subjects, of whatever quality and condition, from carrying off by force or persuasion, against the will of their parents, the children of the said religion, in order to cause them to be baptized or confirmed in the Catholic Apostolic and Roman Church; and the same is forbidden to those of the said religion called Reformed, upon penalty of being punished with special severity. . . .

XXI. Books concerning the said religion called Reformed may not be printed and publicly sold, except in cities and places where the public exercise of the said religion is permitted.

XXII. We ordain that there shall be no difference or distinction made in respect to the said religion, in receiving pupils to be instructed in universities, colleges, and schools; or in receiving the sick and poor into hospitals, retreats and public charities.

XXIII. Those of the said religion called Reformed shall be obliged to respect the laws of the Catholic Apostolic and Roman Church, recognized in this our kingdom, for the consummation of marriages contracted, or to be contracted, as regards to the degrees of consanguinity and kinship.

READING AND DISCUSSION QUESTIONS

1. Why was Henry so intent on "obliterating" memory of "everything done by one party or the other" in the years immediately prior to his coronation as king of France?

2. Is the Edict of Nantes consistent with Henry's aim of increasing the monarchy's and the state's power? Why or why not?

3. Why might Henry's son, Louis XIII, have regarded the Huguenots as "a state within a state"?

4.   Based on the details of the edict regarding ceremonies, property, liter-
      ature, and education, what sorts of practices defined a religion before
      and during Henry's reign? What, if any practices did he consider irre-
      ligious, or purely civil?

DOCUMENT 16-2

JACQUES-BÉNIGNE BOSSUET

Politics Drawn from the Very Words of Holy Scripture

1679

*French cleric Jacques-Bénigne Bossuet's (1627–1704) sermons earned him
the favor of Louis XIV. He preached to the court regularly from 1660 to 1669
and was especially renowned for his funeral orations. In 1670 he was appointed tutor to Louis's eldest son, and thus had the weighty task of instructing the heir to the throne on the duties of a king. The work from which the
following excerpts are taken was composed in 1679 for the Dauphin's
guidance.*

All power is of God. The ruler, [states] St. Paul, "is the minister of God to
thee for good. But if thou do that which is evil, be afraid; for he beareth not
the sword in vain: for he is the minister of God, a revenger to execute
wrath upon him that doeth evil." Rulers then act as the ministers of God
and as his lieutenants on earth. It is through them that God exercises his
empire. . . . Consequently, as we have seen, the royal throne is not the
throne of a man, but the throne of God himself. The Lord "hath chosen
Solomon my son to sit upon the throne of the kingdom of the Lord over
Israel." And again, "Solomon sat on the throne of the Lord."

      Moreover, that no one may assume that the Israelites were peculiar in
having kings over them who were established by God, note what is said in
Ecclesiasticus: "God has given to every people its ruler, and Israel is manifestly reserved to him." He therefore governs all peoples and gives them

From James Harvey Robinson, ed. *Readings in European History*, 2 vols. (Boston:
Ginn, 1906), 2:273–77

their kings, although he governed Israel in a more intimate and obvious manner.

It appears from all this that the person of the king is sacred, and that to attack him in any way is sacrilege. God has the kings anointed by his prophets with the holy unction in like manner as he has bishops and altars anointed. But even without the external application in thus being anointed, they are by their very office the representatives of the divine majesty deputed by Providence for the execution of his purposes. Accordingly God calls Cyrus his anointed. "Thus saith the Lord to his anointed, to Cyrus, whose right hand I have holden, to subdue nations before him." . . . Kings should be guarded as holy things, and whosoever neglects to protect them is worthy of death. . . .

There is something religious in the respect accorded to a prince. The service of God and the respect for kings are bound together. St. Peter unites these two duties when he says, "Fear God. Honor the king." . . .

But kings, although their power comes from on high, as has been said, should not regard themselves as masters of that power to use it at their pleasure . . . they must employ it with fear and self-restraint, as a thing coming from God and of which God will demand an account. "Hear, O kings, and take heed, understand, judges of the earth, lend your ears, ye who hold the peoples under your sway, and delight to see the multitude that surround you. It is God who gives you the power. Your strength comes from the Most High, who will question your works and penetrate the depths of your thoughts, for, being ministers of his kingdom, ye have not given righteous judgments nor have ye walked according to his will. He will straightway appear to you in a terrible manner, for to those who command is the heaviest punishment reserved. The humble and the weak shall receive mercy, but the mighty shall be mightily tormented. For God fears not the power of any one, because he made both great and small and he has care for both." . . .

Kings should tremble then as they use the power God has granted them; and let them think how horrible is the sacrilege if they use for evil a power which comes from God. We behold kings seated upon the throne of the Lord, bearing in their hand the sword which God himself has given them. What profanation, what arrogance, for the unjust king to sit on God's throne to render decrees contrary to his laws and to use the sword which God has put in his hand for deeds of violence and to slay his children! . . .

The royal power is absolute. With the aim of making this truth hateful and insufferable, many writers have tried to confound absolute government with arbitrary government. But no two things could be more unlike, as we shall show when we come to speak of justice.

The prince need render account of his acts to no one. "I counsel thee to keep the king's commandment, and that in regard of the oath of God. Be not hasty to go out of his sight: stand not on an evil thing for he doeth whatsoever pleaseth him. Where the word of a king is, there is power: and who may say unto him, what doest thou? Whoso keepeth the commandment shall feel no evil thing." Without this absolute authority the king could neither do good nor repress evil. It is necessary that his power be such that no one can hope to escape him, and, finally, the only protection of individuals against the public authority should be their innocence.

This conforms with the teaching of St. Paul: "Wilt thou then not be afraid of the power? Do that which is good."

I do not call majesty that pomp which surrounds kings or that exterior magnificence which dazzles the vulgar. That is but the reflection of majesty and not majesty itself. Majesty is the image of the grandeur of God in the prince.

God is infinite, God is all. The prince, as prince, is not regarded as a private person: he is a public personage, all the state is in him; the will of all the people is included in his. As all perfection and all strength are united in God, so all the power of individuals is united in the person of the prince. What grandeur that a single man should embody so much!

The power of God makes itself felt in a moment from one extremity of the earth to another. Royal power works at the same time throughout all the realm. It holds all the realm in position, as God holds the earth. Should God withdraw his hand, the earth would fall to pieces; should the king's authority cease in the realm, all would be in confusion.

Look at the prince in his cabinet. Thence go out the orders which cause the magistrates and the captains, the citizens and the soldiers, the provinces and the armies on land and on sea, to work in concert. He is the image of God, who, seated on his throne high in the heavens, makes all nature move. . . .

Finally, let us put together the things so great and so august which we have said about royal authority. Behold an immense people united in a single person; behold this holy power, paternal and absolute; behold the secret cause which governs the whole body of the state, contained in a single head: you see the image of God in the king, and you have the idea of royal majesty. God is holiness itself, goodness itself, and power itself. In these things lies the majesty of God. In the image of these things lies the majesty of the prince.

So great is this majesty that it cannot reside in the prince as in its source; it is borrowed from God, who gives it to him for the good of the people, for whom it is good to be checked by a superior force. Something of divinity itself is attached to princes and inspires fear in the people. The king should not forget this. "I have said," — it is God who speaks, — "I have said, Ye are gods; and all of you are children of the Most High. But ye shall die like men, and fall like one of the princes." "I have said, Ye are gods"; that is to say, you have in your authority, and you bear on your forehead, a divine imprint. "You are the children of the Most High"; it is he who has established your power for the good of mankind. But, O gods of flesh and blood, gods of clay and dust, "ye shall die like men, and fall like princes." Grandeur separates men for a little time, but a common fall makes them all equal at the end.

O kings, exercise your power then boldly, for it is divine and salutary for human kind, but exercise it with humility. You are endowed with it from without. At bottom it leaves you feeble, it leaves you mortal, it leaves you sinners, and charges you before God with a very heavy account.

READING AND DISCUSSION QUESTIONS

1. If, as Bossuet argued, kings were "the representatives of the divine majesty deputed by Providence for the execution of his purposes," then what need was there for clergymen like him?

2. Bossuet admits that "many writers have tried to confound absolute government with arbitrary government." How does he distinguish between the two, if, as he also claims, the "prince need render account of his acts to no one"?

3. Does Bossuet admit to *any* constraints on royal power?

4. According to Bossuet, the "only protection of individuals against the public authority should be their innocence." What sort of protection would that have been against "absolute" royal power?

DOCUMENT 16-3

JEAN-BAPTISTE COLBERT
Memoir on Finances
1670

Jean-Baptiste Colbert (1619–1683) came from a wealthy family of merchants. He first rose to prominence in the service of Cardinal Jules Mazarin, Louis XIV's political mentor and advisor. Following Mazarin's death in 1661, Louis assumed personal control of France's government, and Colbert served him as both minister of finance and minister of marine and colonies until his death in 1683. He was a staunch proponent of mercantilism, in which the state regulates economic activities in order to increase its wealth. Virtually all of his policies had this aim in view. The memorandum that follows was written for Louis's consideration.

There is only a given quantity of money which circulates in Europe and this quantity is increased from time to time by what comes in from the West Indies.[2] It is certain and clear that if there are only 150,000,000 livres which circulate publicly in France, one cannot increase it by 20,000,000, 30,000,000, and 50,000,000 without at the same time taking the same quantity from neighboring states, a fact which explains the double elevation which has been seen to go on so notably in the past few years: the one augmenting the power and greatness of your Majesty, the other lowering that of your enemies and those envious of you. . . .

I beg your Majesty to permit me to say that it appears to me that since you have taken charge of the administration of finances, you have undertaken a war of money [*une guerre d'argent*] against all the states of Europe. You have already conquered Spain, Italy, Germany, England, and some others in which you have caused great misery and want, and by despoiling them you have enriched yourself, whereby you have gained the means to do all the great things which you have done and still continue to do every

From Colbert, "Memoir on Finances" (1670), reprinted in *Pageant of Europe Sources and Selections from the Renaissance to the Present Day*, ed. Raymond Phineas Stearns (New York: Harcourt, Brace and Co., 1947), pp. 250–251.

[2] **what comes in from the West Indies**: Colbert is referring to shipments of silver from the Spanish empire in the Americas.

day. Only Holland is left, and it fights with great resources . . . Your Majesty has formed companies which, like armies, attack them everywhere. In the North, the company has already a capital of a million livres and 20 vessels; in Guinea, there are 6 French vessels which have begun their trading; in the West, your Majesty has excluded them from all the islands under your authority, and the company which you have formed already furnishes the entire kingdom with sugar, tobacco, and other merchandise which is sold in northern Italy and other foreign countries. In the Orient, your Majesty has 20 vessels employed . . . Those trading in the Levant have a capital of 12,000,000 livres and 12 vessels.[3] Your manufactures, your canal for navigation between the seas,[4] and all the other new establishments which your Majesty makes are so many reserve corps that your Majesty creates to do their duty in this war, in which your Majesty can see clearly that he is winning every year some great advantage.

READING AND DISCUSSION QUESTIONS

1. Why does Colbert equate trading companies like the French West and East India Companies to "armies" that attacked France's enemies, the Netherlands in particular?

2. Why couldn't France increase the amount of money in circulation "without at the same time taking the same quantity from neighboring states"?

3. What does the tone of Colbert's memorandum suggest about his relationship with Louis XIV and about the king's personality?

---

[3] **those trading in the Levant**: State-funded entities established by the Crown to carry on trade across various parts of the globe. "The Levant" refers to the Ottoman Empire and its possessions in the Near East.

[4] **your canal . . . between the seas**: Canal linking the Mediterranean Sea near Narbonne to the Garonne estuary on the Atlantic was under construction at this time. It opened in 1681.

PETER THE GREAT

Edicts and Decrees: Imposing Western Styles on the Russians

1699–1723

Peter the Great's reign (1682–1725) marked Russia's emergence as a major European power. Russia defeated Sweden in the grueling Great Northern War (1700–1721) and acquired a "window on Europe" at the head of the Gulf of Finland, where Peter built a new capital, St. Petersburg. In order to defeat the Swedes, who had routed his ill-trained army at Narva in 1700, Peter had reformed and modernized his military along western European lines. His enthusiasm for western technology and tactics extended also to other realms, including education, dress, and economic programs, as can be seen from the following excerpts.

DECREE ON THE NEW CALENDAR, 1699

It is known to His Majesty that not only many European Christian lands, but also Slavic nations which are in total accord with our Eastern Orthodox Church . . . agree to count their years from the eighth day after the birth of Christ, that is from the first day of January, and not from the creation of the world,[5] because of the many difficulties and discrepancies of this reckoning. It is now the year 1699 from the birth of Christ, and from the first of January will begin both the new year 1700 and a new century; and so His Majesty has ordered, as a good and useful measure, that from now on time will be reckoned in government offices and dates be noted on documents and property deeds, starting from the first of January 1700. And

---

From Marthe Blinoff, *Life and Thought in Old Russia* (University Park: Pennsylvania State University Press, 1961), pp. 49–50; Eugene Schuyler, *Peter the Great*, vol. 2 (New York: Charles Scribner's Sons, 1884), pp. 176–177; L. Jay Oliva, *Peter the Great* (Englewood Cliffs, NJ: Prentice-Hall, 1970), p. 50; George Vernadsky et al., *A Source Book for Russian History from Early Times to 1917*, vol. 2 (New Haven and London: Yale University Press, 1972), pp. 347, 329, 357.

[5] **agree to count their years . . . world**: Before January 1, 1700, the Russian calendar started from the date of the creation of the world, which was reckoned at 5508 B.C.E. The year began on September 1.

to celebrate this good undertaking and the new century . . . in the sovereign city of Moscow . . . let the reputable citizens arrange decorations of pine, fir, and juniper trees and boughs along the busiest main streets and by the houses of eminent church and lay persons of rank. . . . Poorer persons should place at least one shrub or bough on their gates or on their house. . . . Also . . . as a sign of rejoicing, wishes for the new year and century will be exchanged, and the following will be organized: when fireworks are lit and guns fired on the great Red Square, let the boyars [nobles], the Lords of the Palace, of the Chamber, and the Council, and the eminent personages of Court, Army, and Merchant ranks, each in his own grounds, fire three times from small guns, if they have any, or from muskets and other small arms, and shoot some rockets into the air.

DECREE ON THE INVITATION OF FOREIGNERS, 1702

Since our accession to the throne all our efforts and intentions have tended to govern this realm in such a way that all of our subjects should, through our care for the general good, become more and more prosperous. For this end we have always tried to maintain internal order, to defend the state against invasion, and in every possible way to improve and to extend trade. With this purpose we have been compelled to make some necessary and salutary changes in the administration, in order that our subjects might more easily gain a knowledge of matters of which they were before ignorant, and become more skillful in their commercial relations.

We have therefore given orders, made dispositions, and founded institutions indispensable for increasing our trade with foreigners, and shall do the same in the future. Nevertheless we fear that matters are not in such a good condition as we desire, and that our subjects cannot in perfect quietness enjoy the fruits of our labors, and we have therefore considered still other means to protect our frontier from the invasion of the enemy, and to preserve the rights and privileges of our State, and the general peace of all Christians. . . .

To attain these worthy aims, we have endeavored to improve our military forces, which are the protection of our State, so that our troops may consist of well-drilled men, maintained in perfect order and discipline. In order to obtain greater improvement in this respect, and to encourage foreigners, who are able to assist us in this way, as well as artisans profitable to the State, to come in numbers to our country, we have issued this manifesto, and have ordered printed copies of it to be sent throughout Europe. . . . And as in our residence of Moscow, the free exercise of religion of all other sects, although not agreeing with our church, is already allowed, so shall this be hereby confirmed anew in such manner that we, by the power granted to us by the Almighty, shall exercise no compulsion over the consciences of men, and shall gladly allow every Christian to care for his own salvation at his own risk.

An Instruction to Russian Students Abroad Studying Navigation, 1714

1. Learn how to draw plans and charts and how to use the compass and other naval indicators.
2. Learn how to navigate a vessel in battle as well as in a simple maneuver, and learn how to use all appropriate tools and instruments; namely, sails, ropes, and oars, and the like matters, on row boats and other vessels.
3. Discover . . . how to put ships to sea during a naval battle. . . . Obtain from foreign naval officers written statements, bearing their signatures and seals, of how adequately you are prepared for naval duties.
4. If, upon his return, anyone wishes to receive from the Tsar greater favors, he should learn, in addition to the above enumerated instructions, how to construct those vessels [aboard] which he would like to demonstrate his skills.
5. Upon his return to Moscow, every foreign-trained Russian should bring with him at his own expense, for which he will later be reimbursed, at least two experienced masters of naval science. They [the returnees] will be assigned soldiers, one soldier per returnee, to teach them what they have learned abroad. . . .

Decree on Western Dress, 1701

Western ["German"] dress shall be worn by all the boyars, okol'nichie,[6] members of our councils and of our court . . . gentry of Moscow, secretaries . . . provincial gentry, boiarskie,[7] gosti,[8] government officials, strel'tsy,[9] members of the guilds purveying for our household, citizens of Moscow of all ranks, and residents of provincial cities . . . excepting the clergy (priests, deacons, and church attendants) and peasant tillers of the soil. The upper dress shall be of French or Saxon cut, and the lower dress — [including] waistcoat, trousers, boots, shoes, and hats — shall be of the German type.

---

[6] **boyars, okol'nichie**: Nobles of the highest and second-highest rank, respectively.

[7] **boiarskie**: Sons of boyars.

[8] **gosti**: Merchants who often served the tsar in some capacity.

[9] **strel'tsy**: Members of the imperial guard stationed in Moscow.

They shall also ride German saddles. [Likewise] the womenfolk of all ranks, including the priests', deacons', and church attendants' wives, the wives of the dragoons, the soldiers, and the strel'tsy and their children, shall wear Western ["German"] dresses, hats, jackets, and underwear — undervests and petticoats — and shoes. From now on no one [of the above-mentioned] is to wear Russian dress or Circassian coats,[10] sheepskin coats, or Russian peasant coats, trousers, boots, and shoes. It is also forbidden to ride Russian saddles, and the craftsmen shall not manufacture them or sell them at the marketplaces.

DECREE ON SHAVING, 1705

A decree to be published in Moscow and in all the provincial cities: Henceforth, in accordance with this, His Majesty's decree, all court attendants . . . provincial service men, government officials of all ranks, military men, all the gosti, members of the wholesale merchants' guild, and members of the guilds purveying for our household must shave their beards and moustaches. But, if it happens that some of them do not wish to shave their beards and moustaches, let a yearly tax be collected from such persons. . . . Special badges shall be issued to them from the Administrator of Land Affairs [of Public Order] . . . which they must wear. . . . As for the peasants, let a toll of two half-copecks[11] per beard be collected at the town gates each time they enter or leave a town; and do not let the peasants pass the town gates, into or out of town, without paying this toll.

DECREE ON PROMOTION TO OFFICER'S RANK, 1714

Since there are many who promote to officer rank their relatives and friends — young men who do not know the fundamentals of soldiering, not having served in the lower ranks — and since even those who serve [in the ranks] do so for a few weeks or months only, as a formality; therefore . . . let a decree be promulgated that henceforth there shall be no promotion [to officer rank] of men of noble extraction or of any others who have not first served as privates in the Guards. This decree does not apply to soldiers of lowly origin who, after long service in the ranks, have received their commissions through honest service or to those who are promoted on

---

[10] **Circassian coats**: Traditional outer garments worn by the people of Circassia, a Russian territory between the Caspian and Black Seas. The style was evidently adopted by the nobility.

[11] **half-copecks**: One-twentieth of a ruble, the basic unit of Russian money.

the basis of merit, now or in the future; it applies exclusively to those who have remained in the ranks for a short time, only as a formality, as described above.

STATUTE FOR THE COLLEGE OF MANUFACTURES, 1723

His Imperial Majesty is diligently striving to establish and develop in the Russian Empire such manufacturing plants and factories as are found in other states, for the general welfare and prosperity of his subjects. He [therefore] most graciously charges the College of Manufactures[12] to exert itself in devising the means to introduce, with the least expense, and to spread in the Russian Empire these and other ingenious arts, and especially those for which materials can be found within the empire; [the College of Manufactures] must also consider the privileges that should be granted to those who might wish to found manufacturing plants and factories.

His Imperial Majesty gives permission to everyone, without distinction of rank or condition, to open factories wherever he may find suitable. . . .

Factory owners must be closely supervised, in order that they have at their plants good and experienced [foreign] master craftsmen, who are able to train Russians in such a way that these, in turn, may themselves become masters, so that their produce may bring glory to the Russian manufactures. . . .

By the former decrees of His Majesty commercial people were forbidden to buy villages [i.e., to own serfs], the reason being that they were not engaged in any other activity beneficial for the state save commerce; but since it is now clear to all that many of them have started to found manufacturing establishments and build plants, both in companies and individually, which tend to increase the welfare of the state . . . therefore permission is granted both to the gentry and to men of commerce to acquire villages for these factories without hindrance. . . .

In order to stimulate voluntary immigration of various craftsmen from other countries into the Russian Empire, and to encourage them to establish factories and manufacturing plants freely and at their own expense, the College of Manufactures must send appropriate announcements to the Russian envoys accredited at foreign courts. The envoys should then, in an appropriate way, bring these announcements to the attention of men of various professions, urge them to come to settle in Russia, and help them to move.

---

[12] **College of Manufactures**: One of several administrative boards created by Peter in 1717, modeled on Swedish practice.

READING AND DISCUSSION QUESTIONS

1. Why do you think Peter decreed that the nobles, merchants, and townspeople wear German, rather than French, clothes, seeing that the French kings and their palaces were objects of emulation throughout Europe?

2. What does Peter's decree encouraging foreign soldiers and artisans to emigrate to Russia and his Statute for the College of Manufactures suggest about the state of its military forces and economy as of the early 1700s?

3. Why didn't Russia have a navy prior to 1700?

4. What, according to Peter, was wrong with the system of promotion in the Russian army, and how did he intend to redress it? What does his decree on promotion suggest about the power and benefits granted to the Russian nobility?

VIEWPOINTS

The Commonwealth and the State of Nature

DOCUMENT 16-5

THOMAS HOBBES

Leviathan

1651

Thomas Hobbes (1588–1679), the son of a Church of England clergyman, was educated at Oxford University and spent the years between 1608 and 1637 chiefly as a tutor to aristocratic families. Rising religious and political tensions in England drove Hobbes to flee to Paris in 1640, and there he

From Thomas Hobbes, *Leviathan, or the Matter, Form, and Power of a Commonwealth, Ecclesiastical and Civil* (London: George Routledge and Sons, 1886), pp. 64–66, 82, 84–85.

remained until the publication of Leviathan, *which aroused so much anger among English royalists that he was forced to seek protection from Cromwell's republican government. Leviathan originally referred to a biblical sea monster, but Hobbes used it as a synonym for the commonwealth; the frontispiece to his book depicts a gargantuan human figure made up of smaller people (members of the commonwealth) with the head of a monarch. Leviathan itself is based on the premise that without a sovereign authority invested with absolute power, human society is in a state of perpetual violence. Faced with such a prospect, he argued, individuals voluntarily relinquish their personal rights and liberties in return for protection.*

Nature hath made men so equal, in the faculties of body and mind, as that though there be found one man sometimes manifestly stronger in body, or of quicker mind than another; yet when all is reckoned together, the difference between man and man is not so considerable, as that one man can thereupon claim to himself any benefit, to which another may not pretend, as well as he. For as to the strength of body, the weakest has strength enough to kill the strongest, either by secret machination or by confederacy with others that are in the same danger with himself. . . .

From this equality of ability, ariseth equality of hope in the attaining of our ends. And therefore if any two men desire the same thing, which nevertheless they cannot both enjoy, they become enemies, and in the way to their end, . . . endeavor to destroy, or subdue one another. . . .

So that in the nature of man, we find three principal causes of quarrel. First, competition; secondly, diffidence; thirdly, glory.

The first maketh men invade for gain; the second, for safety; and the third, reputation. The first use violence to make themselves masters of other men's persons, wives, children, and cattle; the second, to defend them; the third, for trifles, as a word, a smile, a different opinion, and any other sign of undervalue, either direct in their persons, or by reflection in their kindred, their friends, their nation, their profession, or their name.

Hereby it is manifest, that during the time men live without a common power to keep them all in awe, they are in that condition which is called war; and such a war, as is of every man, against every man. . . .

[*On the "the state of nature":*]
Whatsoever therefore is consequent to a time of war, where every man is enemy to every man; the same is consequent to the time wherein men live without other security, than what their own strength and their own inven-

tion shall furnish them withall. In such condition, there is no place for industry, because the fruit thereof is uncertain, and consequently no culture of the earth; no navigation, nor use of the commodities that may be imported by sea; no commodious building; no instruments of moving and removing such things as require much force; no knowledge of the face of the earth; no account of time; no arts; no letters; no society; and, which is worst of all, continual fear, and danger of violent death; and the life of man, solitary, poor, nasty, brutish, and short. . . .

The passions that incline men to peace, are fear of death; desire of such things as are necessary to commodious living; and a hope by their industry to obtain them. And reason suggesteth convenient articles of peace, upon which men may be drawn to agreement. . . .

And because the condition of man, as hath been declared in the precedent chapter, is a condition of war of everyone against everyone; in which case everyone is governed by his own reason, and there is nothing he can make use of, that may not be a help unto him, in preserving his life against his enemies; It followeth that, in such a condition, every man has a right to every thing, even to one another's body. And therefore, as long as this natural right of every man to everything endureth, there can be no security to any man, how strong or wise soever he be, of living out the time, which Nature ordinarily alloweth men to live. . . .

If there be no power erected, or not great enough for our security, every man will and may lawfully rely on his own strength and art, for caution against all other men. . . .

The only way to erect such a common power, as may be able to defend them from the invasion of foreigners, and the injuries of one another, and thereby to secure them in such sort as that by their own industry and by the fruits of the earth they may nourish themselves and live contentedly, is to confer all their power and strength upon one man, or upon one assembly of men, that may reduce all their wills, by plurality of voices, unto one will: which is as much as to say, to appoint one man, or assembly of men, to bear their person; and every one to own and acknowledge himself to be author of whatsoever he that so beareth their person shall act, or cause to be acted, in those things which concern the common peace and safety; and therein to submit their wills, every one to his will, and their judgments to his judgment. This is more than consent, or concord; it is a real unity of them all in one and the same person, made by covenant of every man with every man, in such manner as if every man should say to every man: "I authorize and give up my right of governing myself to this man, or to this assembly of men, on this condition, that thou give up thy right to him, and authorize all his actions in like manner." This done, the multitude so united in one person is called a "commonwealth," in Latin, *civitas*. This is the generation of that great "leviathan," or rather, to speak more reverently, of that "mortal god," to which we owe under the "immortal God," our peace and defense. For by this authority, given him by every particular man in the commonwealth, he hath the use of so much power and strength conferred on him that by terror thereof, he is enabled to perform the wills of them all, to peace at home, and mutual aid against their enemies abroad. And in him consisteth the essence of the commonwealth; which, to define it, is "one person, of whose acts a great multitude, by mutual covenants one with another, have made themselves every one the author, to the end he may use the strength and means of them all as he shall think expedient, for their peace and common defense."

And he that carryeth this person is called "sovereign," and said to have "sovereign power"; and every one besides, his "subject." . . .

They that have already instituted a commonwealth, being thereby bound by covenant to own the actions and judgments of one, cannot lawfully make a new covenant, amongst themselves, to be obedient to any other, in anything whatsoever, without his permission. And therefore, they that are subjects to a monarch cannot without his leave cast off monarchy, and return to the confusion of a disunited multitude; nor transfer their person from him that beareth it to another man, other assembly of men . . . [he] that already is their sovereign shall do and judge fit to be done: so that any one man dissenting, all the rest should break their covenant made to that man, which is injustice: and they have also every man given the sovereignty to him that beareth their person; and therefore if they depose him, they take from him that which is his own, and so again it is injustice. . . . And whereas some men have pretended for their disobedience to their sovereign, a new covenant, made not with men but with God; this also is unjust: for there is no covenant with God but by mediation of somebody that representeth God's person; which none doth but God's lieutenant, who hath the sovereignty under God. But this pretence of covenant with God is so evident a lie, even in the pretenders' own consciences, that it is not only an act of an unjust, but also of a vile and unmanly disposition. . . .

Consequently none of [the sovereign's] subjects, by any pretence of forfeiture, can be freed from his subjection.

READING AND DISCUSSION QUESTIONS

1. How does Hobbes characterize human existence without the peace and order afforded by a ruler vested with absolute authority?

2. What is Hobbes's view of religious or divine justifications for absolute power?

3. Having placed themselves under the sovereign power of a ruler, what freedom of action do individuals have to govern their own affairs?

4. What options, according to Hobbes, do a sovereign's subjects have in the event that he abuses his power?

DOCUMENT 16-6

JOHN LOCKE

Second Treatise of Civil Government: Vindication for the Glorious Revolution

1690

John Locke (1632–1704) was, along with Thomas Hobbes, one of the two greatest English political theorists of the seventeenth century. Unlike Hobbes, however, who provided a justification for monarchical absolutism, Locke's Second Treatise of Government, *published anonymously in 1690, argued that government is an agreement between governors and the governed. The people submit to governmental authority in return for protection of their life, liberty, and property, and the governors' fundamental task is to provide those essential protections. According to Locke, a government that failed to do so or became tyrannical lost its claim to legitimacy, and could therefore be cast off by the governed.*

87. Man being born, as has been proved, with a title to perfect freedom and an uncontrolled enjoyment of all the rights and privileges of the law of Nature, equally with any other man, or number of men in the world,

---

From John Locke, *Two Treatises on Civil Government* (London: George Routledge and Sons, 1887), pp. 234–38.

hath by nature a power not only to preserve his property — that is, his life, liberty and estate against the injuries and attempts of other men; but to judge of and punish the breaches of that law in others, as he is persuaded the offense deserves, even with death itself, in crimes where the heinousness of the fact, in his opinion, requires it. But because no political society can be, nor subsist, without having in itself the power to preserve the property, and in order thereunto punish the offenses of all those of that society, there, and there only is political society where every one of the members hath quitted this natural power, resigned it up into the hands of the community in all cases that exclude him not from appealing for protection to the law established by it. And thus all private judgment of every particular member being excluded, the community comes to be umpire, and by understanding indifferent rules and men authorized by the community for their execution, decides all the differences that may happen between any members of that society concerning any matter of right, and punishes those offenses which any member hath committed against the society with such penalties as the law has established; whereby it is easy to discern, who are, and are not, in political society together. Those who are united into one body, and have a common established law and judicature to appeal to, with authority to decide controversies between them and punish offenders, are in civil society one with another; but those who have no such common appeal, I mean on earth, are still in the state of Nature, each being where there is no other, judge for himself and executioner; which is, as I have before showed it, the perfect state of Nature.

88. And thus the commonwealth comes by a power to set down what punishment shall belong to the several transgressions they think worthy of it, committed amongst the members of that society (which is the power of making laws) as well as it has the power to punish any injury done unto any of its members by any one that is not of it (which is the power of war and peace); and all this for the preservation of the property of all the members of that society, as far as is possible. But though every man entered into society has quitted his power to punish offenses against the law of Nature in prosecution of his own private judgment, yet with the judgment of offenses which he has given up to the legislative, in all cases where he can appeal to the magistrate, he has given up a right to the commonwealth to employ his force, for the execution of the judgments of the commonwealth whenever he shall be called to it, which, indeed, are his own judgments, they being made by himself or his representative. And herein we have the original of the legislative and executive power of civil society, which is to judge by standing laws how far offenses are to be punished

when committed within the commonwealth; and also by occasional judgments founded on the present circumstances of the fact, how far injuries from without are to be vindicated; and in both these to employ all the force of all the members when there shall be need.

89. Wherever, therefore, any number of men so unite into one society as to quit every one his executive power of the law of Nature, and to resign it to the public, there and there only is a political or civil society. And this is done wherever any number of men, in the state of nature, enter into society to make one people one body politic under one supreme government; or else when any one joins himself to, and incorporates with any government already made. For hereby he authorizes the society, or which is all one, the legislative thereof, to make laws for him as the public good of the society shall require; to the execution whereof his own assistance (as to his own decrees) is due. And this puts men out of a state of Nature into that of a commonwealth, by setting up a judge on earth with authority to determine all the controversies and redress the injuries that may happen to any member of the commonwealth; which judge is the legislative or magistrates appointed by it. And wherever there are any number of men, however associated, that have no such decisive power to appeal to, there they are still in the state of Nature.

90. And hence it is evident that absolute monarchy, which by some men is counted for the only government in the world, is indeed inconsistent with civil society, and so can be no form of civil government at all. For the end of civil society being to avoid and remedy those inconveniencies of the state of nature which necessarily follow from every man's being judge in his own case by setting up a known authority to which every one of that society may appeal upon any injury received, or controversy that may arise, and which every one of the society ought to obey. Wherever any persons are who have not such an authority to appeal to, and decide any difference between them there, those persons are still in the state of Nature. And so is every absolute prince in respect of those who are under his dominion.

91. For he being supposed to have all, both legislative and executive, power in himself alone, there is no judge to be found, no appeal lies open to any one, who may fairly and indifferently, and with authority decide, and from whence relief and redress may be expected of any injury or inconveniency that may be suffered from him, or by his order. So that such a man, however entitled, Czar, or Grand Signior, or how you please, is as much in the state of Nature, with all under his dominion, as he is with the rest of mankind. For wherever any two men are, who have no standing

rule and common judge to appeal to on earth, for the determination of controversies of right betwixt them, there they are still in the state of Nature, and under all the inconveniencies of it, with only this woeful difference to the subject, or rather slave of an absolute prince. That whereas, in the ordinary state of nature, he has a liberty to judge of his right, and according to the best of his power to maintain it; but whenever his property is invaded by the will and order of his monarch, he has not only no appeal, as those in society ought to have, but as if he were degraded from the common state of rational creatures, is denied a liberty to judge of, or to defend his right, and so is exposed to all the misery and inconveniencies that a man can fear from one, who being in the unrestrained state of Nature, is yet corrupted with flattery and armed with power.

92. For he that thinks absolute power purifies men's bloods, and corrects the baseness of human nature, need read but the history of this, or any other age, to be convinced of the contrary.

READING AND DISCUSSION QUESTIONS

1. What, according to Locke, distinguishes "political, or civil society" from "a state of nature"?

2. What, in Locke's opinion, led to the creation of "political, or civil society"?

3. Why does he argue that "absolute monarchy, which by some men is counted the only government in the world, is indeed inconsistent with civil society, and so can be no form of civil government at all"?

4. Why do you think Locke published this work anonymously, rather than publicly claiming credit for what is now generally regarded as one of the classics of Western political theory?

COMPARATIVE QUESTIONS

1. What would Hobbes say of Bossuet's justification for absolute royal authority? What would Bossuet say of Hobbes's?

2. How does Hobbes's "social contract" theory differ from Locke's? How do Hobbes and Locke use "the state of nature" to further their arguments?

3. Compare and contrast how Locke and Hobbes view the scope of sovereign power and authority.

4. What do Henry IV's and Peter the Great's edicts tell you about their attitudes toward monarchy and their role in the lives of their subjects?

5. How would Bossuet, Hobbes, and Locke each respond to Peter the Great's edicts?

CHAPTER 17

Toward a New Worldview

1540–1789

L earning in the medieval period focused on studying ancient texts such as the Bible and Aristotle's writings and then using that knowledge to draw conclusions about the world. The Polish astronomer Nicolaus Copernicus (1473–1543) was one of the first thinkers to dispute effectively archaic ideas about astronomy, spurring a centuries-long challenge to the system of scientific and mathematical thinking that had shaped the Western world since antiquity. By the eighteenth century, the spirit of this "scientific revolution" had spread to human affairs. Philosophers and scientists of the European "Enlightenment," particularly in France, began to question forms of social and political organization. Some thinkers rejected the legitimacy of absolutism and divine right. In the climate of the age, especially beginning in the eighteenth century, even absolutist monarchs made efforts to incorporate new political ideas, though with varying degrees of enthusiasm and success.

DOCUMENT 17-1

NICOLAUS COPERNICUS
On the Revolutions of the Heavenly Spheres
1542

For over a thousand years Europeans widely believed that the earth was the center of the universe, based on the work of the Greek philosopher Aristotle, and his follower, Ptolemy. This view aligned with Scripture and the Christian belief that humans were the center of creation. Copernicus theorized

---

From Nicolaus Copernicus, *De Revolutionibus Orbium Celestium*, trans. A. M. Duncan (Newton Abbot, Devonshire: David and Charles, 1976), pp. 36, 37, 40–41, 43–44, 45–46.

that a sun-centered system made for easier, more precise calculations of planetary and stellar movements, both important accurate calendars, oceanic navigations, and, not least of all, horoscopes. Fearful of how the Catholic Church might react to his theory, Copernicus only published his work in 1542, shortly before his death.

THAT THE UNIVERSE IS SPHERICAL.

First we must remark that the universe is globe-shaped, either because that is the most perfect shape of all, needing no joint, an integral whole; or because that it is the most capacious of shapes, which is most fitting because it is to contain and preserve all things; or because the most finished parts of the universe, I mean the Sun, Moon, and stars, are observed to have that shape, or because everything tends to take on this shape, which is evident in drops of water and other liquid bodies, when they take on their natural shape. There should therefore be no doubt that this shape is assigned to the heavenly bodies.

THAT THE EARTH IS ALSO SPHERICAL.

The Earth is also globe-shaped, because every part of it tends towards its center. Although it is not immediately apparent that it is a perfect sphere, because the mountains project so far and the valleys are so deep, they produce very little variation in the complete roundness of the Earth. That is evident from the fact that as one moves northward from any point that pole [the North Pole] of the diurnal [daily] rotation rises little by little, while the other pole on the contrary sinks to the same extent, and several stars round the North Pole seem not to set, while some in the South no longer rise . . .

WHETHER THE EARTH HAS A CIRCULAR MOTION, AND CONCERNING THE LOCATION OF THE EARTH.

As it has now been shown that the Earth also has the shape of a globe, I believe we must consider whether its motion too follows its shape, and what place it holds in the universe, without which it is impossible to find a reliable explanation of celestial phenomena. Among the authorities it is generally agreed that the Earth is at rest in the middle of the universe, and they regard it as inconceivable and even ridiculous to hold the opposite opinion. However, if we consider it more closely the question will be seen to be still unsettled, and so decidedly not to be despised. For every apparent change in respect of position is due to motion of the object observed, or of the observer, or indeed to an unequal change of both. (Between objects which move equally in the same direction no motion is perceived,

I mean between that which is observed and the observer.) Now the Earth is the point from which the rotation of the heavens is observed, and brought into our view. If therefore some motion is imputed to the Earth, the same motion will appear in all that is external to the Earth, but in the opposite direction, as if it were passing by. The first example of this is the diurnal rotation. This seems to whirl round the whole universe, except the Earth and the things on it. But if you grant that the heaven has no part in this motion, but that the Earth revolves from west to east, as far as the apparent rising and setting of the Sun, Moon, and stars is concerned, if you consider the point seriously, you will find that this is the way of it. And as the heaven is that which contains and cloaks all things, where everything has its place, it is not at once apparent why motion is attributed to that which is contained rather than to the container, to that which is located rather than that which locates it. . . . If this assumption is made there follows another and no lesser problem about the position of the Earth, although almost everyone admits and believes the Earth to be the center of the universe. For if one argues that the Earth does not occupy the center or middle of the universe, not claiming that its distance is great enough to be comparable with the sphere of the fixed stars, but that it is appreciable and significant compared with the orbits of the Sun and other stars,[1] and believing that on this account their motion seems to be variable, as if they were regular with respect to [i.e., revolved around] some center other than the center of the Earth, he would perhaps be able to put forward a not unreasonable account of the apparently variable motion. For the fact that the wandering stars are observed to be sometimes nearer to the Earth and sometimes further away from it necessarily shows that the center of the Earth is not the center of their orbits. It is also undecided whether the Earth veers toward them and away from them or they towards and away from the Earth. It would also not be surprising if in addition to this daily revolution another motion should be supposed for the Earth. Indeed that the Earth revolves, wanders with several motions, and is one of the stars [i.e., planets] is said to have been the opinion of Philolaus the Pythagorean,[2] no mean mathematician. . . .

---

[1] **not claiming . . . other stars**: Copernicus is arguing here that the diameter of the earth's orbit is insignificant compared to the distance of the earth from the "fixed stars," which he, like his contemporaries, believed to be embedded in an invisible crystalline sphere, but is comparable to that of the "wandering stars," i.e., the visible planets.

[2] **Philolaus the Pythagorean**: Greek mathematician and philosopher (ca. 470–385 B.C.E.).

Refutation of the arguments quoted, and their insufficiency.[3]

From this and similar arguments, then, they say that the Earth is at rest in the middle of the universe, and that such is undoubtedly the state of affairs. Yet if anyone should hold the opinion that the Earth revolves, he will surely assert that its motion is natural, not violent. What is natural produces contrary effects to what is violent. For objects to which force or impulse is applied must necessarily be destroyed and cannot long subsist; but objects which exist naturally are in their proper state, and continue in their perfect form. There is therefore no need for Ptolemy to fear the scattering of the Earth and of all terrestrial objects in a revolution brought about through the workings of nature, which is far different from artifice, or what can be achieved by human abilities. Further, why is not the same question raised even more strongly about the universe, the motion of which must be much swifter in proportion as the heaven is greater than the Earth? Of has heaven become so immense, because it is drawn outwards from the middle by a motion of ineffable strength [i.e., centrifugal force], that it would collapse if it were not at rest? Certainly if this reasoning were to be accepted, the magnitude of the heaven will rise to infinity. For in proportion is it is thrown higher by the impulse of the motion, so the motion will be swifter, on account of the continual increase in the circumference which it must traverse in the space of twenty-four hours; and on the other hand as the motion increased, so would the immensity of the heaven. So the velocity would increase the magnitude, and the magnitude the velocity, to infinity. But according to that axiom in physics, that what is infinite cannot be traversed, nor moved by any means, the heaven will necessarily be at rest. But they say that outside the heaven there is no body, no place, no empty space, in fact nothing whatsoever, and therefore there is nothing to which the heaven can go out. In that case it is remarkable indeed if something can be restrained by nothing. But if the heaven is infinite, and finite only in its hollow interior, perhaps it will be more clearly proved that there is nothing outside the heaven, since every single thing will be within, whatever amount of space it occupies, but the heaven will remain immovable. For the strongest argument by which they try to establish that the universe is finite, is its motion. Therefore let us leave the question whether the universe is finite or infinite for the natural philoso-

---

[3] the arguments quoted . . . insufficiency: Arguments by ancient authorities, maintaining that "the Earth was at rest in the middle of the universe as if it was the center."

phers[4] to argue. What we do know for certain is that the Earth is limited by its poles and bounded by a globular surface. . . .

Surely Aristotle's division of simple motion into three types, away from the middle, towards the middle, and round the middle, will be regarded merely as an intellectual division; just as we distinguish between a line, a point, and a surface, although one cannot exist without the other, and none of them without a body. A further point is that immobility is considered a more noble and divine state than that of change and instability, which is for that reason more appropriate to the Earth than to the universe. I also add that it would seem rather absurd to ascribe motion to that which contains and locates, and not rather to that which is contained and located, that is the Earth. Lastly, since it is evident that the wandering stars are sometimes nearer, sometimes further from the Earth, this will also be an example of motion of a single body which is both round the middle, by which they mean the center, away from the middle, and towards it. Motion round the midpoint must therefore be accepted more generally, and as satisfactory, provided that each motion is motion about its own midpoint. You will see then that from all these arguments the mobility of the Earth is more probable than its immobility, especially in the daily revolution, as that is particularly fitting for the Earth.

READING AND DISCUSSION QUESTIONS

1. What justification does Copernicus offer for his opening premise that the universe is spherical? What is his justification for the premise that the earth too is spherical?

2. Why does Copernicus accuse Ptolemy of logical inconsistency?

3. On what grounds does Copernicus argue that the heavens (universe) are of finite extent? Does his logic on this score convince you? Why or why not?

4. What is Copernicus's argument that the earth, like the other planets, is in motion? Why did scientists before him accept the idea that the Earth was stationary?

---

[4] **natural philosophers**: Scientists.

DOCUMENT 17-2

FRANCIS BACON

On Superstition and the Virtue of Science

1620

Trained as a lawyer, Sir Francis Bacon (1561–1626) served in the court of the English king James I (r. 1603–1625) and conducted numerous experiments designed to illuminate the natural world. Bacon argued for a new method of observation and reasoning based on drawing conclusions from specific examples rather than on theory or, worse, on superstition. Most of the scientists (known in their day as natural philosophers) of the seventeenth century were religious men as well, and Bacon was no exception.

There is no soundness in our notions, whether logical or physical. Substance, quality, action, passion, essence itself are not sound notions; much less are heavy, light, dense, rare, moist, dry, generation, corruption, attraction, repulsion, element, matter, form, and the like; but all are fantastical and ill-defined. . . .

The discoveries which have hitherto been made in the sciences are such as lie close to vulgar notions, scarcely beneath the surface. In order to penetrate into the inner and further recesses of nature, it is necessary that both notions and axioms [be] derived from things by a more sure and guarded way, and that a method of intellectual operation be introduced altogether better and more certain. . . .

There are and can be only two ways of searching into and discovering truth. The one flies from the senses and particulars to the most general axioms, and from these principles, the truth of which it takes for settled and immovable, proceeds to judgment and the discovery of middle axioms. And this way is now in fashion. The other derives axioms from the senses and particulars, rising by a gradual and unbroken ascent, so that it arrives at the most general axioms last of all. This is the true way, but as yet untried. . . .

From Francis Bacon, "Aphorisms Concerning the Interpretation of Nature and the Kingdom of Man," in *The Works of Francis Bacon: Popular Edition, Based Upon the Complete Edition of Spedding, Ellis, and Heath*, vol. 1 (New York: Hurd and Houghton, 1877), pp. 70–71, 124–26.

It is not to be forgotten that in every age natural philosophy has had a troublesome adversary and hard to deal with — namely, superstition and the blind and immoderate zeal of religion. For we see among the Greeks that those who first proposed to man's uninitiated ears the natural causes for thunder and for storms were thereupon found guilty of impiety. Nor was much more forbearance shown by some of the ancient fathers of the Christian Church to those who, on most convincing grounds (such as no one in his senses would now think of contradicting), maintained that the earth was round and, of consequence, asserted the existence of the antipodes.[5]

Moreover, as things now are, to discourse of nature is made harder and more perilous by the summaries and systems of the schoolmen; who, having reduced theology into regular order as well as they were able, and fashioned it into the shape of an art, ended in incorporating the contentious and thorny philosophy of Aristotle, more than was fit, with the body of religion. . . .

Lastly . . . some are weakly afraid lest a deeper search into nature should transgress the permitted limits of sobermindedness; wrongfully wresting and transferring what is said in Holy Writ [the Christian Bible] against those who pry into sacred mysteries to the hidden things of nature, which are barred by no prohibition. Others, with more subtlety, surmise and reflect that if secondary causes are unknown everything can be more readily referred to the divine hand and rod, — a point in which they think religion greatly concerned; which is, in fact, nothing else but to seek to gratify God with a lie. Others fear from past example that movements and changes in philosophy will end in assaults on religion; and others again appear apprehensive that in the investigation of nature something may be found to subvert, or at least shake, the authority of religion, especially with the unlearned. But these two last fears seem to me to savor utterly of carnal wisdom; as if men in the recesses and secret thoughts of their hearts doubted and distrusted the strength of religion, and the empire of faith over the senses, and therefore feared that the investigation of truth in nature might be dangerous to them. But if the matter be truly considered,

---

[5] **maintained that the earth was round . . . antipodes**: Bacon refers to an ancient debate relating to the shape of the earth; if the earth was round, some Greek theorists argued, then there would be lands (or ocean) on the side of the world directly opposite the one they inhabited. The debate was largely mooted by the fifteenth-century voyages of European explorers, culminating in the 1492 discovery of the New World. The theorists were proven correct.

natural philosophy is, after the word of God, at once the surest medicine against superstition and the most approved nourishment for faith; and therefore she is rightly given to religion as her most faithful handmaid, since the one displays the will of God, the other his power.

READING AND DISCUSSION QUESTIONS

1. If, as Bacon argues, that moving from specific observations to general truths "by a gradual and unbroken ascent" is the "true way, but as yet untried," what reasons might he have for thinking it is a better way?

2. What reasons would Bacon have for referring to settled arguments instead of ongoing ones in order to make his points?

3. What does Bacon's relationship to religion suggest about the larger relationship between science and faith in the seventeenth century?

VIEWPOINTS

Monarchical Power and Responsibility

DOCUMENT 17-3

FREDERICK THE GREAT
Essay on the Forms of Government
ca. 1740

Frederick II of Prussia (r. 1740–1786) is renowned chiefly for his military genius, but his life and policies reflected his interest in Enlightenment thought. He was a patron of the arts and learning, modernized Prussia's bureaucracy and educational system in accordance with Enlightenment

From *The Foundations of Germany*, trans. J. Ellis Barker (New York: E. P. Dutton, 1916), pp. 22–23.

*principles, abolished torture and corporal punishment, and favored religious
tolerance. He also corresponded with French philosophe Jean d'Alembert
and had a long, if at times stormy, friendship with Voltaire.*

Princes, sovereigns, and king have not been given supreme authority in
order to live in luxurious self-indulgence and debauchery. They have not
been elevated by their fellow-men to enable them to strut about and to
insult with their pride the simple-mannered, the poor, and the suffering.
They have not been placed at the head of the State to keep around themselves a crowd of idle loafers whose uselessness drives them towards vice.
The bad administration which may be found in monarchies springs from
many different causes, but their principal cause lies in the character of the
sovereign. A ruler addicted to women will become a tool of his mistresses
and favorites, and these will abuse their power and commit wrongs of every
kind, will protect vice, sell offices, and perpetrate every infamy. . . .

The sovereign is the representative of his State. He and his people
form a single body. Ruler and ruled can be happy only if they are firmly
united. The sovereign stands to his people in the same relation in which
the head stands to the body. He must use his eyes and his brain for the
whole community, and act on its behalf to the common advantage. If we
wish to elevate monarchical above republican government, the duty of
sovereigns is clear. They must be active, hard-working, upright and honest,
and concentrate all their strength upon filling their office worthily. That is
my idea of the duties of sovereigns.

A sovereign must possess an exact and detailed knowledge of the
strong and of the weak points of his country. He must be thoroughly acquainted with its resources, the character of the people, and the national
commerce. . . .

Rulers should always remind themselves that they are men like the
least of their subjects. The sovereign is the foremost judge, general, finan-
cier, and minister of his country, not merely for the sake of his prestige.
Therefore, he should perform with care the duties connected with these
offices. He is merely the principal servant of the State. Hence, he must act
with honesty, wisdom, and complete disinterestedness in such a way that
he can render an account of his stewardship to the citizens at any moment.
Consequently, he is guilty if he wastes the money of the people, the taxes
which they have paid, in luxury, pomp, and debauchery. He who should
improve the morals of the people, be the guardian of the law, and improve
their education should not pervert them by his bad example.

READING AND DISCUSSION QUESTIONS

1. In what ways do you think Enlightenment principles informed Frederick's views on the duties of rulers?

2. Historians have used the term "Enlightened Absolutists" to describe some eighteenth-century European rulers, Frederick the Great among them. Are the principles enunciated by Frederick compatible with "absolutism"? Why or why not?

DOCUMENT 17-4

CHARLES DE SECONDAT, BARON DE MONTESQUIEU

From The Spirit of Laws: On the Separation of Governmental Powers

1748

The writings of Frenchman Charles de Secondat (1689–1755), better known as Baron Montesquieu (mahn-tuhs-KYOO), were composed as the spirit of the Enlightenment swept over Europe in the early eighteenth century. Montesquieu's political writings, excerpted here, were concerned with the makeup of the state and the effect of a government on the choices available to those it ruled. Rather than turn to ancient writers for evidence — Aristotle had produced a similar work, the Politics *— Montesquieu culled his examples from contemporary European experience. His work was highly influential and was heavily quoted by the American revolutionaries twenty years after his death.*

In every government there are three sorts of power: the legislative; the executive in respect to things dependent on the law of nations; and the executive in regard to matters that depend on the civil law.

By virtue of the first, the prince or magistrate enacts temporary or perpetual laws, and amends or abrogates those that have been already

From Baron de Montesquieu, *The Spirit of Laws*, trans. T. Nugent (New York: Hafner, 1949), pp. 151–152.

enacted. By the second, he makes peace or war, sends or receives embassies, establishes the public security, and provides against invasions. By the third, he punishes criminals, or determines the disputes that arise between individuals. The latter we shall call the judiciary power, and the other simply the executive power of the state.

The political liberty of the subject is a tranquillity of mind arising from the opinion each person has of his safety. In order to have this liberty, it is requisite the government be so constituted as one man need not be afraid of another.

When the legislative and executive powers are united in the same person, or in the same body of magistrates, there can be no liberty; because apprehensions may arise, lest the same monarch or senate should enact tyrannical laws, to execute them in a tyrannical manner.

Again, there is no liberty, if the judiciary power be not separated from the legislative and executive. Were it joined with the legislative, the life and liberty of the subject would be exposed to arbitrary control; for the judge would be then the legislator. Were it joined to the executive power, the judge might behave with violence and oppression.

There would be an end of everything, were the same man or the same body, whether of the nobles or of the people, to exercise those three powers, that of enacting laws, that of executing the public resolutions, and of trying the causes of individuals.

Most kingdoms in Europe enjoy a moderate government because the prince who is invested with the two first powers leaves the third to his subjects. In Turkey, where these three powers are united in the Sultan's person, the subjects groan under the most dreadful oppression.

In the republics of Italy, where these three powers are united, there is less liberty than in our monarchies. Hence their government is obliged to have recourse to as violent methods for its support as even that of the Turks; witness the state inquisitors, and the lion's mouth into which every informer may at all hours throw his written accusations.

What a situation must the poor subject be in, under those republics! The same body of magistrates are possessed, as executors of the laws, of the whole power they have given themselves in quality of legislators. They may plunder the state by their general determinations; and as they have likewise the judiciary power in their hands, every private citizen may be ruined by their particular decisions.

The whole power is here united in one body; and though there is no external pomp that indicates a despotic sway, yet the people feel the effects of it every moment.

Hence it is that many of the princes of Europe, whose aim has been levelled at arbitrary power, have constantly set out with uniting in their own persons, all the branches of magistracy, and all the great offices of state.

READING AND DISCUSSION QUESTIONS

1. What attitude toward representative government — as opposed to monarchy — does Montesquieu display in this excerpt? Hint: the "Italian republics" are the ones with no powerful central monarch.

2. How does Montesquieu's definition of liberty (see the third paragraph) differ from ours today? Does his understanding reflect his status as a nobleman?

3. What reasons might a French author have for discussing political organization and not citing France in his examples?

DOCUMENT 17-5

JEAN-JACQUES ROUSSEAU

The Social Contract: *On Popular Sovereignty and the General Will*

1762

Jean-Jacques Rousseau (1712–1778) was born in Swiss Geneva — not France — and came from the common, not the aristocratic, class. He left Geneva at the age of sixteen; after spending years living on charity and the income from odd jobs, he traveled to Paris seeking to make a name for himself. Rousseau's poverty and origins, combined with his prickly personality,

From Jean-Jacques Rousseau, *The Social Contract*, in *Translations and Reprints from the Original Sources of European History* (Philadelphia: University of Pennsylvania Press, 1898), 5/1:14–16.

made him something of an outsider in Enlightenment social circles. His 1762 work on political theory, The Social Contract, *was part of an extended argument in the seventeenth and eighteenth centuries over who, if anyone, had the right to change the form of government, and from where the government derived its power.*

Since no man has any natural authority over his fellowmen, and since force is not the source of right, conventions remain as the basis of all lawful authority among men. [Book I, Chapter 4].

Now, as men cannot create any new forces, but only combine and direct those that exist, they have no other means of self-preservation than to form by aggregation a sum of forces which may overcome the resistance, to put them in action by a single motive power, and to make them work in concert.

This sum of forces can be produced only by the combination of many; but the strength and freedom of each man being the chief instruments of his preservation, how can he pledge them without injuring himself, and without neglecting the cares which he owes to himself? This difficulty, applied to my subject, may be expressed in these terms.

"To find a form of association which may defend and protect with the whole force of the community the person and property of every associate, and by means of which each, coalescing with all, may nevertheless obey only himself, and remain as free as before." Such is the fundamental problem of which the social contract furnishes the solution. . . .

If then we set aside what is not of the essence of the social contract, we shall find that it is reducible to the following terms: "Each of us puts in common his person and his whole power under the supreme direction of the general will, and in return we receive every member as an indivisible part of the whole." [Book I, Chapter 6].

But the body politic or sovereign, deriving its existence only from the contract, can never bind itself, even to others, in anything that derogates from the original act, such as alienation of some portion of itself, or submission to another sovereign. To violate the act by which it exists would be to annihilate itself, and what is nothing produces nothing. [Book I, Chapter 7].

It follows from what precedes, that the general will is always right and always tends to the public advantage; but it does not follow that the resolutions of the people have always the same rectitude. Men always desire their own good, but do not always discern it; the people are never corrupted, though often deceived, and it is only then that they seem to will what is evil. [Book II, Chapter 3].

The public force, then, requires a suitable agent to concentrate it and put it in action according to the directions of the general will, to serve as a means of communication between the state and the sovereign, to effect in some manner in the public person what the union of soul and body effects in a man. This is, in the State, the function of government, improperly confounded with the sovereign of which it is only the minister.

What, then, is the government? An intermediate body established between the subjects and the sovereign for their mutual correspondence, charged with the execution of the laws and with the maintenance of liberty both civil and political. [Book III, Chapter 1].

It is not sufficient that the assembled people should have once fixed the constitution of the state by giving their sanction to a body of laws; it is not sufficient that they should have established a perpetual government, or that they should have once for all provided for the election of magistrates. Besides the extraordinary assemblies which unforeseen events may require, it is necessary that there should be fixed and periodical ones which nothing can abolish or prorogue; so that, on the appointed day, the people are rightfully convoked by the law, without needing for that purpose any formal summons. [Book III, Chapter 13].

So soon as the people are lawfully assembled as a sovereign body, the whole jurisdiction of the government ceases, the executive power is suspended, and the person of the meanest citizen is as sacred and inviolable as that of the first magistrate, because where the represented are, there is no longer any representative. [Book III, Chapter 14].

These assemblies, which have as their object the maintenance of the social treaty, ought always to be opened with two propositions, which no one should be able to suppress, and which should pass separately by vote. The first: "Whether it pleases the sovereign to maintain the present form of government." The second: "Whether it pleases the people to leave the administration to those at present entrusted with it."

I presuppose here what I believe I have proved, viz., that there is in the State no fundamental law which cannot be revoked, not even this social compact; for if all the citizens assembled in order to break the compact by a solemn agreement, no one can doubt that it could be quite legitimately broken. [Book III, Chapter 18].

READING AND DISCUSSION QUESTIONS

1. What might Rousseau mean when he says "force is not the source of right"?

2. From where does Rousseau see a government deriving its legitimacy, and on what basis?

3. How does Rousseau's concept of the "general will" relate to the concept of majority rule in a representative government?

4. In what way might the concept of dissolving an unrepresentative government be a dangerous one, particularly in a world of hereditary monarchs?

DOCUMENT 17-6

MARIE JEAN ANTOINE NICOLAS CARITAT,
MARQUIS DE CONDORCET

Outlines of an Historical View of the Progress of the Human Mind

1793–1794

Marie Jean Antoine Nicolas de Caritat, Marquis de Condorcet (CON-dohr-SAY; 1743–1794) was a key figure of the later Enlightenment; his views on the equality of the sexes and of races placed him far in advance of most contemporaries. Perhaps more than any other philosophe, too, his thought reflected an unswerving faith in human progress. Those qualities are readily evident in the following excerpts, drawn from his posthumously published Outlines of an Historical View of the Progress of the Human Mind. *Condorcet himself was a victim of the French Revolution. He was denounced as a traitor and went into hiding after criticizing the revolutionary regime's proposed constitution, but was eventually captured and died in prison.*

From Marie Jean Antoine Nicolas Caritat, Marquis de Condorcet, *Outlines of an Historical View of the Progress of the Human Mind* (Baltimore: G. Fryer, 1802), pp. 164–167, 169–171, 223–226, 234, 241–242.

A class of men [the *philosophes*] speedily made their appearance in Europe, whose object was less to discover and investigate truth, than to disseminate it; who, pursuing prejudice through all the haunts and asylums in which the clergy, the schools, governments, and privileged corporations had placed and protected it, made it their glory rather to eradicate popular errors, than add to the stores of human knowledge; thus aiding indirectly the progress of mankind, but in a way neither less arduous, nor less beneficial.

In England, Collins and Bolingbroke,[6] and in France, Bayle, Fontenelle, Montesquieu,[7] and the respective disciples of these celebrated men, combated on the side of truth with all the weapons that learning, wit and genius were able to furnish; assuming every shape, employing every tone, from the sublime and pathetic to pleasantry and satire, from the most labored investigation to an interesting romance or a fugitive essay; accommodating truth to those eyes that were too weak to bear its effulgence;[8] artfully caressing prejudice, the more easily to strangle it; never aiming a direct blow at errors, never attacking more than one at a time, nor even that one in all its fortresses; sometimes soothing the enemies of reason, by pretending to require in religion but a partial toleration, in politics but a limited freedom; siding with despotism, when their hostilities were directed against the priesthood, and with priests when their object was to unmask the despot; sapping the principle of both these pests of human happiness, striking at the root of both these baneful trees, while apparently wishing for the reform only of glaring abuses and seemingly confining themselves to lopping off the exuberant branches; sometimes representing to the partisans of liberty, that superstition, which covers despotism as with a coat of mail, is the first victim which ought to be sacrificed, the first chain that ought to be broken; and sometimes denouncing it to tyrants as the true enemy of their power, and alarming them with recitals of its hypocritical

---

[6] **Collins and Bolingbroke**: Anthony Collins (1676–1729), philosopher and freethinker, and Henry St. John, 1st Viscount Bolingbroke (1678–1751), politician and political theorist.

[7] **Bayle, Fontenelle, Montesquieu**: Pierre Bayle (1647–1706), skeptical philosopher, author of the *Historical and Critical Dictionary*, a foundational Enlightenment text; Bernard de Fontenelle (1657–1757), secretary to the French Academy of Sciences and author of many texts, most notably *The Plurality of Worlds*, which championed the astronomical and mathematical discoveries of Galileo, Kepler, and Newton; Charles-Louis de Secondat, baron de La Brède et de Montesquieu (1689–1755), author of *The Persian Letters* and *The Spirit of the Laws* (see Document 17-4).

[8] **effulgence**: Radiance; brilliance.

conspiracies and its sanguinary vengeance. These writers, meanwhile, were uniform in their vindication of freedom of thinking and freedom of writing, as privileges upon which depended the salvation of mankind. They declaimed, without cessation or weariness, against the crimes both of fanatics and tyrants, exposing every feature of severity, of cruelty, of oppression, whether in religion, in administration, in manners, or in laws; commanding kings, soldiers, magistrates, and priests, in the name of truth and of nature, to respect the blood of mankind; calling upon them, with energy, to answer for the lives still profusely sacrificed in the field of battle or by the infliction of punishments, or else to correct this inhuman policy, this murderous insensibility; and lastly, in every place, and upon every occasion, rallying the friends of mankind with the cry of *reason, toleration, and humanity.*

Such was this new philosophy. Accordingly to those numerous classes that exist by prejudice, that live upon error, and that, but for the credulity of the people, would be powerless and extinct, it became a common object of detestation. It was every where received and every where persecuted, having kings, priests, nobles, and magistrates among the number of its friends as well as of its enemies. Its leaders, however, had almost always the art to elude the pursuits of vengeance, while they exposed themselves to hatred; and to screen themselves from persecution, while at the same time they sufficiently discovered [i.e., revealed] themselves not to lose the laurels of their glory.

It frequently happened that a government rewarded them with one hand, and with the other paid their enemies for calumniating[9] them, proscribed[10] them, yet was proud that fortune had honored its dominions with their birth; punished their opinions, and at the same time would have been ashamed not to be supposed a convert thereto.

These opinions were shortly embraced by every enlightened mind. By some they were openly avowed, by others concealed under an hypocrisy more or less apparent, according to the timidity or firmness of their characters, and accordingly as they were influenced by the contending interests of their profession or their vanity. At length the pride of ranging on the side of erudition became predominant, and sentiments were professed with the slightest caution, which, in the ages that preceded, had been concealed by the most profound dissimulation. . . .

---

[9] **calumniating**: Slandering.
[10] **proscribed**: Publicly ostracized or denounced.

The art of printing had been applied to so many subjects, books had so rapidly increased, they were so admirably adapted to every taste, every degree of information, and every situation of life, they afforded so easy and frequently so delightful an instruction, they had opened so many doors to, truth, which it was impossible ever to close again, that there was no longer a class or profession of mankind from whom the light of knowledge could be absolutely be excluded. Accordingly, though there still remained a multitude of individuals condemned to a forced or voluntary ignorance, yet was the barrier between the enlightened and unenlightened portioned [*sic*] of mankind nearly effaced, and an insensible gradation occupied the space which separates the two extremes of genius and stupidity.

Thus there prevailed a general knowledge of the natural rights of man; the opinion even that these rights are inalienable and imprescriptible; a decided partiality for freedom of thinking and writing; for the enfranchisement of industry and commerce; for the melioration of the condition of the people; for the repeal of penal statutes against religious nonconformists; for the abolition of torture and barbarous punishments; the desire of a milder system of criminal legislation; of a jurisprudence that should give to innocence a complete security: of a civil code more simple, as well as more conformable to reason and justice; indifference as to systems of religion, considered at length as the offspring of superstition, or ranked in the number of political inventions; hatred of hypocrisy and fanaticism; contempt for prejudices; and lastly, a zeal for the propagation of truth. These principles, passing by degrees from the writings of philosophers into every class of society whose instruction was not confined to the catechism and the scriptures, became the common creed, the symbol and type of all men who were not idiots on the one hand, or, on the other, assertors of the policy of Machiavellism. In some countries these sentiments formed so nearly the general opinion, that the mass even of the people seemed ready to obey their dictates and act from their impulse.

The love of mankind, that is to say, that active compassion which interests itself in all the afflictions of the human race, and regards with horror whatever, in public institutions, in the acts of government, or the pursuits of individuals, adds to the inevitable misfortunes of nature, was the necessary result of these principles. It breathed in every work, it prevailed in every conversation, and its benign effects were already visible even in the laws and administration of countries subject to despotism.

The philosophers of different nations embracing, in their meditations, the entire interests of man, without distinction of country, of color, or of sect, formed, notwithstanding the difference of their speculative opinions, a firm and united phalanx against every description of error, every species of tyranny. Animated by the sentiment of universal philanthropy, they declaimed equally against injustice, whether existing in a foreign country or exercised by their own country against a foreign nation. They impeached in Europe the avidity which stained the shores of America, Africa, and Asia with cruelty and crimes. The philosophers of France and England gloried in assuming the appellation [*sic*], and fulfilling the duties, of *friends* to those very negroes whom their ignorant oppressors disdained to rank in the class of men. The French writers bestowed the tribute of their praise on the toleration granted in Russia and Sweden,[11] while Beccaria[12] refuted in Italy the barbarous maxims of Gallic jurisprudence. . . .

[*Having surveyed the progress achieved by the Enlightenment, Condorcet closed his work by speculating on the future of humankind:*]

It has never yet been supposed, that all the facts of nature, and all the means of acquiring precision in the computation and analysis of those facts, and all the connections of objects with each other, and all the possible combinations of ideas, can be exhausted by the human mind.

But, in proportion as facts are multiplied, man learns to class them, and reduce them to more general facts, at the same time that the instruments and methods for observing them, and registering them with exactness, acquire a new precision: . . . truths, the discovery of which was accompanied with the most laborious efforts, and which at first could not be comprehended but by men of the severest attention, will after a time be unfolded and proved in methods that are not above the efforts of an ordinary capacity. And thus should the methods that led to new combinations be exhausted, should their applications to questions, still unresolved, demand exertions greater than the time or the powers of the learned can bestow, more general methods, means more simple would soon come to their aid, and open a farther career to genius. . . .

---

[11] **the toleration granted in Russia and Sweden**: Religious toleration.

[12] **Beccaria**: Italian *philosophe* Cesare, Marquis of Beccaria-Bonesana (1738–1794), whose *An Essay on Crimes and Punishments* (1764) denounced torture and physical punishment, arguing that the purpose of punishments was "no other than to prevent the criminal from doing further injury to society, and to prevent others from committing the like offence. Such punishments, therefore, and such a mode of inflicting them, ought to be chosen, as will make the strongest and most lasting impressions on the minds of others, with the least torment to the body of the criminal."

By applying these general reflections to the different sciences, we might exhibit, respecting each, examples of this progressive improvement, which would remove all possibility of doubt as to the certainty of the further improvement that may be expected. We might indicate particularly in those which prejudice considers as nearest to being exhausted, the marks of an almost certain and early advance. We might illustrate the extent, the precision, the unity which must be added to the system comprehending all human knowledge, by a more general and philosophical application of the science of calculation to the individual branches of which that system is composed. We might show how favorable to our hopes a more universal instruction would prove, by which a greater number of individuals would acquire the elementary knowledge that might inspire them with a taste for a particular kind of study; and how much these hopes would be further heightened if this application to study were to be rendered still more extensive by a more general ease of circumstances. At present, in the most enlightened countries, scarcely do one in fifty of those whom nature has blessed with talents receive the necessary instruction for the development of them: how different would be the proportion in the case we are supposing? and of consequence how different the number of men destined to extend the horizon of the sciences?

We might show how much this equality of instruction, joined to the national equality we have supposed to take place, would accelerate those sciences, the advancement of which depends upon observations repeated in a greater number of instances, and extending over a larger portion of territory; how much benefit would be derived therefrom to mineralogy, botany, zoology, and the doctrine of meteors; in short, how infinite the difference between the feeble means hitherto enjoyed by these sciences, and which yet have led to useful and important truths, and the magnitude of those which man would then have it in his power to employ. . . .

And here we may observe, how much the abolition of the usages authorized by this prejudice, and of the laws which it has dictated, would tend to augment the happiness of families; to render common the virtues of domestic life, the fountain-head of all the others; to favor instruction, and, especially, to make it truly general, either because it would be extended to both sexes with greater equality, or because it cannot become general, even to men, without the concurrence of the mothers of families. . . .

All the causes which contribute to the improvement of the human species, all the means we have enumerated that insure its progress, must, from their very nature; exercise an influence always active, and acquire an extent for ever increasing. The proofs of this have been exhibited, and from their development in the work itself they will derive additional force: accordingly we may already conclude, that the perfectibility of man is indefinite. Meanwhile we have hitherto considered him as possessing only the same natural faculties, as endowed with the same organization. How much greater would be the certainty, how much wider the compass of our hopes, could we prove that these natural faculties themselves, that this very organization, are also susceptible of melioration? And this is the last question we shall examine.

The organic perfectibility or deterioration of the classes of the vegetable, or species of the animal kingdom, may be regarded as one of the general laws of nature.

This law extends itself to the human race; and it cannot be doubted that the progress of the sanative art, that the use of more wholesome food and more comfortable habitations, that a mode of life which shall develop the physical powers by exercise, without at the same time impairing them by excess; in fine, that the destruction of the two most active causes of deterioration, penury, and wretchedness on the one hand, and enormous wealth on the other, must necessarily tend to prolong the common duration of man's existence, and secure him a more constant health and a more robust constitution. It is manifest that the improvement of the practice of medicine, become more efficacious in consequence of the progress of reason and the social order, must in the end put a period to transmissible or contagious disorders, as well to those general maladies resulting from climate, aliments, and the nature of certain occupations. Nor would it be difficult to prove that this hope might be extended to almost every other malady, of which it is probable we shall hereafter discover the most remote causes. Would it even be absurd to suppose this quality of melioration in the human species as susceptible of an indefinite advancement; to suppose that a period must one day arrive when death will be nothing more than the effect either of extraordinary accidents, or of the slow and gradual decay of the vital powers; and that the duration of the middle space, of the interval between the birth of man and this decay, will itself have no assignable limit? Certainly man will not become immortal; but may not the distance between the moment in which he draws his first breath, and the common term when, in the course of nature, without malady or accident, he finds it impossible any longer to exist, be necessarily protracted?

READING AND DISCUSSION QUESTIONS

1. How does Condorcet characterize priests and despotic rulers? Why do you think he employs this characterization?

2. Why does Condorcet argue that gender inequality is "fatal even to the sex it favors"? Do you agree? Why or why not?

3. Surveying humankind's current condition, to what extent do you think that Condorcet's predictions, made more than two centuries ago, have been borne out?

COMPARATIVE QUESTIONS

1. Nicolaus Copernicus and Francis Bacon were separated by a lifetime (Copernicus died almost twenty years before Bacon was born). What similarities can you see between how they thought, and in what ways did they differ?

2. What differences do you see between Montesquieu's and Rousseau's theories about the nature of government and how it ought to interact with its citizens? Where do they seem to be in agreement?

3. Frederick the Great ruled a state in which "the legislative and executive powers [were] united in the same person." What would Montesquieu say to such an arrangement? How do you think Frederick would reply to Montesquieu's charge that under those conditions "there can be no liberty"?

4. Did Frederick the Great have an "enlightened mind" according to the criteria used by Condorcet? Why or why not?

5. What would Frederick think of Bossuet's divine-right monarchical theory (Document 16-2) and why? How would Rousseau respond to Frederick's and Bossuet's views on the monarchy?

Acknowledgments

CHAPTER 1

1-1 "A Mesopotamian Creation Myth." From *Ancient Near Eastern Texts Relating to the Old Testament*, 3rd ed. with supplement, edited by James B. Pritchard, pp. 61, 64, 67–68. Copyright © 1950, 1955, 1969, renewed 1978 by Princeton University Press. Reprinted by permission of Princeton University Press.

1-2 "The Epic of Gilgamesh." From *The Epic of Gilgamesh*, translated with an introduction and notes by Maureen Gallery Kovacs, pp. 4, 6, 51–56, 84–86, 106–107. Copyright © 1985, 1989 by the Board of Trustees of the Leland Stanford Junior University. All rights reserved. Used with the permission of Stanford University Press, www.sup.org.

1-3 "The Code of Hammurabi." From *Ancient Near Eastern Texts Relating to the Old Testament*, 3rd ed. with supplement, edited by James B. Pritchard, pp. 176–178. Copyright © 1950, 1955, 1969, renewed 1978 by Princeton University Press. Reprinted by permission of Princeton University Press.

1-4 The Egyptian *Book of the Dead*: "The Declaration of Innocence." From *Ancient Egyptian Literature: A Book of Readings*, vol. 2; The New Kingdom, translated and edited by Miriam Lichtheim, pp. 124–126. Copyright © 1973 by University of California. Reproduced with permission of University of California Press via Copyright Clearance Center.

CHAPTER 2

2-4 Cyrus of Persia, "Ruling an Empire." From *Ancient Near Eastern Texts Relating to the Old Testament*, 3rd ed. with supplement, edited by James B. Pritchard, pp. 315–316. Copyright © 1950, 1955, 1969, renewed 1978 by Princeton University Press. Reprinted by permission of Princeton University Press.

CHAPTER 3

3-1 Homer, " Odysseus and the Sirens." From "Book 12: The Cattle of the Sun" in *The Odyssey* by Homer, translated by Robert Fagles, pp. 276–279. Copyright © 1996 by Robert Fagles. Used by permission of Viking Penguin, a division of Penguin Group (USA) Inc.

3-3 Archilochus of Paros, untitled poem. From *Greek Lyrics*, translated by Richard Lattimore, p. 2. Copyright © 1960 by The University of Chicago. Reprinted by permission of the University of Chicago Press.

3-3 Sappho, untitled poem. From *Sappho: A New Translation* by Mary Barnard, p. 42. Copyright © 1958 by University of California Press. Reproduced with permission of University of California Press via Copyright Clearance Center.

CHAPTER 5

5-3 "Manumissions of Hellenistic Slaves: The Process of Freedom." From *The Hellenistic World from Alexander to the Roman Conquest: A Selection of Ancient Sources in Translation*, edited by M. M. Austin (Cambridge, UK: Cambridge University Press, 1981), pp. 221–222. Copyright © 2006 by Michel Austin. Reprinted with permission of Cambridge University Press.

5-4 Seneca, "The Sounds of a Roman Bath." From *Roman Civilization: Selected Readings*, edited by Naphtali Lewis and Meyer Reinhold, p. 228. Copyright © 1951 by Columbia University Press. Reprinted with permission of the publisher.